Innovation and Entrepreneurship in the Indie Video Game Industry

Devon Gidley

Innovation and Entrepreneurship in the Indie Video Game Industry

Stories and Practical Lessons from an Eyewitness

Devon Gidley ⓘ
Kassel, Germany

ISBN 978-3-031-80876-0   ISBN 978-3-031-80877-7 (eBook)
https://doi.org/10.1007/978-3-031-80877-7

© The Editor(s) (if applicable) and The Author(s), under exclusive license to Springer Nature Switzerland AG 2025

This work is subject to copyright. All rights are solely and exclusively licensed by the Publisher, whether the whole or part of the material is concerned, specifically the rights of translation, reprinting, reuse of illustrations, recitation, broadcasting, reproduction on microfilms or in any other physical way, and transmission or information storage and retrieval, electronic adaptation, computer software, or by similar or dissimilar methodology now known or hereafter developed.

The use of general descriptive names, registered names, trademarks, service marks, etc. in this publication does not imply, even in the absence of a specific statement, that such names are exempt from the relevant protective laws and regulations and therefore free for general use.

The publisher, the authors and the editors are safe to assume that the advice and information in this book are believed to be true and accurate at the date of publication. Neither the publisher nor the authors or the editors give a warranty, expressed or implied, with respect to the material contained herein or for any errors or omissions that may have been made. The publisher remains neutral with regard to jurisdictional claims in published maps and institutional affiliations.

This Palgrave Macmillan imprint is published by the registered company Springer Nature Switzerland AG.
The registered company address is: Gewerbestrasse 11, 6330 Cham, Switzerland

If disposing of this product, please recycle the paper.

Prologue

What is a crux event? It is a potentially significant event. I define it further at the end of Chap. 1. Each chapter is framed around a crux event. They can feel sprawling with all the different people and organizations involved. I want to give a focused example, so here is my crux event during the fieldwork.

It was a random Friday afternoon, six months into a planned twelve months of fieldwork. I was sitting at my usual desk in the Digital Quarry. There wasn't much going on, so I was contemplating leaving for the day. I decided to quickly write up some notes on Basecamp communication.

I opened Basecamp. Almost everything was gone except for my personal messages to people. I no longer had access. I turned to the video game developer sitting next to me and asked if she had the same issue. She looked on Basecamp, and informed me, "Your permissions have been removed." I had no way to contact the BAT person that had instigated the removal. I asked the developer if she could email BAT on my behalf. Within a minute, she received a reply. The BAT committee wanted to talk to me at BAT headquarters on Victoria Street, if I had time.

I went back to pack up my stuff. I had feared this day would come ever since the first Quarry manager (my gatekeeper) had announced her intention to quit. I turned to the developer, and said, "If I don't see you again in here, it's been an honor working with you." It was one of those kinds of events.

I think the start was a comment I made the week before. I was talking to Felix about some dramatic Quarry meetings I had missed. Here was the exchange:

Felix:	I think Robin recorded the meeting yesterday with the BAT committee because of what happened in the Playroom meeting with Nola. It's illegal to record without someone knowing. It only takes two seconds to announce to people that you are recording.
Ethnographer:	He wasn't the only one that made a recording.

 I didn't have to say that. I know why I did. I had gone a little native. I was gossiping with a participant, one in a delicate complex situation that I knew was evolving. Listening to gossip had been useful for me in the past. It delivered many insights into the Quarry culture and operations. The issue was that the gossip should have been going only one way—from them to me. I made the mistake of sharing some of my own gossip. The consequences? I was about to find out.

 I departed immediately and arrived at Victoria Street ten minutes later. The committee didn't wait long to bring me in. They were faceless nameless arbitrators of my fate. They seated me across a desk from them. Not exactly a firing squad, yet I could feel the authority emanating without even knowing the job titles. John and Jane began the interrogation.

John:	Do you have a formal relationship with BAT?
Ethnographer:	No. I received permission from the former Digital Quarry manager, each of the companies, and the mentors. Everything is being made anonymous.
John:	Do you have a recording from a meeting yesterday?[1]
Ethnographer:	I do, but I haven't listened to it yet.
John:	Do not listen to it. Do you understand me?
Ethnographer:	I will delete it immediately.
John:	Who made it? I want a copy.
Ethnographer:	I'm not sure I can do that.
John:	The recording was made without everyone's knowledge. Because it involves companies and GDPR, it's bad. It should not have been shared.[2]

[1] *Aside—I assumed the meeting was an open-door meeting conducted in the Quarry. BAT had sent over a representative to answer questions from companies.*

[2] *Aside—Appreciate the irony of being asked for a recording that I was just told should not be shared. I believe the recording was made in good faith. The person wanted those that had missed the meeting to know what was discussed. The person knew what was on the recording, so there was less good faith in sharing it with me.*

Jane:	We feel violated.
John:	Everyone in that meeting that didn't know feels violated. People sometimes use colorful language. If they had known they were being recorded, they would have said things differently.
Ethnographer:	I understand.
John:	We could report you to the university.[3]
Jane:	Did you ask someone to make the recording in advance?
Ethnographer:	No. I was sick between Friday and Wednesday. I saw on Basecamp that meetings were happening, but I couldn't be there. I would have been there in person if I could have. I came in on Thursday afternoon. I was told there had been a meeting on Thursday morning that I missed. People told me generally what happened, but I wasn't there. Someone said they had made a recording. They offered to share it with me if I wanted. For accuracy and completeness, I accepted.
John:	Tell me who it was …. I can restore your access to Basecamp …. I know I'm using bully tactics.[4]

My silence prompted John and Jane to digress for a while on BAT's plans and goals. They wanted to correct the misinformation about BAT. They weren't the bad guys. They wanted the Quarry companies to succeed.

John:	How long do you plan to stay?
Ethnographer:	My intention was to follow the second cohort until they left in six months.
John:	I guess it's okay if you continue until March.
Jane:	We wouldn't have had an issue with the recording if it had been announced up front.
John:	Can we guess the person that made the recording? Robin.

[3] *Aside—That was a threat.*
[4] *Aside—I stayed silent. I tried my best to retain a non-threatening poker face. I accepted that my fieldwork was over. If I gave up my source, I would never regain the trust of my informants. I would probably put the person's place in the Quarry at risk. If I didn't give up my source, I would be denied access to the Quarry. Worse case, the committee takes the nuclear option, and my life goes down in flames. To continue the poker metaphor, I was all-in with my opponent knowing more about my cards that I did.*

Ethnographer: I can neither confirm nor deny.[5]
John: We do not give consent for anything in the recording to appear in a report.
Ethnographer: I won't use the recording.
John: Ok. Jane, should we restore his access to Basecamp?
Jane: I think it's fine.

We exchanged some final pleasantries.

BAT restored my access to Basecamp before I reached the street. I spoke to several other informants to try and understand it all better. It only served to confuse me more.

In my crux event, I was faced with essentially three choices: (1) keep or destroy the recording; (2) give up or protect my source; (3) try to continue the fieldwork or quit. The first choice was easy. Nothing good would happen from keeping the recording. Besides, I may not know verbatim the conversation in the meeting, but I had summaries from multiple sources. The second choice was difficult. It may have been easier to save myself by giving up my source, but I never would have been able to return to the Quarry after breaking the trust of my informants. The third choice required courage. Walking away would have been safer. I stayed because I felt that is what an ethnographer would have done. I wanted to believe I could be one.

Do I regret the mistake I made in sharing gossip with an informant? Somewhat. I don't regret it because it all worked out (at least for me). I both regret and don't regret that it put me in the middle of a conflict during the research instead of on the sidelines observing it. It did prevent me from making a bigger (legal) mistake of keeping, listening, and using the recording. I do regret it because I shared information given to me that caused emotional distress to several people, including myself. It's easier in retrospective to consider doing something different. In the moment, I was caught up in the wave of the situation.

For my research, the meeting at BAT was my crux event. How? It was potentially critical to the research—at least it seemed so at the time. It could have changed everything. It could have stopped my fieldwork. This book would have ended after Chap. 5. If I had been so bold and cunning, I might have been able to turn the meeting into greater access. This book would have shown the Wizard as well as Oz. Instead, I tried to ignore it

---

[5] *Aside—They took my answer for confirmation. I felt bad. I can still neither confirm nor deny.*

and pretend that life was normal (in a cautious trust-no-one kind of way). I share the story here and now, so the reader knows that the ethnography is from a participant perspective as well as an observer.

Practical Lessons

1. A crux event may appear at any time and without warning.
2. One of the key points I will make about crux events is that they seem to be potentially significant in the moment. They may not be significant after everything is finished. They may be significant in unexpected ways. In the moment, people make decisions not knowing the future.
3. Know what you want. Make the decisions that will most likely deliver your goals.

Preface

This book is intended for three potential audiences. The primary intended audience is video game and innovation professionals. I provide a brief overview of the industry and innovation spaces in Chap. 1. Chapter 2 surveys interorganizational indie video game spaces around the world (as of 2024). Each story within the ethnographic chapters (3–7) includes practical analysis and insights. Each chapter begins and ends with a summary of the practical lessons in that chapter. The stories in between help you remember. Many of them end with quick lessons—direct analysis and sensible insights from the preceding story. There are 126 or so. The lessons look at the story from multiple perspectives. What is important for a creative developer, a support organization, a student, or general reader? The practical takeaways are synthesized in Chap. 8. The six aggregated lessons focus on membership, resistance, interns, mentors, feedback, and institutional knowledge in the context of business and technology incubators, accelerators, coworking spaces, and video game development. The chapter answers the most common question I received from participants: what did the Digital Quarry do right and wrong?

    The secondary audience is students. This may also include those generally interested in video game development, the creative industries, or what it is like to work as a creative. The book is a raw behind-the-scenes look at some of the processes and challenges of indie video game development. This is not a tale of all indie video game development. The setting (a support program and space) is simply one path, or one tool, that indie developers may use in attempting to produce a game. Additionally, I hope it is obvious to the reader that the ten participating companies and their employees did not have a singular experience. They had varying degrees of success and failure. They became embroiled in drama or flew under the radar. There was no "final answer" or "one thing" that explained it all. Maybe that is the main lesson for those considering a career in game development. There is no "right way" and no guarantees when it comes to creative pursuits. If anyone wants to use this book in a classroom setting, the appendix includes possible seminar discussion questions for each chapter.

The tertiary audience is academics. The book is very ethnographic. It favors practical and commonsense insights. There is not enough grand theory throughout to justify a truly academic monograph. There is some conceptual development. Specifically, the book contributes toward developing theory around potential critical events in the development of innovation spaces and creative industries. These crux events can be used as a framework to understand actions and processes. Crux events are both a theory and a methodology, similar to institutional work (see Gidley, 2021b). I have consolidated the main theoretical aspects into Chaps. 1 and 8; however, each ethnographic chapter highlights a single crux event. The introduction of the chapter explains the crux event simply. The rest of the chapter uses stories to fill in the details.

This book has evolved since the original proposal in spring 2021. The theme has remained the same (how events impact indie video game development), but the structure has changed over the years of writing. It began as a Palgrave Pivot book (~30,000 words) for an academic audience. Next, it evolved into a monograph (~70,000 words) aimed at both academics and professional practitioners. Finally, it morphed into its current form—a book of stories and practical insights that still includes some theory for academics and students.

This book derives from research conducted during my PhD thesis (Gidley, 2021a). How does it differ? First, my thesis was heavily focused on institutional work. I spun off two publications on the subject (Gidley, 2021b; Gidley & Palmer, 2021). I dropped the institutional theory angle from this book. There may be a mention here or there of an institution, but it's not about institutional theory. Second, my thesis was structured as a series of journal-style articles. Despite the lengthy word count, deep ethnographic stories were limited. This book rectifies that oversight by devoting the bulk of the narrative to the findings. Third, my other publications on this research focused heavily on the rapid prototyping section (see Chap. 3). Gidley and Palmer (2022) took a temporal, spatial, and product scales perspective. Gidley and colleagues (2023) looked at the participant experience in an accelerator via the lens of suffering and recovery. Recently, I did publish an article (Gidley & Palmer, 2024) looking at the spaces of the Digital Quarry as a place. I do little of that here. Instead, I use crux events as a means to explore the organizational dynamics of and in the Digital Quarry.

Cast of Characters

I want to introduce the cast of characters to the reader. I used the term "characters" deliberately. They are not real people. The book is based on ethnographic fieldwork, but the "people" named here are characters in a story. Every name of an individual or organization is a pseudonym. The main goal is to make it easier for the reader to follow the story, and therefore to learn something. Below are some background and definitions.

The Digital Quarry has multiple overlapping meanings. The Digital Quarry is the physical coworking space where most of the action in this book takes place. It is also the name of the incubator program located in the space. The Digital Quarry is not an organization in and of itself. From an academic theoretical side, I could refer to it as a proto-institution or an innovation space. So, if an individual says, "I am a member of the Digital Quarry," what does this mean practically? It usually means the individual works inside the Digital Quarry office space. Additionally, since there were no freelancers allowed in the Quarry at the time of the research, the individual worked for an organization that had a relationship with the owner of the space (see below). Less likely, an individual might say, "My company belongs to the Digital Quarry." This basically means the above but with the added implication that the company is part of the video game incubator program based in the Digital Quarry. There was some disagreement on the level of legitimacy conferred by membership in the Quarry. Whether locally or globally, it wasn't clear if membership in the Quarry offered a reputational bonus to participating companies. It did not seem to be a large factor in the everyday life of members of the Quarry. In contrast, participation in some accelerator programs, like the Y Combinator (Pauwels et al., 2016), provides almost a seal of approval in some circles. The Digital Quarry as a physical space could not exist without the Digital Quarry as an incubator program; however, as the reader will see in Chap. 6, the program could be independent of the space. During the research, they were basically synonymous. Finally, it is also known as the Quarry in shorthand.

The Quarry space is divided into thirds. The first third (closest the entry door) has a low ceiling, one story at the most. It almost has the feel of a cave when you walk in. It's darker than the rest of the room. Against the wall is a whiteboard with info on the Wi-Fi password and printer access. Next to it is a big screen TV (50 inches or 1.5 meters) although it was most frequently used to play the radio. The middle third is two stories high. The ceiling is mostly glass, so plenty of light comes down from it. The back half (away from the entry door) contains computers, people on either side. The front half is open and includes the staircase up to a separate organization. Under the staircase and against the wall is the coat rack, a bench, and whiteboards above it. They are being used with timelines (dates/months although mostly empty). Under the stairs are boxes, probably empty from old equipment. The far third is a long corridor, like a galley kitchen. The ceiling is 1.5 stories. There are four large windows providing lots of natural light even with shades pulled halfway or all the down. The columns on either side (separating the room into thirds) have white boards hanging.

The Quarry space is located inside a larger building called the Continental Gymnasium (or the Gymnasium). The building was located in the suburbs of a city in Great Britain. The north half of the Gym was devoted to a classic coworking space (membership simply required paying the fee). The south half contained more diversity. Along with the Quarry coworking space, there were three rooms (Meeting room, Boardroom, Playroom) for use by anyone in the building. Members of the Quarry were promised first access to the three rooms. Additionally, a few other organizations maintained permanent offices in the south half. A kitchen with free coffee and tea was located near the side exit to the building.

BAT (British Artistic Technologists) is the organization managing the Quarry. They are the "owner" of the space (although they lease the office). BAT is a pseudo-public regional arts development agency. Their basic remit is to develop the local creative industries in order to increase investment in the sector. The Quarry was the main aspect of a four-year plan for the video game industry. BAT selected the companies for the Quarry through an application process. BAT did not pay companies directly for belonging to the Quarry, but companies did receive preferential access to certain other funding or programs. They did not control the independent company operations, nor the employees allowed to work in the Quarry.

BAT paid the mentors, consultants, Quarry manager, and two interns. To most people in the Quarry, BAT was an amorphous mysterious entity governed by a committee.

The Quarry Manager works for BAT. She was the physical manifestation of BAT, and the main point of interaction for anyone in the Quarry and BAT. She manages daily operations for the Quarry and serves as an intermediary between the companies, mentors, outside consultants, and BAT. There were two different Quarry managers during the time of the research. The first had experience in the public sector and contributed to the founding of the Quarry. She unexpectedly took another job about nine months after the Quarry opened. The second Quarry manager joined BAT from the private sector. Their management styles may have been different, but they both inhabited the same role.

Up to ten independent digital game development companies worked out of the Quarry. I will use the terms "team" and "company" interchangeably in this book. I have chosen not to provide clear names and biographical details for two reasons. First, this book is more about actions and events and less about individual people, their history, or motivations. I do not believe the reader needs to intimately know the individual to understand the concepts developed in this book. Second, I want to protect the individuals involved in some of the dramatic and contentious events discussed. The video game industry in the region is small. My informants shared private thoughts with me because they believed it would not negatively affect them.

The companies worked for themselves. BAT provided some funding to some of the companies, at different times and for different reasons. The companies had no mandatory relationships with each other. At times, some companies cooperated, such as sharing interns or working on the same contract project. At other times, the companies competed, such as when applying for funding. Overall, most interaction was informal.

The companies were divided into two cohorts. The first cohort consisted of seven companies. All joined at the beginning of the Quarry. The second cohort of three companies started five months later. Each company signed up for one year. The option to extend was implied but also made unclear. Chapters 5 and 6 discuss events around the cohorts leaving.

Four mentors provided services out of the Quarry. BAT paid the mentor consulting salaries to visit the Quarry monthly. The standard rotation was one mentor visiting for two days each week. Each mentor had different expertise: (1) publishing, (2) development, (3) operations, (4) funding. Mentors conducted weekly meetings with the individual companies. Usually, it was the company director(s). In some cases, the full team might attend the meeting. Companies were "required" to attend the weekly meetings, but this rule was not enforced. The mentors met with other local video game developers (not working in the Quarry) on a case-by-case basis.

The ethnographer is the name I use for myself in the narrative. Remember, in the context of this book I am not a real person; rather, I am simply another character in the story. This also allows the narrative to flow smoother (i.e. the reader will not confuse me for a video game developer or someone else). The ethnographer was a PhD student conducting my research on and in the Quarry. He joined the Quarry at the same time as the second cohort. The Quarry managers, companies, interns, and mentors agreed to observations and interviews, but the ethnographer worked for no one and received no payment. He never signed any official paperwork. His relationships with informants were informal. He was a guest of sorts. He had a keycard, so he had access to everything that any other participant did. Further methodological details can be found below (see also chapter two, Gidley, 2021).

A Note on the Ethnography: In Person and in Writing

Ethnographic fieldwork is about immersion in the field (Emerson et al., 1995; Locke, 2011). It requires developing relationships so that people (participants, informants, interlocutors) feel comfortable letting an outsider into their world. Once inside, the ethnographer can participate and observe while at the same time receiving confessions not otherwise available. For this book, I conducted over 800 hours of participant observation, 58 interviews, and collected dozens of material artifacts over the course of 12 months. I was there for most of the important moments, or I defined them as important (because I was there?), in the context of the Quarry as a lived experience, organization, and social space.

I was there for many vulnerable moments. I cannot tell this tale without trying to protect the people in it. Therefore, I have employed several tactics to obfuscate and anonymize the data.

First, I have used pseudonyms—actually, multiple pseudonyms. For some especially vulnerable individuals, I changed their pseudonyms each chapter. The pseudonyms apply to all proper nouns (places, companies, people, products). I have stripped away or changed most biographical details. For example, it's not relevant to the story that one director lost his job and decided to retrain as a video game developer. It adds color but not insight. Alternatively, I may have kept something that seemed relevant to the story. For example, the marketing intern was a university placement student. She does not play a large role in the story, but the use of interns becomes an important practical lesson (see Chap. 7). Furthermore, I use names because it makes it easier to read. Would the reader prefer a mentor meeting between "mentor" and "developer" or between Anthony and Cleopatra?

Second, I have written some detailed scenes and dialogue exchanges. These come from three sources: field notes, interviews, and Basecamp posts. In terms of accuracy, there are different levels. Basecamp was an internal Quarry messaging app (like Slack). All company directors had access, and most posts were available to any member. I recorded these verbatim. In this book, posts are unattributed and paraphrased. Meaning, I have removed any names and rewritten each post (even if they appear in quotes for readability). Some participants agreed to audio recorded interviews. Those quotes are mostly accurate (although I may have redacted sections for various reasons). Many field notes were written in real time; however, this means I probably only caught a quarter of the words (50 typed words versus 200 spoken words per minute). Other field notes were written hours later. Those basically capture the general idea of the conversation. Next, the field notes were edited before appearing in this book. This was done for anonymizing and/or narrative flow. Dialogue was adjusted for clarity or theme. Too vulnerable, hurtful, or compromising details were removed. If it would not substantially change the meaning of a scene, I would sometimes add or subtract a character or change which character said something. By the end, anything resembling a "real person" has been removed. They are characters.

Third, let us not forget the fog of ethnography. Every ethnography presents a certain perspective based on positionality, experiences, and informants. This is one story. It is not the only story. The purpose is not to lay blame or celebrate, to prove individuals right or wrong. There are no heroes or villains. The purpose is to better understand crux events in the shaping of innovation spaces and video game development.

Finally, so it is clear for the reader, here are some notes on dialogue exchanges. As I mentioned earlier, I refer to myself as "the ethnographer."

Other places, I usually write in the first person. I use a theater trick, the term "Aside" (written in different font), to share additional information or perspective with the reader.[1] Usually, this information came at a later moment. These are listed as footnotes. I used two types of dialogue indicators: quotation marks ("") and character name followed by a dash (—) then dialogue. These are for style only. There is no substantive difference because, remember, they are not people being quoted. For example, these are equivalent:

"Do you have an informed consent form?" Hera asked.

Hera: Do you have an informed consent form?

The answer to the above question is in Chap. 2.

Here are a few other notes. First, I am not a video game developer (professional or otherwise), but I have dabbled as a writer, director, and entrepreneur in other creative industries. Second, I am not studying video games as digital artifacts; instead, I am interested in business, organization, and social structure. Styhre (2020) makes similar points and provides a more extensive analysis of ethnographic positioning in his book on the indie game developers in Sweden. Third, I am not from Great Britain, so I may have misconstrued some cultural aspects. Finally, what "actually happened in reality" is less important than what it means and what we can learn from it. The details are only important in that they help us to learn something.

Kassel, Germany   Devon Gidley

References

Emerson, R. M., Fretz, R. I., & Shaw, L. L. (1995). *Writing ethnographic fieldnotes*. University of Chicago Press.

Gidley, D. (2021a). *An ethnographic study of institutional work in a creative proto-institutional place*. Doctoral dissertation, Queen's University Belfast.

Gidley, D. (2021b). Creating institutional disruption: An alternative method to study institutions. *Journal of Organizational Change Management, 34*(4), 810–821.

---

[1] *Aside—for example, ethical approval for this research was granted by Queen's University Belfast.*

Gidley, D., & Palmer, M. (2021). Institutional work: A review and framework based on semantic and thematic analysis. M@n@gement, 24(1), 49–63.

Gidley, D., & Palmer, M. (2022). The impact of video game prototyping in an accelerator as viewed via spatial, temporal, and product scales. International Journal of Innovation, 10(3), 410–433.

Gidley, D., & Palmer, M. (2024). Institutional policing work in a constellation of labels and spaces of place: Video game development management insights. *International Journal of Organizational Analysis*, Vol. ahead-of-print No. ahead-of-print. https://doi.org/10.1108/IJOA-03-2024-4365.

Locke, K. (2011). Field research practice in management and organization studies: Reclaiming its tradition of discovery. The Academy of Management Annals, 5(1), 613–652.

Pauwels, C., Clarysse, B., Wright, M., & Van Hove, J. (2016). Understanding a new generation incubation model: The accelerator. Technovation, 50–51, 13–24. https://doi.org/10.1016/j.technovation.2015.09.003

Styhre, A. (2020). Indie video game development work: Innovation in the creative economy. Springer Nature.

Acknowledgments

I thank the Palgrave team: Alec Selwyn, Jessica Harrison, Liz Barlow, and Esther Rani. They helped bring this book from idea to manuscript. In particular, Alec guided the manuscript from unfavorable peer-reviewed drafts to a publishable stage. I am grateful.

I thank the many anonymous reviewers for their comments on the original proposal, the original draft, and the multiple revisions. I thank again all the other anonymous reviewers of my other works that helped make this one better.

I thank people that helped me while I was at Queen's University Belfast: Dr. Mark Palmer (thesis supervisor), Dr. Mike Crone (thesis supervisor), Dr. Amani Gharib (friend), Dr. Min Zhang (examiner), and Dr. Sabina Siebert (examiner). In particular, Prof. Palmer continued to provide feedback on my academic writing even after I graduated.

I thank my informants in and around the Digital Quarry. They were generous. None of my comments are meant as personal criticism. I mean no harm to any person or organization involved.

I thank my wife Amanda for her support, belief, and encouragement. She is the most important because she is there every day regardless.

I received no additional funding for this research.

I declare no conflicts of interest.

Contents

1 **Theoretical Framework: Video Game Development, Innovation Spaces, and Crux Events**   1
  1.1 *Entrepreneurship, the Creative Industries, and Video Games*   2
  1.2 *Empirical Context*   2
    1.2.1 *Global Games Industry*   3
    1.2.2 *UK Context*   5
    1.2.3 *Indie Game Development*   6
    1.2.4 *Game Jams*   7
  1.3 *Innovation Spaces*   8
    1.3.1 *Accelerators*   8
    1.3.2 *Incubators*   9
    1.3.3 *Coworking Spaces*   10
    1.3.4 *Labeling by Participants*   11
    1.3.5 *Video Game Innovation Spaces Around the World*   12
  1.4 *Crux Events*   17
  References   19

2 **New Players: Introducing Newcomers Leads to Rumblings**   25
  2.1 *Introduction*   26
    2.1.1 *Conceptual Development*   26
    2.1.2 *Practical Lessons*   26
  2.2 *Ethnographer*   27
  2.3 *New Cohort*   30
  2.4 *Original Members*   33

	2.4.1 Original Cohort Welcomes the New Cohort	33
	2.4.2 Original Cohort Interrogates the Ethnographer	34
	2.4.3 A Place in the Quarry	37
2.5	Observers	38
	2.5.1 End of First Week and the First Demo Friday	39
	2.5.2 Scuddled Plans	40
2.6	Conclusion	42
	2.6.1 Reflection on Practical Lessons	42
References		43

3 Next Level: Significant Rule Changes Lead to a New Game — 45
- 3.1 Introduction — 46
  - 3.1.1 Conceptual Development — 46
  - 3.1.2 Practical Lessons — 46
- 3.2 Selling Game Developers on Playing a Real-Life Game — 47
  - 3.2.1 The Presentation — 47
  - 3.2.2 Q&A — 49
  - 3.2.3 Further Reasons Why — 53
  - 3.2.4 Mentor as Strategist or Therapist — 55
- 3.3 How to Build a Game in Four and a Half Days — 58
- 3.4 Six Games in Six Weeks — 60
  - 3.4.1 Week 1: Chilled Out — 60
  - 3.4.2 Week 2: Climate Change — 62
  - 3.4.3 Week 3: Gaslighting — 62
  - 3.4.4 Week 4: Lost (at Sea) — 67
  - 3.4.5 Week 5: Patterns — 69
  - 3.4.6 Week 6: Time and Space — 71
  - 3.4.7 Week 7: Commercial Viability — 74
- 3.5 After the Prototyping — 77
- 3.6 Conclusion — 78
  - 3.6.1 Reflections on Practical Lessons — 79
- References — 79

4 Loading …: The Quarry Manager Leaves a Void — 81
- 4.1 Introduction — 82
  - 4.1.1 Conceptual Development — 82
  - 4.1.2 Practical Lessons — 82
- 4.2 The Unexpected Event — 83

	4.3	*Power Play*	86
	4.4	*Mini-production Funding Cut*	90
	4.5	*The Last Days of Hera*	95
		4.5.1 *Secondhand BAT View on the Quarry*	96
		4.5.2 *The Rebellion*	98
	4.6	*Transition*	101
		4.6.1 *BAT Begins to Solicit Feedback*	101
		4.6.2 *The Rebellion Reignites*	103
	4.7	*After Hera*	108
	4.8	*Conclusion*	109
		4.8.1 *Reflections on Practical Lessons*	109
5	**Boss Fight: Changes in Priorities Lead to a Self-Inflicted Crisis**		111
	5.1	*Introduction*	112
		5.1.1 *Conceptual Development*	112
		5.1.2 *Practical Lessons*	112
	5.2	*The Beginning of the End*	113
	5.3	*Pitching*	116
	5.4	*Aftermath of the First Cohort Exit Interviews*	121
		5.4.1 *Challenging Power*	121
		5.4.2 *Vonn Reverses His Decision*	122
	5.5	*Funding Results*	123
		5.5.1 *The Other 10%*	123
		5.5.2 *Finding Out the Results*	124
		5.5.3 *Disorienting*	127
		5.5.4 *Never Do or Die*	130
		5.5.5 *A Mentor Reacts*	131
		5.5.6 *Congratulations*	133
		5.5.7 *Confused and Frustrated*	134
		5.5.8 *A Part-Time Job*	136
	5.6	*Conclusion*	137
		5.6.1 *Reflections on Practical Lessons*	138
	References		140

6	**Extra Life: New Power Leads to a Change of Direction**	**141**
	6.1 Introduction	141
	6.1.1 Conceptual Development	141
	6.1.2 Practical Lessons	142
	6.2 A New Quarry Manager Begins	142
	6.2.1 First Impressions	142
	6.2.2 How Juno Initially Views the Digital Quarry	144
	6.2.3 Quality Assurance Reset	145
	6.3 Cohort One Shrinks	146
	6.4 Saving the Second Cohort	148
	6.4.1 The Dredges	149
	6.5 A Hybrid Space	150
	6.5.1 An Alternative Quarry	153
	6.5.2 QA Revamp	154
	6.5.3 Moonshot and a Third Cohort	155
	6.6 Game Over: People Abandon the Digital Quarry	158
	6.6.1 Conceptual Development	159
	6.6.2 Practical Lessons	159
	6.7 Waiting	159
	6.7.1 Meeting a Third Cohort Member	159
	6.7.2 Planning to Attend the Game Developers Conference (GDC)	160
	6.7.3 A New Company Joins the Quarry	161
	6.8 Beyond the Quarry	162
	6.8.1 A Mentor Says Goodbye	163
	6.8.2 Decisions on the Future	163
	6.9 A Pandemic Emerges	166
	6.10 Conclusion	167
	6.10.1 Reflections on Practical Lessons	168
	References	169
7	**Postmortem: Practical Lessons in Incubating Creative Development**	**171**
	7.1 Introduction	171
	7.1.1 Membership	171
	7.1.2 Resistance	175
	7.1.3 Interns	178
	7.1.4 Mentor Meetings	179

		7.1.5 Feedback	182
		7.1.6 Institutional Knowledge	184
	7.2	Conclusion	185
	References		187
8	**A Conceptual Crux Events Framework**		189
	8.1	Crux Events	190
		8.1.1 Gateways	190
		8.1.2 Surprises	191
		8.1.3 Crises	193
	8.2	Reactions	194
		8.2.1 Embrace	194
		8.2.2 Resist	195
		8.2.3 Ignore	196
	8.3	Outcomes	197
		8.3.1 Distraction	198
		8.3.2 Questions	199
		8.3.3 Hope	200
		8.3.4 Inspiration	200
	8.4	Conclusion	201
	References		201

Afterword — 205

Appendix — 209

References — 215

Index — 225

List of Figures

Fig. 1.1 Basic crux event framework　18
Fig. 8.1 Theoretical positioning of initial outcomes　198

List of Tables

Table 1.1	Digital game industry estimates	4
Table 1.2	Demographics of digital gamers	4
Table 1.3	UK digital game industry workers	6
Table 1.4	Selected list of incubators and accelerators for video games	13
Table 3.1	Bootcamp summary	59

CHAPTER 1

Theoretical Framework: Video Game Development, Innovation Spaces, and Crux Events

This chapter presents the empirical and theoretical foundation for the narrative in this book. I would encourage all readers to read the section on crux events at the end of this chapter. Otherwise, feel free to skip any section. The rest of the chapter is background information that video game professionals or innovation experts may already know. There are no practical lessons. There are three general sections:

1. An overview of the video game industry:

    (a) Global
    (b) UK
    (c) Indie game development
    (d) Game Jams

2. Definitions and descriptions of incubators, accelerators, and coworking spaces.

    (a) Table of incubators and accelerators for video game development.

3. Crux events.

© The Author(s), under exclusive license to Springer Nature Switzerland AG 2025
D. Gidley, *Innovation and Entrepreneurship in the Indie Video Game Industry*, https://doi.org/10.1007/978-3-031-80877-7_1

The perspective of crux events reveals insights on the Quarry (as a program and a physical space) and other settings—accelerators, incubators, game jams, video game development spaces. In particular, the digital games industry, which sits at the intersection of technology and art, presents the possibility of unique insights into organizing, creativity, innovation spaces, and events. An *in situ* perspective allows the full focus to fall on what happened and the consequences. As such, this monograph seeks to answer the following question: *how do crux events shape an interorganizational innovation space?*

1.1 Entrepreneurship, the Creative Industries, and Video Games

One common definition of the creative industries (Garnham, 2005; Gong & Hassink, 2017) comes from the UK Department of Culture, Media and Sports as industries "based on individual creativity, skill and talent … through developing intellectual property" (DCMS, 1998). The video games industry was one of the 13 "creative industries" designated by the British government using the definition above (Casper & Storz, 2017; Garnham, 2005). Researchers and governments acknowledge the increasing importance of creativity and creative industries, specifically the digital game industry in terms of revenue, employment, and consumers (Parker et al., 2018; UKIE, 2018; Vervoort, 2019).

The companies in the Quarry were micro-sized companies and/or startups. Some researchers use the term creative entrepreneur or entrepreneur in the creative industries (Hausmann & Heinze, 2016; Lee, 2015; Parkman et al., 2012). Participants in the Quarry saw themselves as video game developers, but this book does not analyze them "emergent video game developers" (Malone, 2021). Rarely did they use terms like entrepreneurship or creative industries. The focus in this book is on the events and interactions between individuals and organizations rather than the actions of isolated entrepreneurs.

1.2 Empirical Context

Several features of the empirical field site prove suitable for answering the research question. First, the Quarry was a place housing social actors within the local digital game industry. Based on some informant estimates, the majority of the game developers in the region were housed there. It was a place of confined interorganizational interaction where the lead up and actions of crux events could be observed along with the outcomes. Second, the field site was a relatively new place. The Quarry had not yet developed into an institutionalized space where rules and routines were taken-for-granted. Everything was still in flux. As such, there were more crux events in a short time than in other similar places. Third, the Quarry began as a place to grow the video games industry in the region. It later transitioned to a place trying to actively accelerate this growth (see Chap. 4). Obviously, this was not known at the start of the fieldwork, but that is one advantage of ethnography (Locke, 2011). The field site was partly based on another site in the UK and took additional inspiration from coworking spaces and business accelerators. The hope was to imbue companies with certain professional management practices and then diffuse this outward to the greater region.

The digital game industry is vast, important, and at the same time diverse. In a bibliometric study of academic literature on digital games, García-Sánchez et al. (2019) found business and management the tenth most common field. Therefore, I rely on some industry publications to overview the empirical context. First, I begin with a global view of the industry in terms of facts and figures. Next, I delve deeper into the UK context. Finally, I will discuss some literature around indie game developers.

1.2.1 Global Games Industry

The digital game industry is vast and important. Worldwide, an estimated 2.2–2.6 billion people play digital games, including almost half (32 million) of the UK population; globally, the industry has a worth of approximately 108 billion pounds ($137.9); the industry grew an estimated 13% worldwide from 2017 to 2018 (UKIE, 2018). The UK digital game industry sales and users resembles the worldwide proportions: UK sales were approximately $4.85 billion (fifth largest in the world per the Entertainment Retailers Association); industry growth around 10%, and mobile accounting for around half of sales (UKIE, 2018; Blake, 2019). The UK is a leader in European development of digital games (at least at the time of the research). In 2016, European industry professionals voted the UK the best place to work in games currently and for the next five years (UKIE, 2018). Additionally, the UK digital game industry is unstudied compared with other geographic areas. There are several notable exceptions (e.g. Cabras et al., 2017; Izushi & Aoyama, 2006; Kennedy, 2018; Webber, 2020), but on the whole, much research concentrates on North America (e.g. Harvey & Fisher, 2013; Whitson, 2020) and Japan (e.g. Mikami et al., 2016; Storz et al., 2015).

Digital games are produced and played worldwide. Table 1.1 summarizes industry and Table 1.2 summarizes the demographic details on a global level as well as the UK. Historically, consumer digital games referred to games developed for either the personal computer or various consoles (e.g. Nintendo, Playstation). This was the case between the 1980s until the late 2000s (Johns, 2006). In this time period, competitive advantage lay with publishers and console manufacturers due to the economic and technical restrictions of game development for those platforms (Carpenter et al., 2014; Izushi & Aoyama, 2006). The release of the gaming-capable iPhone in 2007 changed the industry (Nieborg, 2015; Tsang, 2021). Digital game development became more democratized as smaller teams could produce mobile games quicker and cheaper than ever before. Mobile games now account for over half of players and revenue (UKIE, 2018).

Table 1.1 Digital game industry estimates

Revenue	$180 billion (2021 global estimate) and £5.5 billion (2020 UK estimate)
Companies	Approximately 2,000 active UK game companies (2017 estimate)
Platform	Console (25%); PC (24%); Mobile (51%) (2018 revenue estimate)
Employees	Approximately 16,000 FTE (2019 UK estimate)

Source: adapted from UKIE (2018) and Taylor (2020)

Table 1.2 Demographics of digital gamers

	Global	UK
Players	2.6 billion (2017 estimate)	32 million (2017 estimate)
Age	27% under 18; 29% between age 18–35; 18% between 36–49; and 26% over 50	50% age 40 or above (2017 estimate)
Gender	46% female / 54% male (2017 estimate)	42% female / 58% male (2016 estimate)
Time	50% play "most days"	8.2 hours per week average

Source: adapted from Taylor (2020), Thompson and Hebblethwaite (2020), UKIE (2018)

The rise of the Internet and mobile connectivity has led to several other developments. In digital games, industry and consumption seem to change together. Geographically, mobile phones allow people to play games anywhere. While handheld devices (e.g. Gameboy) are not new in digital games, the ubiquitous mobile phone shifted the demographics (Nieborg, 2015). More women now play games, and the typical player is older than previously. The geography of mobile game development has shifted as well. The major shift has been smaller, or distributed remote, studios located outside of traditional game development regions (Pottie-Sherman & Lynch, 2019). For example, both Høvig (2016) and Jørgensen (2019) consider the rise of new game development studios in Norway. Other new developments include esports (Abanazir, 2019), gamification of traditional industries (Rajani et al., 2019), and live streaming of game playing (Johnson & Woodcock, 2019). All these developments represent new patterns of consumption and production; however, different regions developed game industries differently.

1.2.2 UK Context

Game development evolved differently in the UK than elsewhere (for a history, see Tsang, 2021). Izushi and Aoyama (2006) argue the UK digital game development industry rose from the ground via "bedroom-coders" in comparison to the industries in Japan (corporate sponsorships) and America (PCs and arcades). Increasingly, globalization, legislation, and education are impacting the UK industry. In their study of the survival rates of UK game companies, Cabras et al. (2017, p. 312) found "an increasingly globalized market, limiting the effects related to any operation conducted at a local level." The UK industry successfully lobbied for the introduction of a "tax relief" on digital game development (Mac Síthigh, 2014). Starting in 2014, the law allowed companies to claim a portion of development costs as a tax rebate, assuming they could prove the "Britishness" of the game (Mac Síthigh, 2014; Webber, 2020). Some companies in the Quarry took advantage of the tax relief option, if possible; however, I will show their participation in a program and space funded by a quasi-government agency was more important. Finally, digital game development has become formalized within the UK higher education system. Taylor (2020) reports that 27% of workers hold a game-specific university qualification. Comunian et al. (2015) found that digital technology graduates working in the digital game sector had the highest mean salary

Table 1.3 UK digital game industry workers

Age	16% younger than 25, 50% between age 26–35, 34% over age 36
Gender	70% male, 28% female, 2% non-binary
Nationality & Ethnicity	28% non-UK and 10% ethnic minority
Sexuality	21% LGBTQ+ and 79% heterosexual
Health	21% live with chronic health problem and 31% with depression, anxiety, or both
Education	81% undergraduate degree of above
Role	21% programming, 18% operations, 17% sales, 16% art, 28% other

Source: adapted from Taylor (2020)

across the creative industries (£21,100 annually). The salary figures are a few years old, but they are not radically different from the salary of employees in the Quarry. Table 1.3 provides a summary of UK game industry workers from a 2019 survey.

Academic research on the UK digital games industry context has predominantly focused on large studios or quantitative analyses. The high-profile success of some UK-made games led to an interest in "AAA" studios—large well-funded professional studios akin to Hollywood in films (Scarbrough et al., 2015). Others have utilized quantitative surveys, either UK-only (Cabras et al., 2017; Gaudl et al., 2018) or as part of cross-country comparisons (Storz et al., 2015). Recently, several studies have begun to qualitatively explore labor relations (Ruffino & Woodcock, 2020) with Ludic labor becoming a popular topic (e.g. Kennedy, 2018). Following on this and of specific relevance to this book, I must consider the different context of indie game development. In the context of the UK, 99.5% of companies are considered small or medium-sized enterprises with about 88% having 9 people or less (Thompson & Hebblethwaite, 2020).

1.2.3 Indie Game Development

Digital game development companies can be divided into two types: AAA and indie. While this might be reductionist, for the purposes of this book, it helps to differentiate between large and small game development studios. Large studios, such as seen in various studies (e.g. Johnson, 2013; Scarbrough et al., 2015), tend toward departmental compartmentalization and professionalism. In this context, "Job specialization on a game development team means that members are able to 'black box' the work of others" (Whitson, 2020, p. 280). Tasks and expectations draw heavily from professional management practices and are more institutionalized in this context, at least in the sense of projecting a "professionalized image" (Whitson, 2020, p. 282).

On the other hand, smaller studios exhibit fewer taken-for-granted aspects. They may lack "institutionalised forms of game production" common in corporate studios (Guevara-Villalobos, 2013, p. 65). These studios are often called "indie," although "independent" is likely a more accurate term since "indie" implies a cultural element (Jørgensen, 2019; Phillips, 2015). Indeed, several studies have examined the "culture" around indie game development (e.g. Parker et al., 2018). For example, Phillips (2015, p. 150) showed how indie developers have an unwritten "code of honour" when it comes to competition and may use informal networks to regulate creative copying. In an early analysis of the UK context, Guevara-Villalobos (2013, p. 266) differentiated between the stable subsector of corporate game development and the situation of independent developers—"a diverse sector, with a few emerging institutions that are also (to some extent) uncertain." Whether indie or independent, game developers outside the corporate system experience precarity in any number of ways. Programs and spaces like the Quarry aim to support independent game developers. Interestingly, Patten (2016) found that many creative entrepreneurs "may ignore or even avoid the programs set up to support them, feeling instead that, as creative individuals, they are not understood by government agencies" (p. 35). This ethnography offers complex nuance to this perspective.

1.2.4 Game Jams

In Chap. 3, BAT introduces a rapid prototyping program to the Quarry. The program took inspiration from 'game jams'—"a rapid prototyping strategy to deliver innovation and new ideas"—have been known to produce the skeleton of a game in as little as 24 hours (Kennedy, 2018, p. 709). In contrast, the average game development time is 2–3 years (Johnson, 2013).[1] In the traditional game jam, the emphasis is on process, experience, and ultimately the game (Gaudl et al., 2018; Kennedy, 2018).

---

[1] For traditional computer or console games. Mobile games can be developed much quicker.

This is the ideal, but it may not apply to all participants (Kerr, 2020), and organizers might have different goals (Fowler & Khosmood, 2023). The game jam usually has a theme to help inspire and direct participants. There is no need to prove commercial potential or what a finished game would look like. On the other hand, an accelerator aims to fast track and test commercial ideas.

For example, I participated along with several members of the Quarry in a weekend game jam with the theme of "repair." My team interpreted this to mean emotional repair (although our game was so underdeveloped that this wasn't clear to the audience). One Quarry team interpreted this as mechanical repair (in a very polished looking game), and the other imagined physical health repair (in a clever concept with funky art). One final thing to note about game jams. In the region, the biggest financial deal came for a game conceived during a game jam.[2]

1.3 INNOVATION SPACES

Interorganizational spaces and places are physical locations where multiple organizations interact. Trade shows and conferences are examples of temporary interorganizational spaces. In this book, I am interested in the more permanent spaces—ones where people from different organizations interact on a regular or daily basis. Spaces are important for creatives and entrepreneurs, whether science parks (Xia et al., 2020) or Fablabs (Papavlasopoulou et al., 2017). In video game development, spatial proximity (Plum & Hassink, 2014) or creative clustering (Darchen & Tremblay, 2015) can positively influence certain areas of video game development. Three types of interorganizational spaces are relevant to this ethnography: incubators, accelerators, and coworking spaces.

1.3.1 Accelerators

Accelerators are a new organizational form, first appearing in 2005 (Cohen et al., 2019a). Accelerators are generally defined by a formal time-constrained institutional structure with regulation playing a greater role. There is significant overlap between incubators and accelerators (Cohen,

---

[2] In my opinion, the success in securing a publishing owed more to marketing and social media than to the game jam process. BAT appeared to believe the important aspect was the game jam.

2013; Pauwels et al., 2016). Accelerators are defined by three aspects: intensity, cohorts, and duration. As the name suggests, accelerators aim to accelerate business or technological development. They do this through intensive knowledge transfer. Selection is highly competitive, and participants are usually grouped into cohorts (Cohen, 2013; Clayton et al., 2018). The cohorts enter for a fixed time in the program, usually limited to a few months (Cohen, 2013; Pauwels et al., 2016).

The structure of an accelerator can play a significant role in the program. Due to the condensed temporal period, there is less opportunity to make changes to the program—at least within cohorts. The literature usually treats accelerators as having a relatively static organizational structure (Pauwels et al., 2016). For example, Cohen et al. (2019b) discuss different structural choices accelerators make—when to provide mentoring, how participants should share information, and how much to standardized. Even under the topic of whether to standardized or tailor the program to participants, the choice is made in advance. The literature tends to look at how accelerators influence participants (e.g. Hallen et al., 2020) or how accelerator participants might affect each other (e.g. knowledge sharing in Cohen et al., 2019a). There seems to be a general lack of appreciation on how accelerator participants might influence the accelerator. One contribution of this book is to show how, at least in a new accelerator, various social actors interact to shape an interorganizational space.

1.3.2 Incubators

Incubators have evolved over a much longer history than either coworking spaces or accelerators (Leblebici & Shah, 2004). Like other spaces, "no two incubators are exactly the same" (Cohen, 2013, p. 20), but three aspects stand out: development, support, and legitimacy. First, incubators nurture nascent companies until they can survive on their own. There is no predefined exit timeline (Clayton et al., 2018; Cohen, 2013). Second, incubators do this by providing business support. They offer preferential access to formal networking, mentors, and resources (Bruneel et al., 2012; Bueno Merino & Duchemin, 2022). Finally, participation in an incubator confers legitimacy (Leblebici & Shah, 2004; Bruneel et al., 2012).

The incubator model typically offers a long runway. Participating companies may be involved in an incubator for years. Bruneel et al. (2012) found a five-year average for companies listed as first or second-generation maturity. Companies utilized different services (infrastructure, business support, and access to networks) over time (Bruneel et al., 2012). Incubators may focus on the developing the companies, individuals, or projects. Participants in the incubator GameBCN entered with specific video game projects with the goal to develop them over the course of the six-month program (González-Piñero, 2021). The case of a women-only incubator illustrates the difference in structure and tactics (Bueno Merino & Duchemin, 2022). Participants were involved in two phases—deciding on starting a business and creating a business plan. The first phase focused on encouraging "entrepreneurial intention" rather than business skills. Likewise, a women-only video game incubator focused on progress, feedback, and troubleshooting during the sessions (Fisher & Harvey, 2013). All game development work occurred outside of the incubator.

1.3.3 Coworking Spaces

Coworking spaces are a relatively new interorganizational structure, first appearing in San Francisco in 2005 (Spinuzzi, 2012). Coworking spaces are generally defined by a weak structure governed more by norms than regulation. Descriptions of coworking spaces tend to emphasize three aspects: flexibility, community, and collaboration. First, coworking spaces offer flexibility in various ways: membership, space, time, and interaction (Spinuzzi, 2012; Fuzi, 2015; Clayton et al., 2018). Second, coworking spaces feature an informal community of professionals that would not otherwise work in the same place (Spinuzzi, 2012; Garrett et al., 2017). Third, multiple descriptions refer to potential collaboration between members (Bouncken et al., 2018). Others note this does not arise naturally and often requires 'curators' (Fuzi, 2015; Clayton et al., 2018).

Coworking spaces do not necessarily support innovation. That is the main differentiator from incubators and accelerators. They are primarily office spaces (Clayton et al., 2018). Innovation, if there is any, is the prerogative of individual companies. Individual and companies use coworking spaces for a variety of reasons, such as cheaper office space, lack of a home office, and social connections (Spinuzzi, 2012; Garrett et al., 2017). The space owners rarely have a stake in the member companies. So why are coworking spaces often discussed alongside incubators and accelerators?

Modern accelerators, and to a lesser extent incubators, often house participants in a coworking space (Cohen et al., 2019b). BAT did so with the Digital Quarry. The more accurate term might be shared office space since accelerators are diametrically opposed to coworking spaces. There are two arguments for why the Quarry featured a coworking space rather than a shared office. First, the Quarry was housed within a larger coworking building. Quarry members were also members of the Gymnasium. They had the same access and rights as regular paying members of the Gymnasium. This also meant they might interact with coworking space members outside the Quarry but in the same building. Second, the Quarry was physically set up like a coworking space. There were no offices, no cubicles, and no assigned desks. It was open plan—as far as historic buildings allowed.

1.3.4 Labeling by Participants

Much of the literature seems to assume if a place is defined one way by the owners or organizers, then that is it. Ethnography values the terms informants use. At the same time, using a term does not guarantee informants agree on the definition. In the case of the Quarry, this would have meant that how BAT defined the Quarry as a space was the type of space it would be. This is not the situation in practice. In their study of a Toronto incubator, Harvey and Fisher (2013, p. 377) found the incubator "focused on the development of the ideal worker, fully amenable to the flexible, under- or non-paid labor conditions of these industries." In the Quarry case, actors resisted such pressure, either actively or by ignoring rules and demands. Various actors, with different power and resources, worked to shape the Quarry into their desired space. Social actors' work crosses collaboration, competition, and independence. Consequently, actors create simultaneous spaces within the same place. Toward the end of the fieldwork, the future of the Quarry suggested a formalizing of this hybrid nature. It is unlikely this outcome would occur without the various and different work of multiple actors.

How the Quarry was defined and labeled by BAT has policy implications. Defining the Quarry as an experimental space offered flexibility in management and planning. For example, the introduction of the rapid prototyping program (see Chap. 3), while unexpected, was accepted after initial resistance. The success of the pilot program led to a later iteration (run remotely during COVID-19 pandemic). On the other hand, the vague and interchangeable use of labels such as incubator, accelerator, and coworking space created confusion among participants as to the exact purpose of the Quarry.

Labels are important in generating construct clarity and identity around the spaces of a place. Labeling a place as a certain type of space creates expectations from participants. If the expectations are not met, actors may engage in work to remake the space. Additionally, the previous experience of participants with similarly labeled spaces factors into their perception of what a label means. For example, several Quarry participants had previously participated in another "accelerator"; therefore, they entered with certain expectations of the operations. The program would be "hands on" or require copious paperwork. Some found the Quarry to be like other accelerators, but others did not. The initial labeling of the space as for video game developers provided an identity anchor for many companies. Video game development was the core identity of the place. If the Quarry was open to companies in tangential industries, like animation, it might muddle the clarity and identity of the space.

1.3.5 Video Game Innovation Spaces Around the World

This section presents an overview of video game incubators and accelerators around the world. I have ignored solely coworking spaces (like the Indies Workshop in Seattle) since these involve companies paying for participation. The information is current as of July 2024. The information has been gathered from public sources (e.g. websites). This is not an exhaustive list. It is for informational purposes only (not an endorsement). How might this section be used?

Video game professionals and students can use this information in their search for opportunities. This can be a starting point if a team is interested in exploring the incubator/accelerator route. The two main points. First, there are many opportunities out there for video game developers interested in programs to accelerate their development, work beside other developers, or to receive some pre-publisher funding. Second, the programs may run better or worse than the Digital Quarry. The advantage you have in reading this book is knowing that structure does not define everything, things can change at any time, people's experiences are different, and experience is required to know if the format fits you.

Academics should skip this section. Conceptual discussion resumes with "crux events" in the next section (Sect. 1.4).

The above table illustrates several things. First, there is variety. There are incubators and accelerators for video games all around the world. They are funded by different sources (public, private, hybrid). Most focus on

Table 1.4 Selected list of incubators and accelerators for video games

Name	Country	Funding source	Founded	Time	Provides funding	Payback	Pitch
AIE Incubator	Australia	Public	b	b	None	None	Only for graduates of management program
Baby Ghost	Canada	Private	2021	6 mon.	$25,000	None	Worker-centric
Basecamp Malta	Malta	Semi-public	b	b	None	None	Superior office space
Brinc	Hong Kong	Private	b	b	$200,000	4% + $35,000	Cutting edge ideas
Burnout Game Ventures	USA	Private	2014	10 mon.	b	b	"Prepare to risk everything."
Cologne Game Lab	Germany	Semi-public	2014[a]	3 years	None	None	University support
Core Labs Game Accelerator	USA	Private	2015	6 mon.	None	None	Online business training for game studios.
DAE Studios	Belgium	Private	2014	b	b	b	Spinoff of university applies science course
Digital Dragons	Poland	Public	2018[a]	b	80,000 PLN	None	"Take your game to the next level"
Dutch Game Garden	The Netherlands	Public	2008	Flex	None	None	Monthly business training for game developers.
F2P Campus	Spain	Semi-public	2018	3 mon.	Travel / housing	None	Free-to-play games
Flanders Game Hub	Belgium	Hybrid	b	3+ mon.	None	None	Expanding the Flemish market

(*continued*)

Table 1.4 (continued)

Name	Country	Funding source	Founded	Time	Provides funding	Payback	Pitch
Game BCN	Spain	Hybrid	2014	6 mon.	None	None	Knowledge transfer via production and business modules.
Game Founders	Estonia	Semi-public[a]	2012	3 mon.	25,000 Euros	9% equity	Knowledge transfer via extensive mentoring.
GAME.EUS	Spain	Semi-public	1988	[b]	None	None	Basque Country development
GameFounders KSA	Saudi Arabia / Jordan	Public	2022	12 mon.	150,000 SAR	None	Game jam, incubator, accelerator
GameHub	Israel	Semi-public	2022	3 mon.	80,000 NIS	None	Community space and incubator
GameJamPLus	Global	Private	[b]	3–6 mon.	None	None	Multi-stage from game jam to accelerator
Games Incubator SA	Poland	Private	[b]	[b]	[b]	[b]	Producer and publisher. Also runs Game Jams and Unity school.
Games Lift	Germany	Public	[b]	12 mon.	15,000 Euro	None	Supports development and marketing
Games London	UK	Semi-public	2020	3 mon.	None	None	Assisting existing developers
Global Top Round	Global	Private	2015	6 mon.	$40,000	[b]	Accelerating existing games to the next level
Google Play Indie Game Accelerator	Global	Private	[b]	10 weeks	None	None	Mentorship and education
Helika	Canada	Private	[b]	6 mon.	[b]	[b]	Focus on Web 3 gaming
Indie Game Incubator	Japan	Semi-public	2021[a]	3 mon.	[b]	[b]	Japan's first indie incubator

Name	Country	Type	Year	Duration	Funding	Equity	Focus
IndieLabs	UK	Semi-public	2022	3 mon.	None	None	Early to mid-stage
Lawrence Tech	Canada	University	2023	8 mon.	None	None	Focused on Unreal engine
Level Up	Saudi Arabia	Private	b	12 mon.	b	b	Requires existing MVP
Madrid Game Cluster	Spain	Public	2021	b	None	None	A cluster with heavy e-sports focus
Narwhal	Malta	Private	2023	3–4 mon.	$300,000	b	Bridging pre-seed and series A funding
NYU Game Center Incubator	USA	Private	2014	12 mon.	$15,000	None	Transforming projects into games.
Pixelles	Canada	Non-profit	b	2 mon.	None	None	Helping "marginalized gender" people make games.
Prismo	Croatia	Public	2017	b	130,000 HRK	None	Access to tech equipment
RIT Magic	USA	Semi-public	b	3 mon.[a]	$10,000	None	Assisting indie developers
RNG Foundry	UK	Private	2016	b	b	b	Focus on casino games
Scaffold	Canada	Hybrid	2020	b	b	None	Cohorts of game producers
SpielFabrique	Spain, Germany	Public	2016	5 mon.	None	None	Exclusive events and training on managing the business side.
The Game Circle	Türkiye	Private	2021	b	b	b	Incubator, publisher, and investor
The Octopus	USA	Private	b	b	b	b	Sleath company. By invite only.
Tranzfuser	UK	Public	2016	3 mon.	7,500 GBP	None	Grow from graduate to professional.

(*continued*)

Table 1.4 (continued)

Name	Country	Funding source	Founded	Time	Provides funding	Payback	Pitch
Ubisoft	Canada	Private	b	flex	Up to $500k	2.5 times investment	Multiple funding options. Access to AAA support.
Ubisoft	Germany, Switzerland, Austria	Private	2021[a]	12 mon.	< 10,000 Euros	None	Access to AAA support and mentoring for a single winner.
UKIE Creative Enterprise Games	UK	Semi-public	2020	6 mon.	b	b	Focus on art and storytelling
UKIE Mobile Games Growth	UK	Hybrid	b	6 mon.	None	None	In partnership with Barclays
Wulum	Global	Private	2014	b	b	b	Individual consulting

[a] Best guess based on website
[b] Unknown

mentoring or coaching. Many offer funding, or at least potential for funding. Second, there are two general mission types. The ones that include some type of public funding usually are interested in growing the local industries video game ecosystem, organizations, labor, and so on. This is similar to BAT in this book. Private funders, on the other hand, are looking to make a return on their investment, obviously. BAT does this with some of their funding in the form of loans repayable if the project turns a profit. Third, the regional development programs are more likely to include a physical office, like the Digital Quarry. Virtual-only programs probably considered a physical office to be an unnecessary expense or a limit on potential applicants.

1.4 Crux Events

An ethnographic narrative comprises the bulk of this book. The narrative is framed around *crux events*. Crux is derived from the Greek and essentially means "potentially critical." I define a crux event as an event that at the time *seems* like it may significantly impact social actors and spaces. There are three important parts to the definition. First, *event* implies action and process. Something happened. People experienced it. It does not occur in isolation. At the same time, events are discrete with a clearly defined beginning and end. That is not the case here. There is ambiguity—and a lot of it depends on your perspective. Second, *seem* speaks to the experience of the present. In relation to the present, the future possesses potentiality and uncertainty. Things may happen, or they may not. Knowing the ending can influence writing about the past. By using seem, I attempt a perspective that adheres closer to what it was like to be there. I try to put the reader "in the room where it happens" (borrowing from Lin-Manual Miranda in *Hamilton*). Third, *significantly impact* establishes relevance and importance. Simply put, it matters. I have a thousand interesting stories and anecdotes, but few of them were critical to changing life in the Digital Quarry. There is of course value in researching the everyday experiences of people. Most days in the Quarry, people went about their daily work. I wrote an amalgamated "day in the life" in Chap. 2 of my thesis (Gidley, 2021a). But how did these daily routines come about? They were developed and influenced by crux events. Over 12 months of fieldwork in the Digital Quarry, I identified six crux events. Each chapter presents a series of scenes around each event. Events are presented *in situ* as a process in interorganizational development.

In process research (Langley, 1999), the basic form is before-during-after with a heavy focus on the during. While variance research explains the difference between situation A and situation B, process research explains how we started at A, went through something, and ended up at B. This book will argue that crux events and reactions are things that lead from situation A to situation B. In the context of process theorizing, the basic form is current situation (before), crux event and reaction (during), and outcome (after). Figure 1.1 visualizes the framework. I will develop this framework further in Chap. 1. In terms of the ethnography (Chaps. 2–6), I focus heavily on the crux events and reactions. The outcomes can often be seen in later events and chapters. The confined space and time allowed for seeing a series of crux events and their impact over a limited period. The ethnography presents a single spatial-temporal scale (one year in the Quarry), but the concept of crux events can be applied at different scales, like Russian dolls. Take the space race as an example. We could consider crux events in the decades-long global space race between the United States and the USSR, or we could consider a smaller scale such as NASA's attempt to have an astronaut orbit the earth for the first time. Each scale will provide different insight.

It may help to quickly compare crux events to three close cousins: event system theory, critical junctures, and critical events. Event system theory focuses on salient events—ones that meaningfully impact organizations (Morgeson et al., 2015). Events become critical via strength, space, and time. While acknowledging the issue of retrospective definitions, event system theory is concerned with impactful events. Therefore, it lacks the potentiality of crux events. Critical events, or "sparks," are actions that may impact the future (Dorobantu et al., 2017). They may not cascade into something impactful. This aligns with the potentiality of crux events. As utilized by Dorobantu et al. (2017), critical events are examined retrospectively thereby limiting the present temporal perspective. Critical junctures are moments when there is stronger possibly that choices will substantially change things (Capoccia & Kelemen, 2007). Based in path-dependence theory, the focus is on social actors' choices and the juncture

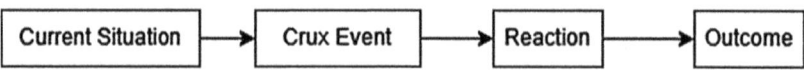

Fig. 1.1 Basic crux event framework

is defined historically. As this ethnography will show, crux events do not necessitate certain reactions or outcomes.

Finally, the main argument of this book is that accelerating creativity and developing a proto-institution hinge on handling crux events properly. Essentially, the book argues for a dynamic, precarious, and uncertain view of innovation programs/spaces and the experience of acceleration on participants. This is tied back to potential critical events as deciding what direction it all goes.

The following chapters present six crux events in a one-year period of the Digital Quarry.

- Chapter 2: BAT introduces a new second cohort of companies to the Quarry.
- Chapter 3: the structure of the Quarry shifts from incubator to accelerator.
- Chapter 4: the founding Quarry manager quits thereby leaving a void.
- Chapter 5: BAT pushes the Quarry into crisis by changing promised funding.
- Chapter 6: a new Quarry manager begins and plans a redesign of the Quarry.
    - The chapter ends with the existential crisis of a global pandemic.
- Chapter 7 presents the practical lessons.
- Chapter 8 develops the theoretical concept of crux events—types, reactions, and outcomes.

References

Abanazir, C. (2019). Institutionalisation in E-sports. *Sport, Ethics and Philosophy, 13*(2), 117–131.

Blake, J. (2019, January 6). How the UK became a major player in the gaming world, BBC. Retrieved from https://www.bbc.co.uk/news/newsbeat-46757989.

Bouncken, R. B., Laudien, S. M., Fredrich, V., & Görmar, L. (2018). Coopetition in coworking-spaces: Value creation and appropriation tensions in an entrepreneurial space. *Review of Managerial Science, 12*, 385–410. https://doi.org/10.1007/s11846-017-0267-7

Bruneel, J., Ratinho, T., Clarysse, B., & Groen, A. J. (2012). The evolution of business incubators: Comparing demand and supply of business incubation services across different incubator generations. *Technovation, 32*(2), 110–121. https://doi.org/10.1016/j.technovation.2011.11.003

Bueno Merino, P., & Duchemin, M. (2022). Contribution of Psychological Entrepreneurial Support to the Strengthening of Female Entrepreneurial Intention in a Women-Only Incubator. *M@n@gement, 25*(4), 64–79. https://doi.org/10.37725/mgmt.v25.4556

Cabras, I., Goumagias, N. D., Fernandes, K., Cowling, P., Li, F., Kudenko, D., Devlin, S., & Nucciarelli, A. (2017). Exploring survival rates of companies in the UK video-games industry: An empirical study. *Technological Forecasting and Social Change, 117*, 305–314.

Capoccia, G., & Kelemen, R. D. (2007). The study of critical junctures: Theory, narrative, and counterfactuals in historical institutionalism. *World Politics, 59*(3), 341–369.

Carpenter, M., Daidj, N., & Moreno, C. (2014). Game console manufacturers: The end of sustainable competitive advantage? *Communications and Strategies*, (94), 39–60.

Casper, S., & Storz, C. (2017). Bounded careers in creative industries: Surprising patterns in video games. *Industry and Innovation, 24*(3), 213–248.

Clayton, P., Feldman, M., & Lowe, N. (2018). Behind the scenes: Intermediary organizations that facilitate science commercialization through entrepreneurship. *Academy of Management Perspectives, 32*, 104–124. https://doi.org/10.5465/amp.2016.0133

Cohen, S. (2013). What do accelerators do? Insights from incubators and angels. *Innovations: Technology, Governance, Globalization, 8*(3–4), 19–25.

Cohen, S., Fehder, D. C., Hochberg, Y. V., & Murray, F. (2019a). The design of startup accelerators. *Research Policy, 48*(7), 1781–1797.

Cohen, S., Bingham, C. B., & Hallen, B. L. (2019b). The role of accelerator designs in mitigating bounded rationality in new ventures. *Administrative Science Quarterly, 64*(4), 810–854. https://doi.org/10.1177/0001839218782131

Comunian, R., Faggian, A., & Jewell, S. (2015). Digital technology and creative arts career patterns in the UK creative economy. *Journal of Education and Work, 28*(4), 346–368.

Darchen, S., & Tremblay, D. (2015). Policies for creative clusters: A comparison between the video game industries in Melbourne and Montreal. *European Planning Studies, 23*(2), 311–331. https://doi.org/10.1080/09654313.2013.865712

DCMS. (1998). *A new cultural framework*. HMSO.

Dorobantu, S., Henisz, W. J., & Nartey, L. (2017). Not all sparks light a fire: Stakeholder and shareholder reactions to critical events in contested markets. *Administrative Science Quarterly, 62*(3), 561–597.
Fisher, S. J., & Harvey, A. (2013). Intervention for inclusivity: Gender politics and indie game development. *Loading..., 7*(11).
Fowler, A., & Khosmood, F. (Eds.). (2023). *Game jams-history, technology, and organisation*. Springer International Publishing.
Fuzi, A. (2015). Co-working spaces for promoting entrepreneurship in sparse regions: The case of South Wales. *Regional Studies, Regional Science, 2*(1), 462–469. https://doi.org/10.1080/21681376.2015.1072053
García-Sánchez, P., Mora, A. M., Castillo, P. A., & Pérez, I. J. (2019). A bibliometric study of the research area of videogames using Dimensions.ai database. *Procedia Computer Science, 162*, 737–744.
Garnham, N. (2005). From cultural to creative industries. *International Journal of Cultural Policy, 11*(1), 15–29.
Garrett, L. E., Spreitzer, G. M., & Bacevice, P. A. (2017). Co-constructing a sense of community at work: The emergence of community in coworking spaces. *Organization Studies, 38*(6), 821–842. https://doi.org/10.1177/0170840616685354
Gaudl, S. E., Nelson, M. J., Colton, S., Saunders, R., Powley, E. J., Ferrer, B. P., Ivey, P., & Cook, M. (2018). Rapid game jams with fluidic games: A user study & design methodology. *Entertainment Computing, 27*, 1–9.
Gidley, D. (2021a). *An ethnographic study of institutional work in a creative proto-institutional place*. Doctoral dissertation, Queen's University Belfast.
Gong, H., & Hassink, R. (2017). Exploring the clustering of creative industries. *European Planning Studies, 25*(4), 583–600.
González-Piñero, M. (2021). How to launch new talent into the video game market? The case of GameBCN. In REDINE (Coord.), *Medios digitales y metodologías docentes: Mejorar la educación desde un abordaje integral* (pp. 165–174). Adaya Press.
Guevara-Villalobos, O. (2013). *Cultural production and politics of the digital games industry: The case of independent game production*. Doctoral dissertation, University of Edinburgh.
Hallen, B. L., Cohen, S. L., & Bingham, C. B. (2020). Do accelerators work? If so, how? *Organization Science, 31*(2), 378–414.
Harvey, A., & Fisher, S. (2013). Making a name in games. *Information, Communication & Society, 16*(3), 362–380. https://doi.org/10.1080/1369118X.2012.756048
Hausmann, A., & Heinze, A. (2016). Entrepreneurship in the cultural and creative industries: Insights from an emergent field. *Artivate, 5*, 7–22. https://doi.org/10.1353/artv.2016.0005

Høvig, Ø. S. (2016). Co-evolutionary dynamics and institutions: Innovation in a guild community in Norway. *Norsk Geografisk Tidsskrift - Norwegian Journal of Geography, 70*, 152–161.

Izushi, H., & Aoyama, Y. (2006). Industry evolution and cross-sectoral skill transfers: A comparative analysis of the video game industry in Japan, the United States, and the United Kingdom. *Environment and Planning A: Economy and Space, 38*(10), 1843–1861. https://doi.org/10.1068/a37205

Johns, J. (2006). Video games production networks: Value capture, power relations and embeddedness. *Journal of Economic Geography, 6*(2), 151–180.

Johnson, R. S. (2013). Toward greater production diversity: Examining social boundaries at a video game studio. *Games and Culture, 8*(3), 136–160.

Johnson, M. R., & Woodcock, J. (2019). 'It's like the gold rush': The lives and careers of professional video game streamers on Twitch.tv. *Information, Communication & Society, 22*(3), 336–351.

Jørgensen, K. (2019). Newcomers in a global industry: Challenges of a Norwegian game company. *Games and Culture, 14*(6), 660–679. https://doi.org/10.1177/1555412017723265

Kennedy, H. W. (2018). Game jam as feminist methodology: The affective labors of intervention in the ludic economy. *Games and Culture, 13*(7), 708–727. https://doi.org/10.1177/1555412018764992

Kerr, A. (2020). Decoding and recoding game jams and independent game-making spaces for diversity and inclusion. In *Independent videogames* (pp. 29–42). Routledge.

Langley, A. (1999). Strategies for theorizing from process data. *The Academy of Management Review, 24*(4), 691–710.

Leblebici, H., & Shah, N. (2004). The birth, transformation and regeneration of business incubators as new organisational forms: Understanding the interplay between organisational history and organisational theory. *Business History, 46*(3), 353–380. https://doi.org/10.1080/0007679042000219175a

Lee, M. (2015). Fostering connectivity: A social network analysis of entrepreneurs in creative industries. *International Journal of Cultural Policy, 21*(2), 139–152. https://doi.org/10.1080/10286632.2014.891021

Locke, K. (2011). Field research practice in management and organization studies: Reclaiming its tradition of discovery. *The Academy of Management Annals, 5*(1), 613–652.

Mac, S. D. (2014). Multiplayer games: Tax, copyright, consumers and the video game industries. *European Journal of Law and Technology, 5*(3).

Malone, N. (2021). *Temporality, selfhood and sociality: Experiences of the emergent indie game developer*. Doctoral dissertation, Edge Hill University.

Mikami, K., Nakamura, Y., Ito, A., Kawashima, M., Watanabe, T., Kishimoto, Y., & Kondo, K. (2016). Effectiveness of game jam-based iterative program for game production in Japan. *Computers & Graphics, 61*, 1–10. https://doi.org/10.1016/j.cag.2016.07.006

Morgeson, F. P., Mitchell, T. R., & Liu, D. (2015). Event system theory: An event-oriented approach to the organizational sciences. *Academy of Management Review, 40*(4), 515–537.

Nieborg, D. B. (2015). Crushing candy: The free-to-play game in its connective commodity form. *Social Media + Society.* https://doi.org/10.1177/2056305115621932

Papavlasopoulou, S., Giannakos, M. N., & Jaccheri, L. (2017). Empirical studies on the maker movement, a promising approach to learning: A literature review. *Entertainment Computing, 18*, 57–78.

Parker, F., Whitson, J. R., & Simon, B. (2018). Megabooth: The cultural intermediation of indie games. *New Media & Society, 20*(5), 1953–1972.

Parkman, I. D., Holloway, S. S., & Sebastiao, H. (2012). Creative industries: Aligning entrepreneurial orientation and innovation capacity. *Journal of Research in Marketing and Entrepreneurship, 14*(1), 95–114. https://doi.org/10.1108/14715201211246823

Patten, T. (2016). "Creative?"... "Entrepreneur?" – Understanding the Creative Industries Entrepreneur. *Artivate, 5*(2), 23–42. https://doi.org/10.1353/artv.2016.0006

Pauwels, C., Clarysse, B., Wright, M., & Van Hove, J. (2016). Understanding a new generation incubation model: The accelerator. *Technovation, 50–51*, 13–24. https://doi.org/10.1016/j.technovation.2015.09.003

Phillips, T. (2015). "Don't clone my indie game, bro": Informal cultures of video-game regulation in the independent sector. *Cultural Trends, 24*(2), 143–153.

Plum, O., & Hassink, R. (2014). Knowledge bases, innovativeness and competitiveness in creative industries: The case of Hamburg's video game developers. *Regional Studies, Regional Science, 1*(1), 248–268. https://doi.org/10.1080/21681376.2014.967803

Pottie-Sherman, Y., & Lynch, N. (2019). Gaming on the edge: Mobile labour and global talent in Atlantic Canada's video game industry. *The Canadian Geographer / Le Géographe canadien, 63*, 425–439.

Rajani, N. B., Weth, D., Mastellos, N., & Filippidis, F. T. (2019). Use of gamification strategies and tactics in mobile applications for smoking cessation: A review of the UK mobile app market. *BMJ Open, 9*, e027883. https://doi.org/10.1136/bmjopen-2018-027883

Ruffino, P., & Woodcock, J. (2020). Game workers and the empire: Unionisation in the UK video game industry. *Games and Culture.* https://doi.org/10.1177/1555412020947096

Scarbrough, H., Panourgias, N. S., & Nandhakumar, J. (2015). Developing a relational view of the organizing role of objects: A study of the innovation process in computer games. *Organization Studies, 36*(2), 197–220. https://doi.org/10.1177/0170840614557213

Spinuzzi, C. (2012). Working alone together: Coworking as emergent collaborative activity. *Journal of Business and Technical Communication, 26*(4), 399–441. https://doi.org/10.1177/1050651912444070

Storz, C., Riboldazzi, F., & John, M. (2015). Mobility and innovation: A cross-country comparison in the video games industry. *Research Policy, 44*(1), 121–137. https://doi.org/10.1016/j.respol.2014.07.015

Taylor, M. (2020). *UK games industry census: Understanding diversity in the UK games industry workforce (Research Report UKIE)*. Retrieved from UKIE website: https://ukie.org.uk/resources/uk-games-industry-census-2021

Thompson, D., & Hebblethwaite, L. (2020). *Think global, create local: The regional economic impact of the UK games industry (Research report UKIE)*. Retrieved from UKIE website: https://ukie.org.uk/resources/think-global-create-local-the-regional-economic-impact-of-the-uk-games-industry

Tsang, D. (2021). Innovation in the British video game industry since 1978. *The Business History Review, 95*(3), 543–567.

UKIE. (2018). *UK video games industry fact sheet* [white paper]. The Association for UK Interactive Entertainment.

Vervoort, J. M. (2019). New frontiers in futures games: Leveraging game sector developments. *Futures, 105*, 174–186. https://doi.org/10.1016/j.futures.2018.10.005

Webber, N. (2020). The Britishness of 'British Video Games'. *International Journal of Cultural Policy, 26*(2), 135–149. https://doi.org/10.1080/10286632.2018.1448804

Whitson, J. R. (2020). What can we learn from studio studies ethnographies?: A "Messy" account of game development materiality, learning, and expertise. *Games and Culture, 15*, 266–288. https://doi.org/10.1177/1555412018783320

Xia, S., Xiong, Y., Zhang, M., Cornford, J., Liu, Y., Lim, M. K., Cao, D., & Chen, F. (2020). Reducing the resource acquisition costs for returnee entrepreneurs: Role of Chinese national science parks. *International Journal of Entrepreneurial Behavior & Research, 26*(7), 1627–1657.

CHAPTER 2

New Players: Introducing Newcomers Leads to Rumblings

*Drawing by PhDcartoon (illustration used with permission)

2.1 Introduction

In this chapter

- The ethnographer joins the Quarry and deals with identity issues.
- The new cohort of companies tries to fit in.
- The original cohort deals with trust issues.
- The observers attempt change and fall short.

2.1.1 Conceptual Development

The *introduction of newcomers* is identified as a crux event. It is not all newcomers. An individual company hiring an additional person or BAT adding a new intern does not feel potentially significant. On the other hand, introducing a new cohort of companies feels different for several reasons. Increasing from seven to ten companies means more complexity. Intergenerational knowledge and dynamics come into play. Moving beyond the original cohort also signals a desire to create something lasting as opposed to a one-off event.

2.1.2 Practical Lessons

As you read this chapter, consider the following practical lessons:

1. First impressions (sometimes) reveal much.
2. *Imposter syndrome.* In this case, it is a PhD student entering the field for the first time as an ethnographer. It could be starting your first job in video game development. It could be entering an accelerator after a successful application.
3. In a shared space, people want to find their place. Often it starts with a shared identity, such as indie video game developers.
4. Someone probably wants to steal your game idea (if it's good). It's probably not the person next to you. It probably won't happen until after it's successful.
5. A change in cohort *should* have been a good time to make other changes. Why did it fail?

2.2 Ethnographer

I present my perspective first—that of a PhD student and novice ethnographer. Conveniently, my perspective serves to introduce the reader to the Quarry and the digital game industry. I was a newcomer to both. As such, I did not fit squarely in an identity box. In contrast, the game developers in the second cohort, and any visiting industry consultants, clearly had specific industry roles. Trust was an issue. What was my role? I am sure that Holly was not the only one to think I was a "spy" for BAT—something she only confessed to me after ten months. Later, the reader might notice the similarities with the experience of the two BAT interns (one experienced in the industry, and one not).

The Gymnasium is a renovated concrete building built in a post-WWII architectural style popular in England. Renovation brought it into the twenty-first century. Krieger told me, "I've worked in offices for big companies that haven't even been as nice as this to be honest." Asphalt parking lots and modern glass and steel buildings tower over the old community gym. The heavy front doors lead to an entryway. On the left, the first keycard locked door leads to the main coworking space. The swinging doors straight ahead lead to another waiting room. A single piece of old exercise equipment from a bygone era sits on display. No one uses it. A second keycard locked door leads to the north side and further on, the Quarry. An old avant-garde documentary had been filmed here. Collins showed me a short video clip once. Few of the developers knew of this forgotten history. They were too young.

On my first day, I tried the north side door. It was locked. I know it leads to the Quarry since I attended an event sponsored by an English industry association a few months ago. I was a couple minutes early at most. No one was around. I realized I didn't have the Quarry manager's phone number. Mobile reception was spotty, but I managed to email him. I waited outside for what felt like forever, refreshing my email.

A few minutes later, heels clicking on tile flooring, Hera appeared from behind the locked doors. She wore a blue "power suit" and oversized hoop earrings. After some awkward excuses and explanations, we went through the coworking side to a six-seat coffee shop in the building. She ordered a flat white. I got the same having no idea what it was. I figured it was easiest just to copy. She paid. As we waited, Hera mentioned that she had been in contact with the local university about student placements for a marketing internship. We took the coffees back to the north side and settled into the keycard accessed the Playroom—one of the three extra rooms Quarry members had right of first booking on. It was dark (as always). We sat down and the interrogation began, or maybe it was the darkness making the conversation more atmospheric than it should have been.

Hera:	Do you have a contract for the research, or would you be willing to sign one? Like a release form.
Ethnographer:	I don't have one, but sure.[1]
Hera:	Do you have an informed consent form?
Ethnographer:	Sure. I can email it to you.[2]
Hera:	The Quarry operates under Chatham House rules.[3]
Ethnographer:	I plan to make everything anonymous and won't reveal confidential information.
Hera:	What can you deliver to these companies?
Ethnographer:	I'm not doing action research. It is participant observation. I can help out and offer my services, but I don't want to influence the interorganizational outcome.[4]

Hera pitched me on what she wanted: go over the developers' business plans by "tearing them down." She wanted to accelerate the process. She believed they were mostly creative types, and only a few had business acumen. She said they needed to focus more on selling and the retail side. Hera believed that unless a game was featured in the app store, it would get lost. After her pitch, and my non-committal agreement, we settled on a 12-month deal. Hera would introduce me at an event on Friday.

Hera:	I need you to sign some sort of contract so that BAT has the option of kicking you out if needed. Not that I anticipate that, but I need to protect BAT.

She never did have me sign anything.

Hera took me down the short hallway, passed the bathrooms. The Quarry was oddly quiet despite most of the computers having someone

---

[1] *Aside*—Whatever it took to get access.
[2] *Aside*—I rushed to make one up immediately after the meeting.
[3] *Aside*—Like Vegas—what happens in the Quarry stays in the Quarry. Although at the time I had no idea what this was. I gathered the general gist.
[4] *Aside*—How naive, like most early career researchers.

sitting in front of them. Most have headphones on. I expected hustle and bustle based on my one time here. That was the event atmosphere, not 11 in the morning on a random Tuesday. Hera showed me to my desk. It was against the far wall. My back would face the rest of the Quarry. There was no chair, so I took the one next to it. There were five empty chairs to my right and three to my left. Hera handed me a white plastic keycard. Nothing identified it, but it allowed me access to the Quarry.

The next day, Hera invited me to the app Basecamp. It appeared to communicate events and information to the members of the Digital Quarry. There were 30 people on it (including me). Hera sent out an announcement of research along with the consent form and information sheet that I made up yesterday.

In summary, I became a member without fanfare. It seemed like I slipped in the backdoor, but as I will show in the next section, my experience was not unusual. This reinforces the "inherently dialogical nature of ethnographic research" (Rodgers, 2007, p. 444). Hera and I negotiated my access as well as my entry into Quarry. She did the introduction like she did others. In my personal narrative, especially in the context of the PhD journey, joining the Digital Quarry was a crux event. For everyone else, including the Quarry as an organization, it was footnote.

Quick Lessons

1. Come prepared. Hera and I were not for our first day. I didn't have her phone number. I didn't have any participant information forms. She didn't have anything for me to sign. Then again, we were both figuring it out along the way.
2. Written agreements are professional. Hera and I began a relationship without any explicit rules. Six months later, she was gone, and I was sitting in front of the BAT committee with nothing proving that I belonged in the Quarry. Written expectations and responsibilities would have made everything clearer (if not easier). Then again, as you will read later, written agreements in the Quarry were rarely followed or enforced.

2.3 New Cohort

In several ways, the new cohort of three companies was "a different beast," according to a mentor, from the existing seven companies. The new companies were newer and smaller companies but run by older individuals coming from non-industry backgrounds. There was an uncertainty of place and an eagerness to connect.

It was day two, and already the second cohort was coming in late. Hera observed, "It's amazing, but no one else from the second cohort is here." In their defense, they were gamers, and it wasn't even noon yet. There was no mention on Basecamp of a new cohort starting right up until the day they started. The Basecamp post had the subject line: "Starting Today! New Cohort!" Several original cohort members reflected on the introduction as follows:

Davy: I heard they were doing interviews. One of my friends interviewed but didn't get in.
Aslani: The first I heard was that the applications were live online. Someone emailed me and asked how best to apply. I was like, 'I have no idea.' It felt rushed. It was just like—surprise! We're bringing in a second cohort because there are not enough butts in the seats.
Titus: I just remember it being rushed. They announced it and then they were here.
Aslani: We didn't do anything for them in advance. There was an induction on the first day. They showed up and asked where to sit? [Shrugging.] We just pointed to the empty seats in the back.

All three companies from the second cohort were seated to my right. An orange post-it note with a woman's name on it slowly peeled above a seat near me. Printer paper–sized sheets spelling "Yerbe," the name of one of the new companies, hung next to it. Neither looked very permanent. The area was certainly the leftovers. Capone, a second cohort member, observed:

> I don't feel like we've got a proper desk if I am honest. The best seats are over there, you know where the first cohort are. They've got the best seats cause they got a desk that kinda faces each other. We're just like a bench on the wall. Facing the wall. It's not as, not as attractive ... it's a small detail,

but I think it's important. You know, instead of everyone kind of facing inwards almost, we're not.... There's a bit of a divide. So that's unfortunate. But I don't know what they can do because the pillars are there.

Over the next few hours, the introductions to my neighbors in the new cohort were quick. We barely exchanged names at first. They all asked if I was part of one of the new companies. When they found out I was not, they went back to talking amongst themselves. For example:

Holly: I think the Queen of Dragons will win the throne.
Capone: I want the Night King to just wipe them all out.

A while later, on my way to get some fresh air, I saw a man sitting on a chair in the entryway wearing a Digital Quarry lanyard. It was Thorne, a member of the second cohort. I barely recognized him, so I apologized. I asked him more about himself. He was the sole person in his company. He had finished one mobile game and had it in pre-release. Not too many people had play tested it. He said he planned to ask the Quarry members to test it for him since he could play it "blindfolded." I didn't offer to playtest, but I assumed that I would at some point. He had started working on the second game. We talked:

Ethnographer: How was the induction ceremony yesterday?[5]
Thorne: Almost half the event was devoted to GDPR [Greater Data Protection Regulation]. I know a lot more about it now. There are fines up to 20 million Euro per instance. Coke has been fined like 80 million Euro for breaches relating to their prize giveaways.

The focus on GDPR reminded me of the 25 or so policy documents Hera had sent me earlier. There was a full presentation on GDPR in addition to the boilerplate policies on discrimination, privacy, conduct, and so on. The Digital Quarry induction sheet was very brief. It listed the terms and conditions of Quarry membership and associated responsibilities (including attending various meetings and making quarterly reports on progress). The rules were rarely, if ever, enforced. In time, most people forgot exactly what they were.

[5] *Aside—I made it sound like a cult or elite group.*

Thorne: I just wanna make games, you know, and it takes money to make games, and it takes a team to make games, and you have to pay the team. That's one of the reasons why I want it to be sustainable. It's just so we can actually hire people in or keep them and literally make games and that'd be a bit of fun.

Capone would echo the theme in talking to a pair of Italian student interns shared by two companies from the first cohort. He explained to them his motivation for joining the Quarry: "I like to play games. In English we say, 'a means to an end.'"

The next morning, I arrived early and spoke to a member of the new cohort alone. She had purple streaks in her hair, glasses, and the only dress on in the room. I asked her about her background. She had planned to go to university in England to study computer animation, but the advisor[6] there said that she would be better off going to the Netherlands. So, she did. At the university, Celeste worked on a game focused on incidental representation. The team never finished it because the programmer got a job at an AAA studio. She just started working on the current project two weeks ago after meeting her boss at a games award show.

Celeste: It's weird working in a two-person team.
Ethnographer: There are several two-person teams in the Quarry.
Celeste: Yeah, but they are together. Partners. I'm freelancing. It's his game. I don't feel the same ownership. But at the same time, with two people, everything you see is my work, so if it's not good looking, everyone will know who did it.

In summary, the second cohort shared an identity with members of the first cohort. They were all gamers even if they were at different stages of being game developers (Phillips, 2015). They were able to make a connection. Identity did not determine motivation—for making games or for being in the Quarry. Some were embracing the opportunity while others were feeling paradoxical about it. The same experience leading to different reactions and outcomes is a key feature of the crux event perspective.

---

[6] A *man*, she says, with what I can only term disgust.

Quick Lessons

3. The second cohort was an afterthought. Their arrival was announced at the last minute. They received the worst seats in the house. For individual members, joining the Quarry was a significant step. The Quarry did not treat them that way.
4. There is a difference between making *a* game and making *your* game. Pride of work should not be confused with ownership. People may feel motivated by working in a small team, but hired hands can jump ship at any minute. Without direct ownership, people are liable to take a better job offer.
5. Game developers are usually gamers first.

2.4 Original Members

I asked Ruby what she thought the purpose of the space was. She replied, "Cooperation, I guess," before adding that she skipped all the meetings. She was just there for the "free desk." She compared it to her previous job at an animation company. They were both quiet, but the main difference was that the animators all had the same schedule. They came in at the same time and took the same lunch breaks. Here, everyone sets their own schedule.

The original members of the Quarry had different reactions to the introduction of the second cohort and the ethnographer. Some went out of their way to welcome the new cohort. Others were distrustful of the ethnographer.

2.4.1 *Original Cohort Welcomes the New Cohort*

When I came back from lunch, Aslani called me over. She introduced me to her team (Titus—designer, Maryann—the artist). She mentioned that she was due to join a research laboratory before backing out to go to the Quarry and make games.

Aslani:	Don't be shy about coming over.
Ethnographer:	I don't want to impede on anyone's space or work.
Hera:	People are not that formal here.

Aslani: I feel weird having new people in the room. I worry about them.

Before I got a chance to ask "how so," Thorne walked by. Aslani stopped him to introduce herself and her team.
Aslani: Have you been to the kitchen at all? You're allowed to use it.

The above story illustrates how some of the original cohort helped the new cohort settle in socially. Another member would later tell me other ways his team helped:

> We've really like mentored a lot of people, especially when the new group came in. We've done a lot of helping those guys with all sorts of stuff, business things that they just don't know. Advice. Technical stuff. You know, most of the teams are using Unity. Some of them don't have the technical skills. They'll have problems. We're able to advise them on that and just things in general like game design stuff, our process.

Other members ignored the introduction of new members. It was possible to treat the new cohort as similar to new hires. For some, it didn't fundamentally change the Quarry. An increase from seven to ten companies was interpreted as a quantitative change and not a qualitative one.

> **Quick Lesson**
>
> 6. Social connections matter. The original cohort may have expressed mixed feelings about the new cohort, but at least some people were willing to make them feel welcome. BAT could have done a couple things differently. They could have informed the original cohort sooner about the new arrivals. They could have utilized the existing members to create a more welcoming atmosphere.

2.4.2 Original Cohort Interrogates the Ethnographer

After lunch, Hera took me over to Noah—a director of one of the original cohort companies. He was absent on my first day. I gave him my research pitch.

Noah:	What information are you going to record?
Ethnographer:	Events and interactions. How things change over time. People's views and feelings about the space.
Hera:	What about anonymity?
Ethnographer:	Yes, I can do that. Even in my notes I am using pseudonyms.
Noah:	The Quarry needs some sort of feedback forum that is anonymous. It can't be the same person complaining every time.
Hera:	I agree that we need something where we can respond immediately to certain issues. Devon's project is more long term.
Noah:	I'm concerned about the information you might record. Like client details and so on.
Ethnographer:	I am not really interested in names.
Noah:	I want to speak to you privately for five minutes.
Hera:	Can Devon listen?
Noah:	Ah … [He hesitates.]
Hera:	I probably shouldn't have put you on the spot.
Noah:	It's about something else.
Ethnographer:	I don't need to. If there is ever anything you don't want me to write down, just let me know.

They left to talk privately. This was the first example of the Quarry members acting as independent companies. They resisted outright or failed to comply with certain requests. They also didn't like surprises, of which there were many in the life of the Quarry.

I wandered over to another member of the first cohort. I introduced myself and explained I was having a hard time figuring out the exact composition of the companies. Wallace explained it, but I was still confused. His company shared freelancers and/or student interns with about three other companies. He was short a person but waiting for the next round of BAT funding before bringing someone in. He thought it would be about six weeks later. He asked about my research:

Wallace:	What are you doing about confidentiality?
Ethnographer:	I'm making everything anonymous with pseudonyms.
Wallace:	Do you have an NDA [non-disclosure agreement] set up with the Quarry or anyone else?

Ethnographer: No. I don't, but I'm okay with it as long as it doesn't interfere with my research.

Wallace: I've had problems in the past. I have multiple NDAs in effect, and I have to be careful what I mention in passing.

The ironic thing is that months later, a member of the first cohort would tell me:

> I overhear Wallace on the phone like doing, like talking big numbers or something … me and [my partner] will be like we need to like get our shit together. It's just competitive in that sense. It's not competitive in the sense of like I found out about this and I'm not going to tell them because I want us to win over them.

Wallace never asked me for a non-disclosure agreement or redaction. He simply redacted himself.

The two company directors offer an interesting contrast. Noah chose to resist disclosing information. Wallace simply redacted himself. At the same time, Wallace didn't seem to worry about the rest of the Quarry overhearing sensitive information. It is interesting that the game developers seemed more wary of non-developers (outsiders, like the ethnographer) than of other developers. It could be explained, as we will see below, that despite working in the same industry and nominally fighting for the same funds, Quarry companies did not see themselves in competition with each other. Many seemed to share the ethos of the indie developer—us against the world (Phillips, 2015).

Quick Lesson

7. Resistance comes in different forms. This is a lesson for the powerful and powerless, for the resistors and the resisted. Open direct resisting makes the most noise. It can be the most dangerous for all involved, but it may not be the most effective. Non-conformance or limited conformance is less obvious, but they can be more successful. Very little of this book features Wallace since he mostly chose to avoid engaging with me.[7] On the other hand, Noah became a valuable informant after our awkward beginning. His reluctance nearly disappeared by the end.

---

[7] Even in our formal sit down interview six months later, Wallace managed to talk while saying very little.

2.4.3 A Place in the Quarry

In the kitchen, I took a tea break with a first cohort member. Leon regaled me with his pondering about life in the Quarry for fifteen minutes.

Leon:	Everyone hands in what is needed. Everyone is a generalist in SME [small medium enterprises]. There are not enough resources to specialize. That's my experience and the experience of people I've talked to. There would not be much work if you only wanted to do modeling, for example. There is aspiration for bigger companies, by pulling in indies the hope is to get to an AAA company someday. That's just my interpretation.
Ethnographer:	By one rising to the top or by combining companies?
Leon:	I don't think there is competition in the Digital Quarry or in the industry in general. The Digital Quarry is an opportunity to join forces, to bring applicable skills from different companies into one space. There is a nurturing atmosphere. People will be like, "can you give me advice?" There is an absence of protectedness because it is a small local office space. Everyone knows each other. There is trust. If it was bigger, it would not be as strong.
Ethnographer:	Is that because people here knew each other before the Digital Quarry or is it because of the Digital Quarry?
Leon:	Most people knew of each other before the Digital Quarry, or at least of the work, if not personally. Once we were in the space, met in person and worked in the same space, we came to know more. It was more real. There was a lack of isolation. Everyone is in a team of 2–4 people, so it has created a familiar standard. We all have the same curiosity—everyone wants a feel for what others are doing and how it compares to what they are doing. I was not in the industry before this job. I wouldn't have known about the industry otherwise. It's not my solo ambition to work in games, but it feels more like it after being in the space. Everyone in here started from humble beginnings.

> **Quick Lessons**
> 8. Indie game development is different than AAA development. This should be obvious, so the important thing to note is the role of specialization. In a small team, you must be able and willing to do many things. In a big studio, you will get the smallest piece. Really, this applies to any industry.
> 9. Physical proximity can reduce competitive feelings. Bringing developers together in a confined space created a "nurturing atmosphere." Leon did not put a number to it, but the size of the group mattered. We could consider the Quarry as an anthropological band (Britannica, 2016). Above this number (30–50 people), trust based on everyone knowing each other would break down, thereby allowing increased feelings of competition. Later, as some teams grew and not "everyone is in a team of 2-4 people," divisions developed.

In summary, the original cohort was surprised by the introduction of the new cohort and the ethnographer. Some members welcomed the newcomers socially while others resisted new requests. On the whole, the new arrivals were mostly ignored. Whereas the original cohort members were familiar with each other's work, the new companies were less connected and less known in the local industry.

2.5 Observers

Observers included mentors, BAT, and the Quarry Manager. The introduction of newcomers offered the chance to implement change. Some happened, but due to absences, further change did not. One mentor reflected:

> The mentors and BAT in general came at it with a different viewpoint. I think because with the first cohort we had not experienced that cohort as a living beast. And so of course you learn what they're like and then the second cohort you're perhaps thinking a little bit more about you know, the value those companies can bring in a collaborative way and maybe different ways where they can spread learning amongst, you know, the two cohorts combined.

2.5.1 End of First Week and the First Demo Friday

On Wednesday of my first week, a post went up on Basecamp:

> We need to see more demoing and gameplay of what people are working on. I want this to be a regular thing every two weeks. We'll start this Friday. It should be a great introduction to our new members as well. We'll start at 4pm and crack open some beers.

At 3:59 on Friday, Holly asked me if I knew when the demo testing would start. I said things appeared to start on time or late. The Quarry buzzed with people milling about. I scanned the crowd for Hera. She was answering a question for Aslani. The beer arrived. Hera interrupted the chatter to get the event started.

Hera: I want to introduce the new people. I didn't prepare at all.

The introductions to the new cohort were short and awkward. Thorne was not there. My intro was two sentences.

Hera: Maybe the old cohort can do short demos of their projects.

Aslani volunteered to go first. There was lots of clapping before and after. A couple members of the new cohort asked questions. None of the original cohort members said anything.

Hera: We plan to launch a QA internship with a student from one of the local universities. I'm open to how you want the sessions to be run, but I want to focus on code and playable versions.

No one suggested anything different. Three other members of the first cohort presented their games. The first demo day fizzled out.

The promise was there, as months later, one member of the first cohort reflected:

> Something the Digital Quarry possibly should have done is focus a bit more on that sort of Friday showcase thing they did once or twice where everyone kind of looked at each other's games cause there's such a breadth of knowledge in there. It would make sense for people to actually critique each other's work a little bit. Some people don't like having their little projects critiqued, but like at the end of the day, I think it makes things better.... I

honestly think that will actually improve the games coming out of there just because it's actually like free critique essentially. You know, you can't pay for experienced game developers to look over your project and study it. So even if you could get ten minutes with like ten people looking at it, that's amazing. You normally have to like, you know, pay people 30 quid and some pizza to get them in for the day to look at your game. Not that, that's terrible. It's just, while it's there, it'd be really good for the teams, I think.

The Quarry manager used the introduction of the second cohort to launch a new event—Demo Friday. She attempted to leverage the change of membership into a change of routine. The entry of new members served as a gateway, but the first Demo Friday fell flat. In an accelerator, the demo day is a graduation style event (Cohen, 2013). Demo Friday's purpose wasn't clear. Was it a form of peer feedback? Was it a way for BAT to check up on product development? Did it aim to encourage community bonding? It could have been any number of things. Attempting to introduce the new cohort and a new routine at the same time muddled both introductions. Demo Friday lasted only two weeks. The concept was incorporated into the rapid prototyping program (see Chap. 3), and there it made sense.

2.5.2 Scuddled Plans

The second week for the second cohort promised big things. The plans did not work as expected. There was a message on Basecamp about canceled meetings. Two people were supposed to come in. Over the weekend, the week's mentor had canceled. The mentor had a large network of contacts and planned to bring in an investor from France for a business plan pitch event. Then, Monday morning, the investor had called in sick after arriving in the city. I was talking to Aslani when Hera walked up to us.

Hera:	Things are a little chaotic. He must be really sick to not come in.... Devon, maybe you could go over Aslani's business plan and see if you could help.
Ethnographer:	I know nothing. Just like this investor. It can be pre-practice practice.
Aslani:	I don't have anything right now. I'll find you later this afternoon.

Hera: The investor is supposed to ask some tough questions. But I don't know exactly if the investor is serious or what role he is taking. Quarry companies are used to pitching projects, but this would be new. They would be pitching their business.

The absent mentor was spearheading the effort. Hera had not talked to him yet, so it was all vague. Hera shrugged a lot, as if to say it's up in the air and she didn't have all the answers.

Aslani never found me. An investor connected to the mentor eventually returned six months later.

In summary, the Quarry manager attempted to use the introduction of the second cohort to launch other initiatives. The Friday Demo days did not work out. The canceled investor meeting offered perspective. People were not actively against the idea in either case; however, the lack of communication and planning did not achieve any buy-in. Quarry members were content to let the opportunities pass, so it ended as a distraction.

Quick Lessons

10. New initiatives should have a clear and simple purpose. Friday demos were a great idea. The messaging around them was unclear, and the execution was lackadaisical. Here is how it could have gone:

    - Messaging: Receive free feedback and help from gamers and game developers in a safe space.
    - Execution: One team a week presents a game demo or a problem. Everyone else provides feedback or help. BAT provides refreshments, so it's causal.

11. Good ideas can become lost opportunities. The Friday demos were one lost opportunity, and the sick investor was another. The plans ran into an issue, and the issue (sickness) led to a complete collapse. Could BAT have run the event as practice? Could companies have sought feedback on what they planned to present? In both cases, they did not.

2.6 Conclusion

The introduction of the second cohort was a crux event. It was the first time new members had joined the Quarry. It never rose to the level of changing things. There was nary a reaction from existing members. The Quarry manager did try to use the change to begin a new initiative—Friday Demos. It did not last. One might have expected a feeling of hope and possibilities with the introduction of newcomers, but there was none. The introduction did create two cohorts—which in the UK echoes the class system (Dacin et al., 2010). This would subtly influence things over the next months (see Chaps. 5 and 6).

2.6.1 Reflection on Practical Lessons

1. Structure does not have total influence. The place becomes a living thing. Resistance is not always plainly visible. Look at the examples of non-conformance: developers did not pursue Demo Fridays, Aslani never followed up with me (nor I with her). These things seem small at this point, but the same techniques will be leveraged to greater effect later.
2. Social aspects are required to create a community of help. If people only stay with those they know, then it limits the feedback and help they can receive. It starts with small things—welcoming newcomers, sharing a tea break. It evolves to discussing games and problems.
3. Change can fail despite good timing. The example of Demo Friday suggests several reasons.

    (a) Magnitude—the change was excessive. It required more than people were willing to give.
    (b) Execution—the implementation was poor. Even good ideas require skill in action.
    (c) Apathy—people didn't care. Change goes smoother if people support it.

REFERENCES

Britannica, T. Editors of Encyclopaedia (2016, January 18). *band. Encyclopedia Britannica.* https://www.britannica.com/topic/band-kinship-group

Cohen, S. (2013). What do accelerators do? Insights from incubators and angels. *Innovations: Technology, Governance, Globalization, 8*(3–4), 19–25.

Dacin, M. T., Munir, K., & Tracey, P. (2010). Formal dining at Cambridge colleges: Linking ritual performance and institutional maintenance. *Academy of Management Journal, 53*(6), 1393–1418.

Phillips, T. (2015). "Don't clone my indie game, bro": Informal cultures of video-game regulation in the independent sector. *Cultural Trends, 24*(2), 143–153.

Rodgers, D. (2007). Joining the gang and becoming a broder: The violence of ethnography in contemporary Nicaragua. *Bulletin of Latin American Research, 26*(4), 444–461.

CHAPTER 3

Next Level: Significant Rule Changes Lead to a New Game

*Drawing by PhDcartoon (illustration used with permission)

3.1 Introduction

In this chapter

- The Quarry manager pitches a rapid prototyping program (RPP).
- Some individuals attend a bootcamp for game making.
- Teams (mostly) produce six games in six weeks.
- The companies try to figure out commercial viability and prepare for Gamescom.

3.1.1 Conceptual Development

A month into the fieldwork, the Quarry manager announced a new "rapid prototyping" program for Quarry companies. The program would turn the Quarry into an accelerator. While technically optional, several companies were strongly encouraged to participate. The *forced change in the organizational rules* is identified as a crux event. The rule change impacted all teams and the Quarry as a whole. Consider what Krieger said of the Quarry compared to an accelerator: "in here it's a little less hands-on or a good bit less hands-on. We don't have as much structured criteria to meet." The Quarry went from a coworking/incubator space to an accelerator with an emphasis on acceleration. It became nearly all-consuming for those involved.

3.1.2 Practical Lessons

As you read this chapter, consider the following practical lessons:

1. If you change the rules to benefit yourself, don't expect other people to jump on board without a fight.
2. What is the purpose of bootcamps? To indoctrinate people into a new way of thinking (military), to push people beyond their chosen limits (fitness), and to convey information rapidly (coding). How did the rapid prototyping bootcamp fit into this?
3. The same theme can lead to different games. The same applies to the experience of rapid prototyping. Within the same structure, people will experience and produce differently.

4. What role does commercial potential have in creativity? Does it arise before everyone is committed to an idea? Where is the dividing line between commercial and not? A million dollars, Euros, pounds? Profitability?

3.2 Selling Game Developers on Playing a Real-Life Game

The Quarry manager posted a notice on Basecamp about possible funding to be discussed in a meeting on Monday morning. It was to be held in the boardroom—a place with six to nine seats usually. When I arrived a few minutes before the start, people were already dragging in extra chairs to line the walls. Hera had a visual slide presentation started on the wall mounted TV.

Hera: It's amazing how when you say you have funding, how many…

She left it unfinished since it was obvious: she was referring to the full room. Every company had at least one representative present. The only person I didn't recognize was the co-director of a first cohort company. A couple people took out notebooks or laptops to record notes.

3.2.1 *The Presentation*

Hera spoke as she flipped through the slideshow presentation:

> It's a new financial year, and we have more money to deploy. BAT did an internal review and wants to reset based on feedback. The only currency Quarry people have is their ability to generate ideas. You are here for a short period of time. We need to make you credible. A win for BAT is for people to independently source funding after they leave the Quarry. This is a training type space. Afterwards, you have to stand on your own two feet. Some people are already doing that. There is lots of momentum from previous programs. The newer companies are starting from a lower base…. BAT is invested in the space, mentors, the time. We need to prove it. BAT will back the winners. That is how BAT operates. The goal is to develop 1-2 companies to grow into a different tier of company. I always hated this phrase—aim for the stars and you might hit the moon. That's not how rocket science works. Over ambition will kill you. You need the right level. I've seen projects hang on for too long and then come back like zombies. [We all laugh.] We're here to de-risk things, but we don't want people taking money and

not delivering. We are here to support the sector, but it's not acceptable to not deliver on agreements. The key is project management. If you don't manage the project, the wheels will come off. 70% of the value in all startups is delivered by the project manager.

The next slide appeared on the screen: *How (do they propose accomplishing all these goals)?*

BAT wants to get into rapid prototyping. BAT says that not enough IP [intellectual property] has been generated in the Quarry. Three to four people in a company can generate a magnitude of ideas. How can we set time aside for you to generate ideas? It was flagged as a concern. If you are not putting the player first, then you are not thinking about who is playing your game. Anyway, so it's based on a book. We won't make you read it. Stage one. We will recreate this experiment. It's something different. Usually, we fund a project and it's very specific. The new idea is to fund a team at living wage cost to generate ideas. The goal is to take something to the mini-level production. There have not been enough ideas produced in the Quarry so far. Next year might be a ghost period, and we don't want that. Prototype like crazy and take them forward. The aim is for projects to come out in Q1/Q2 2020. A good time to launch an indie game.[1] It's not a lot of money—£65,000 total. Grow and gain speed. There is £15,000 for the first stage. £50,000 is for stage two. The aim is not to sustain you for a year.

The next slide appeared on the screen: *Kill your darlings.* Everyone laughed.

You have to self-eval. It's hard to know what to bring forward. BAT wants you to have a war-chest of ideas. BAT is not interested in tech. It's all about gameplay, story, theme, narrative, the world, and aesthetics. You're not going to be competing with EA and Ubisoft. You don't have the technical capability to do that. Think steppingstones…. They want you to take things from here outside of the Quarry. I think a week is feasible. BAT is not looking for 'mega-big' games. The delivery date is for BAT, but if a publisher comes along, then that is a win for us.

---

[1] Obviously, no one anticipated a global pandemic at this point.

Quick Lessons

12. Too many explanations confuse things. In just the opening paragraph, Hera tried to cover:

    - Why there was additional funding?
    - Why BAT was about to propose something new?
    - The Quarry raison d'être.
    - How BAT operates?
    - What BAT expects from the companies?
    - Why the companies would fail (overambition and project management)?

13. Professionals don't like to be told they are working in a "training like space." It makes them feel like students.
14. Project management is a necessary evil, a hindrance to creativity, or the only way to finish a creative product? Or all three? Two company directors came from traditional industry backgrounds (e.g. construction) and valued project management. The rest were creatives (artists or programmers).
15. The rapid prototyping was a project management exercise disguised as creative idea generation.
16. Lean into the indie. The triple A studios are always going to have sharper graphics, smarter AI, and bigger worlds. They do not have a monopoly on innovative gameplay, compelling storylines, and cute visuals.

3.2.2 Q&A

Hera: Any questions?
Mario: How much control does the company have?
Hera: You have to prove the viability of the idea. It will be agreed between developers, mentors, and market research. Aim to develop six prototypes, then take one or two to Gamescom. Working with the mentors, they will be able to guide you. Not all six will work. Hopefully one good idea comes out of it. If not

	one good one comes out, we'll figure it out. BAT will not fund something they don't think will succeed.
Larissa:	So we need to find a team within two weeks?
Hera:	This phase is about idea generation. It's not going to start until mid-June, so you have a month. BAT just needs applications in quick. The format will be different than the usual BAT application. They want to work like a game jam. There will be themes.

The next slide appeared on the screen: *How to build a game in seven days.*

Beatriz:	That should say five days.
Larissa:	We need some time off [laughing].
Beatriz:	I don't know how we are going to do six weeks of seven days.
Hera:	BAT is not going to monitor you daily. Recently, the most successful regional games have come out of game jams.
Imani:	We're busy.
Beatriz:	All my company is working on our new game and getting to Gamescom.
Hera:	It's not for everyone. You have to make a call. This is kinda pitched to new companies. It's up to you.
Collins:	Could they not use the current game and prototype?
Imani:	Our game would literally never be done.
Collins:	You could try [laughing].
Beatriz:	Publishers want a real slice [of the finished game]. I'm not sure we can deliver.
Percival:	I agree. That's the same problem.
Hera:	That's where £50,000 comes in [during stage two].
Larissa:	If we do this, what can we show at Gamescom?
Hera:	A playable prototype. Creative gameplay that's R&D oriented. There's a big risk with overstretching. Once you have gameplay knocked out, go to development. Not everyone is in the same boat. It's just an offer.
Wallace:	The prototypes will be themed based? At least on thematic level, it will be similar?
Hera:	Things work best when things are competitive. Well, friendly. You can push each other. I totally get it. It's an experiment.
Wallace:	Are we encouraged to NOT talk with other companies?
Hera:	No. I didn't bring you into this space to not talk.
Larissa:	If we hit gold in two weeks, do we continue?

Hera:	Yes.
Wallace:	How does the £50,000 work?
Hera:	BAT is going to be really tough. The game will have to stack up. It's not a massive amount of money, but it's enough to get something done. You have a small window of time. We want you to have credibility at the end of the Quarry experience.
Beatriz:	I really want to avail of this, but I don't know how it would work with our current plans.
Imani:	I agree.
Hera:	We can chat.
Collins:	Can you just like not do one week?
Hera:	No. But we're not your keepers. It's your own business.
Akira:	So every Friday, we all play each other's games?
Hera:	Yeah, there could be good feedback. The mentors have been saying there is not enough reviewable code. The best advice in the games industry—start with something simple and add complexity. Worry less about the money and more about how you can use resources to grow.

The meeting broke up. Vincent closed his notebook without writing anything. A few minutes later, out in the hallway, Hera spoke with Beatriz, Percival, and Imani. They were three of the most vocal about being too busy to participate. During the conversation, the directors were persuaded, via bribery or coercion, to participate in the rapid prototyping.

Quick Lessons

17. Opportunity cost is the cost of what you forgo by choosing a path. BAT had a very specific plan for the structure of the rapid prototyping. To participate was to go "all-in"—no skipping weeks, no dropping out, no reusing projects. Participation meant putting other projects on hold—in the months leading up to Europe's largest video game expo. The opportunity cost was the untouched projects—either the ones already in development or the ones not yet imagined.

(continued)

(continued)

18. BAT needed participants. The second cohort alone was not enough. In pressuring teams from the first cohort to participate, BAT muddied the relationship. BAT wanted the companies to be independent but to also produce certain things. Offering funding was (surprisingly) not enough.
19. The rapid prototyping program was crunch—nonstop work until it was done. It is not sustainable. There are ways to limit stress.

- Start by restricting working hours.
- Don't let sick people work.
- Make clear what is due by the end of each week (4pm Friday).

There were multiple ambiguities and misunderstandings involved in the RPP. One informant told me that he knew another company was obliged to participate. Another said that he was encouraged, then discouraged, then encouraged again. Mentors, as surprised as everyone else about the announcement, were not consistent either. One mentor said he could not fully support the rapid prototyping concept and later told someone else it was daft *not* to do it. In the below exchange, Akira (developer) considers the best-case outcome, and Kwame (mentor) accepts the possibility while hedging his bets.

Akira: Going back to prototyping. Is there value in it? Best case, I come up with some brilliant prototype. Polish it. I have two backups. Best case, I will speak to some publishers, they will express interest but tell me to keep working on it.
Kwame: Yes. In that scenario, you have an excuse to stay in touch with them.
Akira: Get something validated one way or the other. Quick feedback [snapping fingers].
Kwame: Yeah. Everyone will be polite.
Akira: You have to read between the lines.
Kwame: I think you know if you got something.

> **Quick Lesson**
>
> 20. Mentors were as surprised by the rapid prototyping announcement as the companies. Hera claimed the rapid prototyping was partly in response to feedback from the mentors. It could be argued that BAT did not need to consult the mentors on introducing the rapid prototyping. It was less excusable to not inform them a little in advance and achieve their buy-in to the idea.

The introduction of the rapid prototyping program was a crux event at its most pure. The change in organizational rules threatened to go from one extreme to another. While incubators, accelerators, and coworking spaces share similarities (Clayton et al., 2018), they are also opposites. It was philosophical and existential. What was the point of the Quarry? Companies had thought it was one thing (build sustainable businesses, often through contract work), and now it was becoming something else (an idea factory betting on the most speculative of creative games). What say did most participants have in the change? Not much. The mentors were obliged. Some team directors resisted the initial proposal, and they were overcome. Those that did not participate were still affected by proximity. What did it seem like at the time? It seemed very likely that it would significantly change things.

3.2.3 Further Reasons Why

A week later, Hera and I sat down to further discuss the rapid prototyping program. She explained that participating companies would attend a mandatory "boot camp"—all day for five days. A combination of new and existing consultants would be giving talks. The camp aimed to show a process for (1) generating ideas, (2) turning those ideas into reality, and (3) developing communication, marketing, and profit around it. The camp was not solely about making games but also about selling those finished ideas to BAT, publishers, and others. The takeaway from the week was the "process" rather than the ideas.

Hera:	Monetization and retention are both dirty words whenever I mention them to developers, but retention is there to measure the effectiveness of the game. Are people continuing to play it? And obviously monetization is about staying in business.
Ethnographer:	How do you know if the prototyping program is a success?
Hera:	It's a failure if none of the [seven participating] companies come up with anything. I don't think that will happen. I think at least each company will come up with something. The best idea might not be the most commercial. BAT will push for the idea they want most. BAT will be the judge essentially.
Ethnographer:	A mentor said that one week's work and showing a non-playable concept might not be enough for a publisher.
Hera:	The developers are learning a design sprint. One week is the minimum time they have to be able to schedule and manage. How can they do a two-week sprint or hit milestones if they can't manage a week of work?
Ethnographer:	So you're teaching them design thinking?
Hera:	I don't like that term. It's one of my triggers.
Ethnographer:	So what is the model?
Hera:	In game jams, people go in with preconceived ideas and then they try to fit the ideas to the theme or requirements. I don't want this prototyping to be like that. I want new ideas. The first week might be a train wreck.

The rapid prototyping program changed the Quarry quantitatively and qualitatively. BAT wanted more ideas. They also wanted commercial games. It wasn't enough to have a good idea. The concept had to be sellable.

In the end, seven companies "chose" to participate in the rapid prototyping program. It was mandatory for the three companies in the new cohort. At least two companies at first felt pressured to do it.

- Hera promised one company that they could use two of the weeks to develop something for their main game.

- For Larissa, it was "rare to get that much freedom, and money, and it's not client work. It's only six weeks of our time here. It will be tough, but I'm excited. I've won some hackathons."[2]
- For Wallace, he had nothing better to do.
- One company did not do it because they were signing a publishing deal.
- For Akira, "I'm not going to do six games jams in a row by myself. I'm not doing one by myself." He told himself that if he couldn't find a programmer, he wouldn't do it. Despite the difficulty of finding available gaming programmers in the region, Akira found a person with a CV that included a released commercial game.

> **Quick Lessons**
>
> 21. It takes learning and practice to make a good game. I once heard John Romero talk about the dozens of (unreleased) games he made before *Wolfenstein 3D*. His advice? Make a lot games.
> 22. Selling the first copy begins on day one. To BAT and Hera's credit, they knew that a successful game requires thinking about the gamer every step of the way. The gamer may be sitting in his mother's basement, or she may be standing in the grocery store checkout line, or they may be riding the school bus.
> 23. The bootcamp was a great idea. In some ways it seemed like it tried too much. It reminded me of an intensive language course where you are dumped in the country to survive afterward.

3.2.4 Mentor as Strategist or Therapist

The developers used the mentor (Sandy) that same week to process the plan. First, Thorne explained to Sandy why he was going to make only mobile games.

---

[2] A hackathon is like a game jam for solving software or hardware problems. For example, see Lifshitz-Assaf et al. (2021).

Thorne: That's the area I want to get in. I don't want to change everything for just six weeks.
Sandy: What happens at the end of the period?
Thorne: If you can prove commercial viability…
Sandy: Big if.
Thorne: I will take the prototype to Gamescom. Whatever the best one is. At least if it's presentable.
Sandy: That's very difficult. Best case scenario, you've worked on it for three weeks. You're a small studio. You don't have a team of 20 to deploy. It's a big challenge.
Thorne: I won't have time to do the iOS until after the rapid prototyping.

Building only an Android version did not change Sandy's opinion. Thorne still needed to produce a presentable game in three weeks.

In the next meeting, Collins and Sandy discussed the philosophical reasons behind the new program.

Collins: I don't know if six is a magic number for some unknown reason or whether they just picked it out.
Sandy: I don't know. For a while we wanted people to do service work and be plugged into the rest of the UK. People like you are doing service work, and now they want the opposite. It's like whack-a-mole. I think we are moving in the right direction, but it's squeezing you out.
Collins: What started out as a good thing [the Quarry] is now getting cramped.
Sandy: You have any ideas? Have you done any game jams?
Collins: No. I know the ethos behind it. I think working 48 hours on something is a bad attitude to foster on someone. This feels like a school project.
Sandy: Can you park your current projects?
Collins: We're waiting to hear back. We're not chasing work right now since we have this luxury.
Sandy: I do worry that a week will be quite rapid for you. Like you said, it's against your ethos.
Collins: The idea is not to be afraid of failure. But I know what the industry is like. There is a mentality. To do six projects back-to-back, that is draining. Kill Friday…. It's all good, but two

	things. Because of the time frame, there will only be certain types of games made. As an experimental team, we will fail.
Sandy:	I guess it depends on the core of the idea. It might work against experimental games unless you have the nub of something easily understood.
Collins:	Try to make six toys. It takes a different mindset. It's not high level.
Sandy:	It's going to be a different approach for you. It's going to be a challenge for you.
Collins:	We always like exploring the new. But because of the tight deadline, does anything new or experimental get left behind? It could go—"We can't do six weeks of that because we will be too defeated."

After the mentor meeting, I continued the conversation with Collins. I asked about the emphasis when he first got here.

Collins:	It was about making the companies sustainable and the best way to do that was contract work, so you don't have to go to BAT with hat in hand. It's a false economy. I'm not sure that is the right word.... Generating your own content is a risk. Now it seems like they want to see just IP content. Every mentor meeting is about IP, about content creation. Every meeting with Kwame is about promoting the company.
Ethnographer:	What does promoting your company mean?
Collins:	It's the same as getting your game out there, finding client and partners, making others aware of you.... The friction for me in here—there are ten companies. Hera sees the majority behaving a certain way. Here is a path for them, but we are an edge case. She is not asking any company to do this exact path. It's there as one potential path. My concern is that if we don't follow that path, are we being seen as a failure? Lots of the time, she talks in the opposite direction of what we are doing. She probably doesn't see it that way.

> **Quick Lessons**
>
> 24. You can build a mobile game fast. You can focus only on one platform (iOS or Android). It will be especially tough to stand out in the market after a few weeks. No publisher is really going to care until you can prove retention metrics. Then, there is a good chance they would just copy the game instead of partnering with you.
> 25. There are all kinds of game developers. The Quarry couldn't be everything to everybody. BAT focused on the majority and the most commercially minded. An experimental company must find their own way.

Thorne and Collins offer two different perspectives on the rapid prototyping program. Both felt that the RPP challenged their ethos as indie video game developers. For Thorne, this meant not changing what he was doing philosophically but rather working within the accelerated timeline by doing less work. It was a partial embrace. For Collins, the change to acceleration threatened to isolate his company. He felt he could neither outright resist nor ignore the change in organizational rules. At the same time, he worried about the consequences for himself and the Quarry. The RPP tested indie video game development culture (Phillips, 2015).

3.3 How to Build a Game in Four and a Half Days

It wasn't even nine yet, and people were already complaining about the time commitment.

Beatriz: The boot camp doesn't need to be five full days.
Percival: You can't take up a week of our time without consulting us. If it was two days, we wouldn't be happy, but at least it's not an entire week lost. Or even if the speakers were across a couple of weeks. It's at the worst possible time for us.

The main boot camp sessions were held in the Playroom. More chairs were brought in. Some people were still sitting on the floor. Attendance peaked during the morning session on day two and declined throughout the week. Table 3.1 summarizes the sessions.

3 NEXT LEVEL: SIGNIFICANT RULE CHANGES LEAD TO A NEW GAME   59

Table 3.1 Bootcamp summary

Session	Short description
Day 1 morning	Kwame gave a presentation on player types. The categorization was straight from a publisher, his previous employer. Kwame gave the same talk last year. Several attendees had heard it before.
Day 1 afternoon	Finch gave a presentation on player motivation based on self-determination theory and Quadratic Foundry model.
Day 2 morning	Prince gave a rambling talk nominally about storytelling (e.g. an old red brick failed to make the impact of Chekhov's loaded gun).
Day 2 afternoon	We used paper prototyping to create a game. Larissa—"I am convinced by the paper prototyping. More paper."
Day 3 morning	Usman and Viper told us how to do rapid prototyping (based on techniques used at Sony). My team came up with a real estate game based on a cross between *Mad Max: Fury Road* and *Sim City*. I wanted it to be good, but it wasn't.
Day 3 afternoon	Usman and Viper presented on monetization. An informant noted that the last time he heard them talk, they were focused on licensing IP and crowdfunding. That was nowhere to be seen today.
Day 4 morning	Armstrong began the first of four sessions. Armstrong—"You always think that EA knows what they are doing, but then you work with them and realize they don't…. There is no magic bullet…. If you follow the template and process, you will deliver a game on time. But if it's good, that's up to the creatives…. Project management is so boring, but I get a kick out of it. If you don't plan your budget, you will run out of money. If you sign a contract with the publisher, and run out of money, the IP will go to them."
Day 4 afternoon	Armstrong—"If you don't have fun making games, how are people playing your games going to have fun? Most of us do it just for the fun of it."
Day 5 morning	Armstrong—"The biggest thing in the industry is knowing people. Not a single one of you hit me up on LinkedIn last night."
Day 5 afternoon	Armstrong—"Even over a five-day period, you should have a person or collective that tracks how you are doing. No one wants to be Ringo, but you need that beat to keep going."

Quick Lessons

26. See days four and five above.
27. Player stereotypes (categorizations, archetypes, motivations, groupings) help even if they seem wrong.
28. More consultants meant more ideas on how to make games. This scattershot approach gives people more options; however, BAT might have been better served with a singular vision (see week 3).

Overall, the consensus seemed to be that the bootcamp was overly long and repetitive. It was a distraction for many people. The best talk happened over the final two days by which time attendance had fallen in half.

3.4 Six Games in Six Weeks

3.4.1 Week 1: Chilled Out

Week one theme was "chilled out," and the Quarry was the exact opposite. Hera noted it immediately, "It's the most activity I have ever seen in here." Although she was surprised:

Hera: I don't know where Dylan went.
Jabari: I think he is operating from home now. Some people can't handle the noise. You can't please everyone.

Dylan had removed his desk and equipment. His colleague left after week one and only returned after Gamescom. Dylan never returned to the Quarry.

The other major noticeable absence was a pair of company directors. They were initially resistant to the RPP. I asked their artist about it. He said they were not doing week one due to "personal issues." He planned to work on some ideas himself.

Zeek: It is nice to work on something new after so many months of working on the same thing. Having no restrictions is easier.

Friday afternoon at 3:30, someone brought out beers and leftover cake. Each of the first six teams got up to present their prototype. The format was announced at the time—"a five-minute presentation and then people can play at their desk." One team had a full PowerPoint. The rest improvised.

After the demos, the Quarry Manager went up to question the only team not to present a prototype. Percival explained that they had work to do for a client. He ended, "There is no choice. We warned you about this…. I appreciate your understanding."

The tension was palatable across the room. Percival and Hera both laughed, but a few minutes later the two directors and Hera left for a private meeting in the boardroom. It lasted one hour.

One informant reflected on the experience:

I messaged Percival on Discord right away, like, what, why did you do that? You can't just talk to her like, ugh. And then I went and found Hera and then she was like 'boardroom now.' And I was like, 'Aw man, we are so fucked, we're off the program.' This is just like, of course we are. This is just hell week, this, of course, this is so typical. But they actually kind of actually like emotionally hugged it out and had like a great hour-long chat. Then it was very cathartic, and Hera was all rightly really annoyed. And then Percival just said to her like, 'I'm not okay. I'm really not doing okay. I shouldn't even be in.' And I think Hera like realized like you know, okay shit, like he's not playing about. It's not like just shit or whatever. It's a whole combination of a lot of things. So, it ended up being fine. When we find out Hera was leaving.... I was terrified that was like the straw that broke the camel's back—that incident. And Percival, as soon as he got Hera on his own is like 'you're not leaving because of me, are you?' Hera, she's like, no.... But, by the end, they shook hands and that and all.... So, I think it was a good pressure release. But yeah, regrettable that it sort of unfolded publicly in front of everyone. But shit happens.[3]

Quick Lessons

29. The presentation/game demo format should have been announced in advance. Game developers are not natural salespeople. Talking about a game, let alone pitching it, requires different skills than making a game. In retrospect, the bootcamp probably should have included a session on talking about games to different audiences.
30. The structure should have been consistent—whatever it was.
31. Conducting an accelerator in a coworking space affects everyone. An accelerator creates activity and noise. Participants can surf it like a wave. Bystanders may be crushed.

In summary, the first rapid prototyping week went from "really good game dev hustle today" to not delivering on Friday. There was some surprise—"I thought people would be frantic and working until the last

---

[3] *Aside—Another informant observed about the interaction, "When you're under pressure, every mistake becomes a big one.... If you take their money, you have to jump through the hoops."*

minute, but maybe it's not as frantic as a traditional games jam.... I'm thinking of challenges we can throw into the week if you keep on telling me how easy it is." Almost no one was prepared to present on Friday—"A week is not a long time to come up with an idea, design the game, build it, and test it. There is no time for a presentation." One team didn't deliver, raising questions around the sustainability of the concept. The cracks applied even to the Quarry manager—was the first week's less than ideal opening a reason for her eventual departure (see Chap. 4)?

3.4.2 Week 2: Climate Change

The week started off with a presentation by a North American consultant on "discoverability" in games. The idea behind discoverability is how to stand out in a crowded marketplace (see for example, Vu & Bezemer, 2021). His main argument was that indie developers should "design for discoverability." He was preaching to the actively hostile. As Hera noted at the end of the week, "There was a massive rejection from what Bob was saying early in the week? Was that conscious? Were your ideas fully formed?" Imani was the only one to answer directly—the team had fleshed their idea out after demo day last Friday. It was the rejection of discoverability.

> **Quick Lesson**
>
> 32. Discoverability is an underappreciated and underutilized concept. It is also difficult to achieve since the online world moves fast.

3.4.3 Week 3: Gaslighting

Monday morning at 8:55, Hera called an all (RPP) company meeting for 11am. No one was ready for it. People were "scattered everywhere." Only four companies managed to send representatives. I asked Hera about it. She explained:

> Different speakers at the boot camp are influencing people and we're not getting what we want.... I've told one person, and then I get the same question from someone else. I assumed that they would have passed it on. That's

not how communication works.... Part of the investment process is putting the shackles on.

In the meeting, Hera will try to redirect prototyping efforts toward more commercial concepts and more singular ideas. The attending company directors will push back. In particular, Larissa finds it difficult to reconcile the evolving relationship with BAT. Now that she has taken the money and a place in the Quarry, they seem more and more like clients. Hera will not agree to this directly, but she does want the companies to know what BAT thinks after two weeks.

Hera: The question keeps popping up. What are we doing? Why are we doing these crazy things? Obviously, the answer comes down to money. Commercial development. It should be in the back of everyone's minds. You should be pitching toward another production budget.... For publishers, a lot of games are being shared and discovered on Twitter and stuff. There is some really interesting potential. I'm worried that some of these things are drifting out of sight.... We've seen some very ambitious things go down and they haven't worked. A week is not a long time. If you only focus on one or two things, you can get to your differentiation faster.

Larissa: Maybe I should have asked this earlier. We have more ambitions for the game, but the time frame doesn't allow it. We are doing mini games because for this we can get there sooner. We're enjoying it, but what do you recommend?

Hera: It's about proven gameplay, a proven distinct feature. If story is your thing, then I expect a really fleshed out story. I want character arcs and narratives. If you're going to pitch a story game, it better be the best story game ever.

Larissa: You said play with gameplay, but there is definitely a market for walking simulators. Do you want to see it in a PowerPoint, or in a working game?

Hera: Identify the market.

Larissa: I don't mean to be taking over the meeting. I'm just having a hard time fitting it into what we have been asked for.

Hera: Here's an example game—*What remains of Edith Finch*. This company is very niche.

Beatriz: So how do people get published by them?

Hera: I don't know.
Larissa: I just wish I had more time. I felt like everyone had a meeting that I wasn't a part of.
Wallace: I didn't have a deck either.
Beatriz: When we do the demo, it would be good if there was a timer and more structure.
Wallace: It's more valuable to get feedback instead of talking.
Hera: I want people to play more stuff. In an ideal world, I would rather have real players playtest the games. They will be more honest than your fellow developers.
Wallace: I don't know how many of us are picking these things back up after the weekend. As soon as the next week starts, I'm on to the next one.
Larissa: I would have liked to know that it was more of a pitch than a demo.
Hera: It's a case that you should always be pitching.... Everyone is up against that same challenge—very early-stage game companies. Our goal is to build credibility for everyone. If you came from a Triple A studio, that gives you carte blanche to work on a story game. If you don't have that, how do you build credibility? The stuff that Bob covered about discoverability, he's not a fan of narrative games, but he mentioned *Lost*. If you are going to do that, you need to create shareable moments … these weeks don't lend themselves well to new tech or new gameplay.
Larissa: I feel like there is some conflict between what I am expected to do in this project and the overall goals of my company. I invested my money in the company, and I want to please the funders, which is you, but I don't want to lose my vision, especially since I have had people interested. I'm getting mixed messages. I've gotten such a great response from Sandy. Everyone else is responding to everything else … we're getting contradictory messages. Clarification would be nice. It's not all negative. This has been a great way to onboard a new employee. If we are going to Gamescom, I want to represent my company and not BAT. Does that make sense?
Hera: I'm not sure what your concerns are.
Larissa: The prototypes are not our strongest thing right now. I understand I am a difficult person. I'm ambitious.

Hera: We're not prescriptive, but there are caveats and traps. We're not here to give money as a charity.

Larissa: I know there is a market for the stuff we're pitching. It's tough to get into VC. Only 1% of women are funded. You don't like my vision. Maybe I'm wrong.

Hera: Your business is what got into here. I don't think anything has changed. It's working out the details.

Larissa: We're not trying to make games for just women, but it is a growing market. It's underserved.

Hera: Ultimately that doesn't matter. That's like saying that writers -

Larissa: I know. But the counter argument is a lot less efficient if you have to do a ton of research for a group that you are not a part of and you will make more mistakes.

Hera: I don't know if it's true.

Larissa: We're not just interested in farming 99p from people over and over again for years. Our USP is our identity and our ethos, not our ability to make an addictive game.

Hera: We are in the entertainment business.

Larissa: The examples you were showing in different markets had the same numbers as Edith Finch.

Hera: They have limited publishing slots.

Larissa: I'm just uncomfortable. I've felt it from the first week. You're my client.

Hera: You're not working for us. You're working for the market.

Larissa: I love that we are doing this. It's establishing credibility. I'm afraid that we are establishing credibility in the wrong area. I just want to make sure there will be support for those people that are not into perpetual games.

Hera: We're agnostic. I've said that a lot. You have to prove these things are viable.

Larissa: I feel like the goal post shifted a little bit. We're learning. It's only six weeks. It's our first Gamescom. We may not get another chance. The mentors have told us that we're not going to have a publisher interested because we worked on a prototype for three weeks.

Hera: It's all about validation.

Larissa: I'm sorry. I'm just trying to figure this out.

Hera: We're trying to give you process and techniques and best industry practices. If you ignore it, that is up to you.

> **Quick Lessons**
>
> 33. If you let people make what they want, they will make what *they want*.
> 34. Structure is one part. What people do within the structure is the other part. After the first two weeks, BAT decided that the structure needed to change to accommodate the actions happening within it.
> 35. There is inherent conflict in an accelerator. What benefits the accelerator may not benefit individual companies. Accelerator organizational goals are not independent company goals.
> 36. There is not an inherent conflict in game development between good ideas and commercial ideas. They may overlap. They may not. If you have one or the other, you consider making the game. If you have both, you should definitely make the game.
>
> - "The issue is that the companies with commercially viable games did not explain why it was. We could, but should we invest if we have to tell the teams how to sell it? They have to take some responsibility.... They believe they are competing with each other. But really, they are competing with the marketplace" (Hera).
> - Hera thought two prototypes were commercially viable and three were good ideas. Not necessarily the same games.

The meeting was ostensibly about the prototypes created and the Friday pitches. Underneath, it was about the impact of the existential change in the structure of the Quarry. Members did not understand what that meant immediately. BAT had a vision, and they were taking a more active hand in bringing it about. The consequences played out over time. It created confusion around expectations. Were participants there to develop good ideas or make money? It created confusion around relationships. Now that BAT was directly funding some companies, how did that shift the duties and responsibilities among all parties? I leave the reader with this thought. The Collins Dictionary defines gaslighting as an "attempt to manipulate (a person) by continually presenting them with false information until they doubt their sanity."

Creatively, the teams interpreted this into one realistically terrifying domestic abuse game, gaslighting gas lamps, gas giant lights in space, a trickster adventure from mythology, a multiplayer memory game, and (in my opinion, the best ideas of the lot) two very different ghost games.

3.4.4   Week 4: Lost (at Sea)

Lost in the first week's chaos was an announcement about a new marketing intern (Kasumi). She was from a local university and would be starting during week two. Hera asked for ideas about tasks and a schedule for her. Imani replied on Basecamp that she wanted to see the intern develop "community engagement tips specifically for games," understand crowdfunding and how it related to games, routes to market, digital distribution platforms, examples of communities, and "anything that makes conversations as efficient as possible and streamlines the process—especially with all of us being crazy busy from now until forever." She was the only one to reply. This surprised me since I assumed developers could use the help.

It reminded me of a conversation with Larissa where she admitted that joining the Quarry had been tough as a new member.

Larissa:	Now I'm being forced to do things I don't want to do.
Ethnographer:	Like what?
Larissa:	Mostly admin to run the business. I just want to make games. I would like to have someone to do it for me, but my team size is not big enough. The mentors are great, but I would rather have someone to do actual work. Even half a day a week would help.

During week 4, Hera went over to Kasumi and asked how she was doing. Kasumi had met with each company and was working on the marketing plans for their feedback.

Hera:	I would like to get a tracker going to see who you are meeting with and what you are doing. It would be more useful if it wasn't a timetable, but like a spreadsheet that lists what you are doing for each of them. So, if stuff isn't getting done, we can go after it.

In the present, it seemed the marketing intern was lost in the bustle of the rapid prototyping. Teams did not have time or mental capacity to avail themselves of her help. It could be compared to the first attempt at Friday Demo days during the first week of the first cohort. Alternatively, it could be compared to the later experience of the QA intern. He started in week five (see next section), and companies did not fully utilize him. In BAT's defense, the marketing intern arrived on a university placement schedule. It was bad luck that her time coincided with a time when companies were focused on the present and game making rather than business and brand building.

Quick Lessons

37. Many creatives (including game developers) hate marketing and selling. They also wanted people (laborers) to do things (as opposed to just giving advice). Combining those two thoughts, I expected them to embrace the interns. They did not. Only four companies chose to engage with the marketing intern. One possibility was that she was lost in the activity of the rapid prototyping program. On the other hand, none of the three non-participating companies worked with her. Another possibility is that her gender or age or being a graduate student subtly disinclined some people.
38. If you hate something, hire someone that loves it. Here are a few areas that people could have hired: marketing, social media, community relations, finance and accounting, business development.
39. One informant preferred a different metaphor to the storm-tossed sea. Akira reflected, "It's a roller coaster. Stress increases each week. It's stressful Monday then lower on Tuesday then increases by Friday. By the end of Friday, you just like crash and feel relief. Fucking brilliant."

3.4.5   Week 5: Patterns

Hera removed a laptop from a closet in the corner of the Quarry. I hadn't realized there was a door there.

Hera:	We have a new person [Felix] starting today. I mentioned it to people previously but never really updated them again.
Ethnographer:	What will this person be doing?
Hera:	He will mostly be reviewing game builds and maybe doing some QA testing for the companies on the side.
Ethnographer:	So he works more for the benefit of BAT than the companies.
Hera:	Well, technically he is part of an employee exchange with a sister organization in Scotland. It's for cross-training purposes. Anyway, I don't have time to review everything, like all the prototype games. I want someone to review them and write up a report. Also, it would be good to get an external perspective. I don't know where he is going to sit.
Ethnographer:	I guess I will be moving again.
Hera:	We're running out of space. I don't know how to reign it in. We were empty for so long, so it wasn't a problem, and now it's a problem.

Akira came up to us to ask about Felix.

Akira:	Do you have more of plan with him than with Kasumi?
Hera:	I have a plan... He will keep a log of defects, so BAT can track how people are doing.
Akira:	What about the students that Vincent used to QA test?
Hera:	His QA testing started out as UX [user experience] and quickly shifted to functional QA testing. If we do the rapid prototyping again, we might spend two weeks having people build user profiles. It would be great if we could get some real users in here. It would have to be hyperlocal.
Akira:	No one in this room is my audience. I am my audience.
Hera:	Then you need to find one of you to bring in.
Akira:	What benefit would they get?

Hera: We would pay them. Maybe 20 quid. It would have to come out of your production budget. If money was no object, we would probably hire a new user researcher. Someone that would just go find users and build a database.

Akira: How would you do that? How do people here usually get them? Isn't that why you go to consumer expos so people can test your game? But it's just a one off.

Hera: You could just go down to the video game shop and post a flyer asking for people. They would fill out a user profile. We might do it. Not for this year, but maybe next fiscal year.

> **Quick Lessons**
>
> 40. Don't be afraid to share your early game. Find a trusted player (professional or friend) and solicit their opinion before it is too late to change it. Felix could do UX on the prototypes because they were early in development. At that point, QA (bug testing) was pointless. The prototypes were too raw. In his main work with games near completion, it was all about bug testing. He could point out all the bugs and smooth out the experience, but that didn't mean he thought the game was fun. It was too late for changes to UX.
> 41. User experience testing and marketing share one thing in common. They require thinking about the player as someone other than yourself. As Akira stated, "No one in this room is my audience. I am my audience." This does not come naturally to some game developers. It is a skill worth cultivating.

Another intern started during the rapid prototyping, and the pattern was repeated. It seemed likely that a UX researcher would have been ignored as well. In my year in the Quarry, I observed little play testing, and little of it was outside of the development teams. Felix ended up doing most of his work playtesting for the two companies with nearly complete games. It was by default. He was the only one to play all the rapid prototyping games (that were submitted to him). His evaluations became part of the decision-making process in deciding to fund the next round of development.

3.4.6   Week 6: Time and Space

Akira asked me to join his team in the Playroom. Iris and three interns were already there.

Iris to Akira: So now you're trying to recruit Devon?[4]
Ethnographer: How does your selection process work?
Akira: A democracy.

He pitched 11 different games and wrote the title on a white poster board. His team had come up with all the ideas that morning. He asked for my feedback on the ideas.

Akira: Just give me your top two or three.
Ethnographer: All my opinions are anecdotal. The title of number nine is fantastic. My top choice is probably number six if it was done correctly. Number ten sounds insanely difficult, and I don't do difficult games.

The team discussed if they should "cull" some ideas or just vote for the top three. They basically agreed to vote on the top three. Everyone handed the marker around. Each person examined the board and took a few minutes to decide how to allocate their votes. They each gave three, two, and one vote to a game. They began voting partly based on what other people had already marked.

Akira: Maybe we should have done a secret ballot.

Carlos was torn between what he would want to play and what he would want to develop. Akira joked that I could break any tie. I declined. Three games ended up with most of the votes. Game number four had the most votes at six with game number one and number nine at five. They kept coming back to whether the game would be "fun." Akira eliminated the bottom four, each received less than one vote. Daisy suggested taking the top three, but Akira really wanted a different one. He refused to eliminate a game with four votes because it meant eliminating one with three votes that he wanted. He complained that if he had known that Daisy wanted number two so badly, he would have voted for it too.

[4] *Aside—He probably was. In week 4, he had solicited my feedback on his preferred idea since the team did not favor it. I didn't respond to Iris's comment.*

Akira: Why didn't you speak up earlier?
Daisy: Because it was already on the list, so I didn't think I needed to.
Akira: I want to revote.
Iris: We should just do whatever game you want.
Akira: Imagine what the game will look like in a week.... What can we accomplish?

There was no discussion about a final game or what the game would look like if they pursued it further. The interns stared at the list. Akira worked two laptops at once. Iris drew artwork on her iPad the entire time. She appeared sick, pale and nursing a cough drop. Akira didn't seem to want to make the top vote getter. He pushed for the game he didn't vote for—number two—that had five votes. He compelled Daisy and Carlos to state their top choice.

Iris: I don't care anymore. Three of us voted for the top game. I don't know why it hasn't won.
Akira: Because it's close.

Two hours in, Carlos asked how much longer they had on the room reservation. Another hour.

Akira: I hope the next people don't come for it. I have to make a phone call. I leave you half an hour to decide how [number four] would play. If not, then we will do number nine. I think it's worth spending an hour trying to figure it out instead of not doing it. Last week, we were in that room until five.

Akira left the room.

Daisy: Yea, OT [in a fake enthusiasm voice].

In the end, they went with number nine. Akira explained, "We couldn't come up with a compelling level for number four.... At least in the time we had."

At the end of the week, Akira was not happy with the prototype.

For students, I have included the above story to illustrate one example of how early game making can progress. It was "messy" (Whitson, 2020). It wasn't a straight line. People were working sick (or appeared to be). The boss pulled rank. It all felt longer than necessary. No one was happy at the end of it. They made the game anyway.

Quick Lessons

42. Games are made cooperatively, but very few are made democratically. Akira wanted to run his game development process as a democracy. He discovered that it is hard to spend your own money on something you don't want to create. On the other hand, Imani and her team made prototypes by two junior team members for two of the prototypes. One would be released. What was the difference? Akira made people choose from a large selection of ideas. There were twice as many ideas as team members. Therefore, most votes were cast for ideas that were *not anyone's* top choice. Each week, the idea people disliked the least emerged—the one "everyone could live with." In contrast, Imani let someone passionate about an idea lead the way. The next week, it was someone else. The passion remained.

43. The above development process is not typical. It might most closely resemble building a game during a school course. It will be different in the commercial world. If you work with your friends, you all need to find an idea that stirs passion in all of you. If you work for someone else, you will be expected to do what you are told. They probably won't ask for your opinion.

    - Carlos reflected on the process: "Monday was kinda relaxed but then it was four days of rushing. I thought about it all the time. I would leave my computer but still work on it in my head. I couldn't have kept that up. It was exhausting after six weeks."

44. One level does not make a game. On the other hand, if you can't come up with one level, then you can't make an entire game out of it.

There is an entire (unpublished) paper on the process of rapid prototyping a game. The above story illustrates one example of the early stages of development. Quarry members were not short of inspiration. On a single Monday, one team quickly came up with numerous ideas. A handful of them sounded like they could be good games. The difficulty was in choosing the right idea and executing. A good idea did not guarantee a successful prototype. If they had more time, would they have succeeded?

3.4.7 Week 7: Commercial Viability

After making six prototypes, companies were told (surprise!) that they needed to perform a market analysis. The goal was to determine the most "commercially viable" prototype. BAT never defined commercial viability. The closest they came was a Basecamp post: "We require projected return on investment of 4 to 1 (tax and distribution costs)." How they determined which game(s) to take forward varied. The important factors were budget (in order to secure the £50,000 promised by BAT for a commercially viable project) and potential in the marketplace (in order to secure a commercial publisher). All the companies had to make some of the numbers up, as one participant admitted during a presentation. Several teams had discussions with the mentors on the best option. One team (Akira, Daisy, Carlos, and Iris) discussed all the games internally before making a decision. They did not do it sequentially. Instead, they jumped around.

Akira:	Let's just go through and discuss each game one by one.
Daisy:	I'm not sure how much legs the week six game has.
Akira:	It's missing a lot of fundamentals.
Carlos:	Compared to the other five, week six is the most immediate fun. Week two game is fun, but it takes a while to get into.
Daisy:	I could pick it up and play it right now.
Carlos:	I like the idea of week five game, but I don't think we have the gameplay yet. We need to scale it back. One suggestion I didn't make while we were making it…. I'm not sure we could get it done in three weeks.
Iris:	It just needs something.
Akira:	It's very novel. It's the most novel idea we have.
Carlos:	We could get to the end of the three weeks and realize this isn't fun.
Iris:	What do you need us to have at the end of the three weeks?
Akira:	It's very open ended.
Iris:	Do you want a vertical slice? A video? A game design document?
Akira:	I'm thinking of September onward. If we had £50k, what would we do? What game could we make? I'm not really worried about Gamescom. I'm not going to Gamescom to get funding. No one is going to give it to me.

Iris:	£50k would only get you a vertical slice.
Akira:	I want to build a game with £50k.
Carlos:	If you want to build a game with £50k, then you need to rule out week three game.
Iris:	The only game you could really make with £50k would be week six game. I don't see any of the other games coming in under £50k.
Carlos:	I think maybe you could do week five game depending on what we do.... In three weeks, it's tough.
Akira:	If you think about six months, how about week two game?
Carlos:	It's like week six game. It's set in design. We just need to do more.
Akira:	I'm totally open to your suggestions on how we should proceed.

The conversation continued on in the same vein as the team attempted to agree on mythical visions of the final game.

The following week, the company director picked up the same conversation thread in a mentor meeting.

Akira:	I had to scale up quickly. They were offering the funding and with the time constraint, I had to. I think we came up with some really good prototypes.... The idea people liked the most was the week three game. I'm thinking about September. It's probably too big a project for me to take on now. It's not easy to build. It's like project number two. It's something I would do next year.

Sandy agreed that week three game was his favorite. Akira moved on and tried to explain the week five game. He pulled up a video on his computer. He tried to use *Game of Thrones* analogies to help explain the idea.

Sandy:	It's cool, but you don't have the core of how it's going to work yet. There has to be some reason besides being cool to have that in there.
Akira:	We're still trying to iron out the kinks.
Sandy:	I think what you're doing is absolutely right. Throwing out prototypes.
Akira:	The week five game is deliverable.
Sandy:	It's smaller and doable.
Akira:	BAT is talking about delivering a game in the next eight months. I know we can do a version of it in that time.

Sandy: I don't think it's wrong being where you are.

Akira: We spent four days on it. We came in here Monday morning. It was one of six or seven ideas. Then it got the most votes. So, it was one o'clock on Monday and we didn't even know how it would work. The programmer was hitting his head against the wall. We decided to go with [a feature] just to make it simple so it could work for the demo. We turned it into a twin stick shooter last week. We worked on it for a couple days. Then we got stuck and decided to leave it for now…. I didn't come into games to make safe games.

Quick Lessons

45. What is commercial viability? Here are a couple options:

    - Target audience x sales potential > budget.
    - A sequel to an already successful game.
    - License of intellectual property with an existing fanbase.
    - A great marketing concept.
    - Anything that people with money are willing to finance.

46. How do you calculate the cost to make a game? Here's a basic idea. There are three basic aspects: people, time, and the game elements.

    - (People needed x living cost) x (time / game element)/ (game elements x size of game) then add another 25% for contingencies.
    - Example #1: BAT calculated three person teams at 20,000 GBP each for one year to produce a full game (size undetermined). This figure came from the second version of the rapid prototyping program (see Chap. 6).
    - Example #2: Akira calculated three-person team at 24,000 GBP each for eight months could produce a full game. Iris argued he would not get a full game for this. He probably did not intend to pay himself, so that was zero cost work. It might also have been a small game. Based on actual results, it seems more likely that Iris was correct.

In the end, companies were trapped in three ways. Participants had to decide between their most creative product and their most commercial product. They were not necessarily the same thing. Second, participants had to decide how the potential final compared to current version. Finally, companies had to pitch versions to both potential commercial publishers and to BAT for the £50,000 mini-production funding.

3.5 After the Prototyping

The prototyping program represented a philosophical change from slow incubation to rapid acceleration. It changed the space, and it changed the companies. BAT wanted more from the Quarry. In some ways they got it—40 prototype games. For additional details, see my other work (Gidley & Palmer, 2022; Gidley et al., 2023). How the companies reacted to the crux event varied. I conclude with three separate reflections on the experience.

Reaction #1

Collins: By week six, I was fucking shattered. But damn if it didn't work.

Reaction #2

Larissa: After the rapid prototyping, we had to pay for an extra month out of our pocket so we could have a demo-able prototype at Gamescom. BAT didn't take that into account.... [Quarry mentor's publishing company] is really interested in the game.

Ethnographer: Does Kwame have insider knowledge?

Larissa: It's their type of game. Kwame keeps on telling us we need to send them a playable version. [Publisher] is also interested. They want to see all the playable features in the vertical slice. The AI was harder to program than we expected.... Not every company here can be a million-pound company. I told Hera that. She was saying that one viral tweet can get you a million-pound deal. It's not that simple. A lot goes into that.

Reaction #3

Three months after the end of the original prototyping, the director for one of the prototyping teams posted on Basecamp:

> Hey all! We loved doing the rapid prototyping program, so we decided to do our own every three months. We finished our first one this week. Come to the Playroom at 4pm on Friday to check it out. We would love the feedback rather than just guessing what people might think!

The demo seemed like a promising concept at the start of the presentation. After 42 minutes of feedback from the other developers, I was no longer convinced. The team did not pursue the prototype further.

> **Quick Lessons**
>
> 47. Rapid prototyping is intense. Like an intensive language course, you may learn a language, or you may be overwhelmed.
> 48. Rapid prototyping is very early-stage game development. It's getting out of the starting blocks on a long track race.
> 49. Rapid prototyping is a gamble. You place a bet and wait for the dice or cards or ball to stop. Sometimes it works, sometimes it doesn't.

3.6 Conclusion

The introduction of the rapid prototyping program was a crux event. It changed the rules of the game. It turned the Quarry from an incubator slash coworking space into an accelerator (for the seven participating companies). The initial reaction was resistance from some members and acceptance from others. The RPP was pitched as "six weeks of game jams." It ended up consuming the teams from the bootcamp through Gamescom, a total of almost 12 weeks. The RPP presented a vision of the Quarry as launchpad to accelerate creative development. By itself, the launch was not enough to propel teams to releasing a game.

3.6.1 Reflections on Practical Lessons

1. The rapid prototyping was not sustainable. I've written about this elsewhere (Gidley et al., 2023). I mean unsustainable in several ways:

    (a) The program could not continue indefinitely. It needed to stop so people could recover. In the end, did it speed anything up or just frontload it?
    (b) It allowed for building teams and teaching lessons, but the teams mostly broke up afterward (see next chapters). Organizations hate that. They train an employee and then the employee leaves. For BAT, if the people stayed in the region, it wasn't a complete loss. Individuals retained some of the knowledge from the experience; however, any teambuilding and coordination were lost.
    (c) BAT somewhat fixed this with the second version by funding people for a year (see Chap. 6).

2. Bootcamps (in the military and coding) are conducted at the beginning with novices. The idea is to break down the individual before inducting them into a new social structure and to teach them new things. It works because the participants are not veterans. The experienced video game developers in the Quarry were (generally) not interested in being taught a new way of making games. Plus, the Quarry did not have a social structure that needed induction.

References

Clayton, P., Feldman, M., & Lowe, N. (2018). Behind the scenes: Intermediary organizations that facilitate science commercialization through entrepreneurship. *Academy of Management Perspectives, 32*, 104–124. https://doi.org/10.5465/amp.2016.0133

Gidley, D., & Palmer, M. (2022). The impact of video game prototyping in an accelerator as viewed via spatial, temporal, and product scales. *International Journal of Innovation, 10*(3), 410–433.

Gidley, D., Palmer, M., & Gharib, A. (2023). Suffering, recovery and participant experience in a video game development accelerator. *Journal of Organizational Ethnography, 12*(1), 31–45. https://doi.org/10.1108/JOE-07-2022-0023

Lifshitz-Assaf, H., Lebovitz, S., & Zalmanson, L. (2021). Minimal and adaptive coordination: How hackathons' projects accelerate innovation without killing it. *Academy of Management Journal, 64*(3), 684–715.

Phillips, T. (2015). "Don't clone my indie game, bro": Informal cultures of video-game regulation in the independent sector. *Cultural Trends, 24*(2), 143–153.

Vu, N. Q., & Bezemer, C. P. (2021). Improving the discoverability of indie games by leveraging their similarity to top-selling games: Identifying important requirements of a recommender system. In *Proceedings of the 16th international conference on the foundations of digital games* (pp. 1–12).

Whitson, J. R. (2020). What can we learn from studio studies ethnographies?: A "Messy" account of game development materiality, learning, and expertise. *Games and Culture, 15,* 266–288. https://doi.org/10.1177/1555412018783320

CHAPTER 4

Loading …: The Quarry Manager Leaves a Void

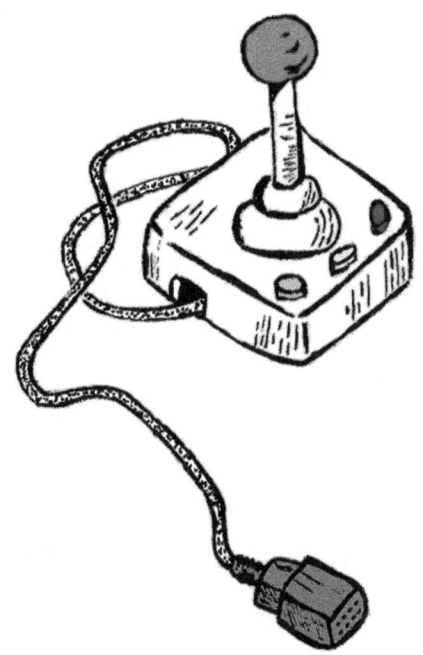

*Drawing by PhDcartoon (illustration used with permission)

4.1 Introduction

In this chapter

- The rumor mill reveals the Quarry manager is leaving.
- BAT cuts the mini-production funding.
- Social norms break down in the void.
- The Quarry manager is missed.

4.1.1 Conceptual Development

Nine of the Quarry companies sent at least one representative to Gamescom. The only exception was a company with an existing publishing deal. Back in the quiet of the Quarry, I stumbled across a social media post by one of the mentors. It said that BAT was looking for a new "interactive entertainment manager." At Gamescom, several members found out that the Quarry manager had accepted a new job. The *unexpected departure of a dominant social actor* is identified as a crux event.

It was unexpected for everyone for several reasons: the manager had been with BAT for several years, no one knew she was looking for another position, and she had been influential in founding the Quarry less than a year before. In retrospect, it seemed that none of us imagined a Quarry without her—perhaps because we took her for granted (with all that implies). The Quarry manager was the central actor in the Quarry—the conduit between BAT, the Quarry, mentors, and the companies. She was the dominant social actor in the Quarry due to her formal interactions with all others and her everyday active presence.

4.1.2 Practical Lessons

1. Surprises are like fires—spontaneous and violent. They can bring warmth, light, burn, or destroy. The two surprises in this chapter were different fires. The first (Hera leaving) was a wildfire. It wasn't managed at all. The second (funding cut) was an intentional controlled burn. The two mixed and threatened to start a third (a revolt against BAT).
2. To some people, a powerful organizational figure is a barrier. Remove the figure (like they take another job) and remove the barrier. It becomes an opportunity.

3. Expectations influence how someone reacts. Losing the opportunity for money can feel like losing money.
4. People don't blindly accept dictates from unseen authorities. Sometimes they react loudly and publicly.
5. Useful feedback is hard to acquire. It is usually worth the effort.

4.2 THE UNEXPECTED EVENT

The surprise departure came as everyone stood at the Cologne airport gate waiting to fly back to London. One informant remembered:

> I saw [the Quarry Manager's] job on Facebook. People were coming up to her and asking her about it. She didn't make an announcement. In all her meetings, she seemed to be in it for the long run. Valentine and I knew. Everyone found out Friday morning and then they came to ask Valentine about it. Yohan went right up to Hera and asked. Loads of us were just sitting there. I think they were all quite shocked. I don't think they expected it at all. Loads of them thought it was another position, that they were hiring another person, not that Hera was leaving. She said it was due to the pay. They were advertising her job at higher pay. I think she decided because she was wanting more money. If there was some internal thing going on, I don't know.

Another informant explained later that Hera was "doing two jobs" because she had to manage the Quarry and do her other job for BAT. Her final day was two months later, but she had some annual leave stored up. It was not clear how much Hera would be around over the final weeks.

Even with Yohan publicly confronting Hera about her departure, there was confusion in the weeks afterward. It was two weeks after Gamescom before I finally got the chance to ask Hera about his leaving.

Hera: Another year would have been good. But I think I can write it all up and pass it off on to somebody.... I get bored quite easily. The opportunity came up to build something like the Digital Quarry but bigger. It will be an adventure. I've never lived in Denmark. Plus, it paid more money.

We were joined by Kofi, the week's mentor. His schedule was relatively empty.

Hera: People have been slow to sign up. Felix wanted to meet with you. He is our new intern, but I want to give him some assistant producer or project manager training. He is quite junior, so I don't want to bombard him with too much.

Kofi: We have a meeting tomorrow with BAT to plan out your succession.

Hera: Valentine will be the point of contact now, at least for the mentors. Although she is busy with her own work.

Yet the confusion over Hera leaving continued. The following week, three weeks after Gamescom and the initial rumor of her leaving, Hera met with Felix. She admitted Felix needed more structure in his job.[1] She spoke about a plan for him going into the following year. Hera didn't mention she was leaving at all, so Felix was unsure if she was staying until then. There never was an official announcement. It was just that everyone heard the rumor and had it confirmed by someone else.

Quick Lessons

50. It's a terrible idea to deny a salary increase request. It's a worse idea to then advertise for a replacement person at the higher salary.
51. If someone asks for a raise, and you don't give it to them, prepare for them to leave. BAT did not (or so it appeared).
52. Hera should have formally announced her leaving to members of the Quarry. It would have avoided confusion, such as with Felix (one of two people she directly managed). She might have thought everyone already knew, but she overestimated the social connections in the growing Quarry. Also, an important person should say goodbye.

Below are two reflections on Hera leaving and what would happen next.

The first reflection comes from Collins. He found out at the airport departure gate.

---

[1] A few days later, Felix explained his job to Thorne as "helping everyone and monitoring their progress. Nobody told me about the monitoring part."

Collins:	If you want to be cold, she doesn't owe us anything. We don't work for her, and she doesn't work for us.
Ethnographer:	What do you think will happen, like change, once she is gone?
Collins:	The new person might consider just getting rid of the whole lot of companies and bringing fresh ones in.
Ethnographer:	I don't see how the new person could find enough companies to fill the space.
Collins:	I wonder if she left because of the people in the Digital Quarry. Maybe dealing with all their shit for nine months was too much.
Ethnographer:	What do you think about me doing the job? Or trying to do it part time—just the Quarry part.
Collins:	It would only take 1–2 hours per day to run the Quarry. You can rely on mentors for the contacts, so you don't need them yourself. I saw the job advertised. It doesn't pay much. They might want someone younger. Sandy and them have been around for a while in the industry. Hera wasn't trained to manage the Digital Quarry. She probably wanted to do what she originally did at BAT.... Everything makes more sense looking at it from the perspective that the person in charge has checked out.

The second reflection comes from Vincent. He found out from another company the week after Gamescom. Vincent:

> Most qualified people are running game companies, but they can't do it.... I think Hera was underqualified when she was hired, but the industry was young, and she was able to grow with it.... BAT need to look further afield, but that takes longer and costs more.... Games are at an interesting intersection. It's hard to get creative people to understand business. It's hard for the technical people to understand that the industry is changing all the time. It's like fashion. Things are popular this month, and you just have to follow it.... I've never seen a schedule around here that was valid for more than a month.

Collins and Vincent offered two differing views on what the Quarry needed. For Collins, the Quarry could run itself. The next manager could take a *laissez-faire* approach. It might even help avoid burnout. For Vincent, a more experienced hand was required. Games sat at an intersection that required a certain personality type—one operationally flexible and comfortable with ambiguity.

4.3 Power Play

A few weeks after Gamescom, Valentine posted a mandatory meeting for company directors. Six teams attended the meeting. They were surprised by the meeting topic. A team of researchers from a local university had secured funding to conduct leadership training sessions, and members of the Quarry would be the trainees. The three training sessions would occur the following month. The researchers solicited feedback on the start times. The dates and program were set. The researchers noted that few teams had filled out the intake surveys. At the time, there was little active resistance. That would change as it became a flashpoint for BAT dictating events to Quarry members. The workshop series would end up canceled. Even still, it would remain a point of contention. It was a proxy for other issues, one amplified by Hera's absence.

> **Quick Lessons**
>
> 53. Just because it's free doesn't mean anyone wants it. Like all the mentorship and consultant sessions in the Quarry, the leadership workshop series was free to members. More members tried to get out of it than showed interest in attending.
> 54. People want to be consulted early in the process. Telling them that they will be getting X on Y date and then asking what time they want to start is like giving loose change as a tip. It's a token and an insult.
> 55. Quarry members didn't respect "mandatory" requirements. Rule enforcement was not consistent; therefore, companies chose to ignore ones that were inconvenient. This seemed especially prevalent when it came to BAT administrative tasks, like meetings.
> 56. It's all connected. A wrong choice here, a slip of the tongue there, and everything spirals out of control. It's more work to fix it than to prevent it in the first place.

The leadership information session led into the afternoon mentor sessions. I sat in with Yohan (developer) and Kofi (mentor) and later spoke to both separately. Kofi stood the whole time. He was the first person I observed using the whiteboard in the boardroom—which he did extensively.

Yohan:	This is maybe above my paygrade. This job that is becoming vacant, are you thinking about applying?
Kofi:	I can't do it. I want to be able to have various interests.
Yohan:	Conflict of interest.
Kofi:	I think what may happen, between me and Sandy, Hera's boss will ask us to keep it ticking while they find a replacement.
Yohan:	I know it's none of my business. I just saw you taking over in the last meeting [leadership information session].
Kofi:	I was here at the beginning. I had to get Hera to persuade BAT to get this going. She rolled the dice with me. This is where we ended up. I think the change of regime will be good. We need to make some changes for next fiscal year.
Yohan:	You don't happen to know when the £50,000 is happening?
Kofi:	It's not a question of money. It's a question of process. We don't always know what the process is to award the money. Hera and I have an idea what we want to do with the £50,000. We need legal people to say yes. Hera will be gone by then. It will probably be Sandy and I presenting it to people. We will make it substantially harder.
Yohan:	It's going up from £50,000?
Kofi:	Yes.[2]
Yohan:	I'm trying to keep my team together. I am paying some people out of my pocket.
Kofi:	I have a meeting with Hera and her boss and her boss's boss. It's expensive to have me come back, but I can get you through October. If they say that they don't want to do this before the new person is in place, it will be mid to late November. If not, it will be mid to late October.

After the meeting, I stayed to talk further with Kofi. I asked his view on a few Quarry members.

Kofi: Thorne might learn in 4–6 months what everyone else is taking a year to. He could be out of here soon. You only have to tell him once. Then he comes back having done it and giving feedback. I wonder whether BAT got lucky

---

[2] Remember this. It will actually end up in the opposite direction.

	with him or whether their screening process was better. I want more like him.
Ethnographer:	What about some of the first cohort?
Kofi:	Noah and Titus are getting worried about leaving. Their teams and Vincent definitely need to go. I suspect BAT will make me do it [kick the teams out]. I will be the bad guy. I will be Beelzebub before Christmas. It sounds cruel, but the better you are, the less you need to be here. People are proving their way out of the place. I'm friends with Titus and Aslani, but if someone asked me, I would tell them that they are the first to go. They have come the furthest. I told them that at the end of the cohort they couldn't stay.
Ethnographer:	What do think is going to happen to the Quarry?
Kofi:	I want to change the entire structure of the program. I want to model it on a different place. I would get rid of the 1-year cohort. People would only be around for as long as they are getting something out of it. I want to reduce it from ten teams down to six. The money would go from £40,000 per team up to £100,000 per team. They would only be around long enough that they succeed. I expect about eight applications and four to be acceptable. That would then leave the three weakest teams from first cohort in the Quarry. The weakest ones can stay…. The day they are no longer getting anything out of the mentors is the day they need to leave. BAT can't do anything to me because I'm a consultant, but I need to protect Hera from an audit. If they came in here and audited us, we can't have them say that we were just making it up as we went along. I want to create a document that lays out my plans. It will be interesting to see where the resistance comes from…. In the early days, people were against Hera because they thought she was empire building.

Kofi mentioned something about the first cohort that would come up later:

first we have to kick them out and then we can bring them back in. There's legal reasons. It would set dangerous legal precedence if they let them stay. The others would use it as an excuse for why they should stay. If some want to come back, then they can go through a submission process. They will be extended on a fix-term deal. Maybe six to eight weeks to start or three months.

In Chaps. 5 and 6, the end of the first cohort becomes a point of contention. The absence of Hera, more so than "legal reasons," dictated the outcome.

Quick Lessons

57. Someone will try to fill a power vacuum. Hera leaving removed a barrier to change in the Quarry. Hera was the only non-developer with everyday practical experience of working with the Quarry members. Everyone else was there for a few hours or few days.[3] Without Hera, any proposed changes would go through a distant BAT committee. Kofi was the only one interested in using this void to implement his vision.
58. The Quarry could have become a training, coaching, and mentoring program. Companies or individuals would come in, receive their knowledge transfer, and exit (through the gift shop). The physical space would have been a byproduct. Collaboration, comradery, and competition would have been incidental or excluded. The goal was to get to MVP—minimum viable people.
59. Power is an illusion until you try to use it. At that point, you understand how much you can influence. Kofi had grand plans—some of which he laid out to Robin. He talked a "big game." When he tried to implement the plans (following chapters), he discovered his influence was less.
60. Be wary of "things that may happen." Little is certain. This applies especially to creative development. One of the main points of this book is that at the time things may seem more significant than they ended up being.

---

[3] I'm ignoring the interns. Kasumi was temporary and Felix had just started.

Kofi had strong opinions on members of the Quarry—even people he had just met. Few impressed him. Therefore, Hera's leaving represented an unexpected opportunity to make changes. Kofi embraced the chance to remake the Quarry in his own vision. As he told Robin, he did not want to do it directly by becoming the Quarry manager. He preferred to work behind the scenes. With the Quarry manager on the way out, Kofi expected to have greater influence. The first move was to raise the mini-production funding amount and the criteria for awarding it. Kofi did not convince BAT; instead, they went the opposite way.

4.4 Mini-production Funding Cut

Three weeks after Gamescom and Hera's departure announcement, a meeting was held to discuss the "mini-production funding." In the initial RPP kickoff meeting, teams were told that £50,000 was available for successful prototypes. Unfortunately, Hera had "bad news." Only directors from three teams attended.

Hera: I suppose the rumor mill has been filtering through. The funding levels have changed. There were cold feet. On the corporate level, they are not comfortable making the £50,000 award. We can do £30,000 then followed by another £20,000 application. Does anyone have a publisher?

Aslani: Nearly [she holds up her fingers with an inch between them].

Imani: Ah, not yet.[4]

Hera: Ok.

Aslani: So the £30,000 is not match funding? It's just a lump sum.[5]

Hera: Yes. This is just the prototyping. When you get lost in the heat of the project, this is your anchor point. It needs to be rock solid. It's your base foundation. I think this will catch everyone out. You need to spend time addressing major risks. Everything from the boot camp that we covered with Armstrong, you should look back over that.

---

[4] *I was a little surprised by this.*
[5] *Lump sum means they get the money and don't need to put up any of their own.*

Collins: Do you have a set schedule in mind? You start at the end of October then you have a game in January?

Hera: We want to see something released. It can be early access build. Release dates are a commercial decision. For indie games, traditionally it has been bad to release in the second half of the year. This is structured to accommodate that. This is also where a digital marketing schedule would be useful. We want to see how you will promote this. How will you build a community? I think one thing we missed out on the prototyping was promoting it externally. We didn't build a community around it. We are keen to build a following. If you go it alone, we want to see you can tap into an audience. It just gives more reassurance to the project.... I don't care about buggy builds. It has to be in the build. It can't be a bunch of pieces that will eventually come together. Between now and this starting, you need to put in the systems to make this work.

Aslani: I really like that. It's a lot of work but it's good to be doing at the same time. It's like a game, Hera. Very cool.

Hera: What we want for this program is actual projected sales. If you get a letter of intent, they say they want X, Y, Z, that if you deliver that, you can take it to the next stage. That reinforces the value.

Noah: Like an official letter of intent?

Hera: Like an email. It doesn't need to be official. If publishers don't think it's ready to go to committee, they will give you feedback. It's these indications of interest.

Noah: So the more of these we can get, the better?

Hera: Don't hold back. This is not the point to hold back. BAT are looking to be strict. It's a big risk on BAT's behalf. They are cagey. Cagier than when we started this. There will be another Quarry manager. The mentors will help out. Are there any questions?

Aslani: Is there a maximum number of companies that can avail of this?

Hera: Everyone can apply. I've been told if there are justification for all, then they could do it. But I have been told other things before that didn't happen. Nothing is guaranteed. It has to go through the process. The market interest will be real critical. The idea is that there are enough people that can judge it.

Aslani:	So, obviously, you are going. Between you leaving and us doing this, who can we go to with questions?
Hera:	All questions can be sent to Valentine.
Valentine:	I don't know the answers, but I will disseminate them. A BAT committee will handle them.
Titus:	In this transition period, can we expect things to go more slowly?
Hera:	I would very much expect that. The mentors are there. They are on access. If you have more business-related questions, talk to the mentors. Kofi is not always as reliable. I haven't mentioned this to Sandy yet, but we want to bring him on for more time. Maybe not fly him over but have him available.
Titus:	Kwame is good at emailing you back if you have questions. He was emailing us this weekend.
Hera:	Everything we have outlined here, if you do this, it's generally smooth sailing. If you can make our lives easier, that is great.
Titus:	Do you know when your replacement will come through?
Hera:	They have some people. Maybe November, but more realistically January.
Imani:	So there will be no replacement before we leave for our 12 months?
Hera:	I will tell you on Thursday. I think the program ...
Aslani:	Is it still going to exist?
Hera:	Yes, it will still exist. BAT will continue to support this. It's in the strategic plan. There is a lot of value in this. That argument is over.
Titus:	So BAT are not leaving the games industry?
Aslani:	But it's not going as fast as they like?
Hera:	It may sound that way on the phone. I'm oftentimes the translator for these things.... No matter what happens with the next stage of the Digital Quarry, it's not about cutting you loose. It's about providing more people with opportunity. I would advise you to read the strategy document. The new person will have in their inbox working out on what the next corporate strategy will be.

The meeting wrapped up. When I returned to the Quarry, I found Robin and Holly sitting at their desks. I asked why they weren't in the meeting. Robin thought it was Thursday. He went to talk to Hera and reported she "didn't seem upset" about the missing teams. A few hours later, Robin found me sitting idly in the entryway to the north wing. He wanted to complain to me after hearing from someone else about the change in funding. Robin commented:

> I don't know what they expect. Does anyone in that organization know about games besides Hera? They cut the funding by 40%. That's almost no funding. How do they expect anything if they don't invest in it? That's double the paperwork, double the admin, double the time, and it's not even guaranteed. I'm not even sure about this anymore.

The next day, Hera held a meeting with Robin and Thorne to discuss what they had missed yesterday. Robin took the chance to confront Hera about the reduced funding.

Hera: It comes with strings attached.
Robin: Doesn't it always?
Hera: Maybe barbwire.
Robin: I wish BAT would justify their case to us about their spend in games.
Hera: The games sector here is small. It's a million per year. That is more than our other sector priorities. The more you thrash at these things, the less it's going to help.
Robin: Are we going to be judged by the same criteria as Aslani and Noah? They have been here a year, and we haven't.
Hera: You will be judged against them. You are going to be judged by every game in the marketplace.
Robin: I just think for an accelerator—
Hera: We're not here to give you a leg up.
Robin: I'm just not convinced. The goal posts keep shifting. The investments don't seem wise.
Hera: Things change. They change all the time.

Quick Lessons

61. Funding cuts are devastating. The financial impact is obvious, but the Quarry teams also demonstrate the emotional impact. It hurt. It made multiple people question their decision to make games.

    - Obviously, less money means changes to the final product. BAT still expected a completed game. This seemed especially challenging. Teams already debated if the original amount was enough.
    - Splitting the potential funding means doing everything twice, as Robin noted. This ended up not being an issue because BAT never held a third round.
    - Publishers had already heard the original amount. Even if the funding cut was not related to any individual team, a publisher could view the cut as a lack of confidence in the project.

62. Cold feet can be justified. Hera said there was only "one commercial prototype" among the 40. Would more time (via more funding) have made any of them more commercial?

    - Then again, she said there were two "commercially viable prototypes" after week three. Was one downgraded upon reflection? Did the undefined definition of "commercially viable" change? Was one statement Hera's personal view and the second statement the official stance?

63. Accepting or resisting the funding cut changed nothing.

The exact reason for the surprise cut in funding was never discovered. Was it just "cold feet" as Hera said in the first presentation? Was it related to Hera leaving as Robin implied? Was it a reaction to the early prototype demos? Was it independent of anything to do with the Quarry and tied to other BAT financial issues? Most company directors seemed to accept the funding cut without protest. The surprise barely made an impact on them.

4.5 The Last Days of Hera

Hera's last days arrived more quickly than some expected. Perhaps because she had about a week to go, Hera sought no privacy for an hour-long phone call with someone at BAT. She sat at her desk where anyone in the Quarry could overhear if they desired.

> I advise a break of at least one week before allowing anyone from cohort one back in. We need a clean break. I need to work on the application process, dates and times and processes. I need to get on that right away. The first application was based on a business plan. I think we should have an interview. We should bring some mentors in because they are business focused.... The problem is we have different types of companies. The new ones won't be at the same level as the current ones. We have talked about doing a boot camp with half of the grant. In our business plan, we have stage one, stage two, and stage three companies. A company that stays in the Digital Quarry for a second year, they would be a stage two. There is a need to handle them differently than a stage one. The stage one companies that are coming in are just starting up. They need to be handled differently. They should be judged differently. To get to an equilibrium, we should be letting five companies in, whether that is five new or a mix between new and old. The original plan was to offer ten companies three seats each. There are 30 in here. What happened over the summer was that everyone increased. It has died down a bit. There are about 15 people milling around right now. While getting to capacity looks good.... Some of them are beyond our help. There is not a great enough need for them to be here. Others seemed to have their own things going on.... If we did the rapid prototyping again, it would be up to £10,000. £15,000 or £20,000 was too much. It was like, spend the money and now that we have spent the money, it's like, what have you done?

The Quarry manager leaving complicated how to handle the first cohort. The original plan had not worked out. Companies had not clearly progressed to the next stage, as defined by BAT. All the goals of the prototyping had not been achieved. Everything was still in flux on the eve of Hera's departure.

Quick Lessons

64. The Quarry as ladder differed from other views. Hera imagined the Quarry as a community where companies grew through stages. It contrasted with the mentor's plan for the Quarry as brief knowledge transfer school.
65. Some companies were no longer a good fit for the Quarry. Both Kofi and Hera agreed on this—but for different reasons. Should BAT have taken a more active role in curating the Quarry culture? In some ways, being agonistic about creative development made the Quarry more inclusive. Teams were not initially excluded because they didn't fit a certain type. It also meant that the benefits the Quarry provided were not evenly distributed. The companies that fit BAT's vision received preferential treatment—some intentional, some subconscious.

4.5.1 Secondhand BAT View on the Quarry

Valentine arranged a surprise going away party. The marketing intern's last day was the same as Hera's. BAT sent over a manager to give a speech. It was self-deprecating.

BAT: For mentors, talk to Valentine. For everything else, email [someone else]. Don't expect an answer because they don't have it.

Several people from BAT spent 30 minutes reassuring Felix about his job. After giving me knowing looks all day, I followed Felix outside for an exercise break. Felix liked to lift weights throughout the day, specifically a pair of 20-kilogram dumbbells he stored by his desk. The symbolism wasn't lost on us as we stood at a side door to the Gymnasium. He confessed to me at length about his experiences and conversations recently.

> My interpretation of my job matches what BAT bosses told me. They told me that Hera was miscommunicating what it was.... There don't seem to be any rules about coming in. People are not using the space or services.

Hera is afraid to put pressure on them. She told me to ignore Wallace, Robin, and Collins, but BAT told me not to do that. I've only been working with three companies. BAT told me that I need to report on all of them. They have been left behind.... The companies don't realize that delivering stuff to me is delivering to BAT. Not talking to me hurts them. I just want to help people make games.... Like Jabari's team asked me to come to a mentor meeting, but I was only involved in ten minutes of the meeting. The team claimed that all these features were in the game. I played it for three months. They lied.... Maybe it was miscommunication. The mentor was asking me about the features. I had to get the question repeated because I didn't understand.... It makes me look like I don't know what I am doing. They were probably trying to say all the features were there because it would get them more funding. Once I called them out, there were no consequences. But they now communicate with me more. They have funding, so are set in their ways.... I didn't know who I was supposed to report to. I now know that BAT management wants me to report to BAT directly. That won't be an issue with Hera leaving. I was told there would be big changes over the next month.... They think it's their baby [he cradles a dumbbell like an imaginary baby]. They won't let anyone see it.... Hera just takes people at their word. It's easy to take a screenshot or a short video and make it look like a good game. When I play the game, it's easy to see they haven't done much work.... There should be a weekly reporting of what has been done by each team. They don't realize that giving me nothing looks bad on them.

Even though the manager gave two months' notice, the organizational norms of the Quarry began to break down. Roles began to change. Hera had given Felix instructions based on how she wanted things done (e.g. ignore some teams). Now, BAT wanted Felix to do more and different things. There was more "monitoring"—a term he used elsewhere. Whereas before Hera was the filter between the Quarry and BAT, Felix would now take on that role. He would have a direct link to BAT, which in turn meant he would have more power and influence in the Quarry. His role would enlarge to fill some of the void left by Hera. The primary function was not to manage the Quarry but rather to report on the happenings.

> **Quick Lesson**
>
> 66. Expectations and communication define and shape a role. The quickest way to get a reaction is to go against expectations. (This is the foundation of comedy or joke-telling.) When it comes to a job, the unexpected is often negative.
>
> - Felix wanted clarity and to do the job outlined in the description. Or, in his words, "I just want to help people make games."
> - Hera wanted Felix to do two things: be a second set of eyes and to help some Quarry members—the ones that wanted help (in Hera's view).
> - BAT probably didn't think of Felix until Hera's announcement. Afterward, they needed him to serve as a conduit between the Quarry and BAT as well as between Hera (the present) and the next manager (the future).
> - The Quarry companies didn't know what to do with Felix. They treated him like an intern. Admittedly that is what Hera had called him. He wasn't a placement student (like Kasumi finishing her master's degree). He wasn't there for a short few months stay (his one year transfer from the sister company would see him outlast all the Quarry companies). He wasn't inexperienced (he was a hardcore gamer with a game development undergrad degree). They squandered his talent and time because of unclear expectations.

4.5.2 The Rebellion

Dissent began brewing with Hera's unexpected departure. Her impending absence created a "vacuum" (to quote one developer). Whereas previously upper management at BAT had been nearly absent from the Quarry, several people became slightly more involved. The reduction in mini-production funding intensified the issue. People brought the issue to Hera, but they knew she had no ongoing stake in the game. With the seeds of rebellion sown, sprouts continued to emerge in different places.

A new week brought a different mentor. I sat in with Robin and Kwame for their first meeting post-Gamescom. After a quick update, Robin shifted the topic to the funding cut.

Robin: Someone should talk to BAT.... I don't think talking with BAT will change anything. I don't see anyone else doing anything. I am at the point where I am like, should I even continue here?

Kwame: I see your frustration. The spending—it's a government thing. Games have never gotten the respect. I think we will be in a better place in 12 months once we have a slate of games published.

Robin: If we can get anything published. I'm not going to hire a team for less than student wages.

Kwame: No, you shouldn't do that.

Robin: I try to do a 32-hour work week for my staff. They don't always do that, but that's the games industry.

Kwame: Another perspective: If I was a publisher, and I was told the funding was going to move from 50 to 30, and I really wanted the game, I don't think that would matter.... I think for 30,000 to get something releasable is ambitious.

Robin: I feel like they are setting us up for failure.

Kwame: I don't think they are setting people up to fail on purpose.

Robin: I have to decide if I am going to stay here. I gave up my life to pursue what I wanted to do. I am pretty upset right now. Honestly, I just want to make games. I don't want to fight for this.

Kwame: Sometimes you have to say things, so people will stop and take notice.

In the end, Robin decided to meet with BAT despite Hera still being in the building. He said, "I know they are going to punish me for this. It won't be in a visible way, but they will. I don't want to be the sacrificial lamb. I don't see anyone else speaking up. They are willing to tell me in private."

Robin communicated with other members of the Quarry first:

> I have a meeting with BAT management next week. The key issue will be funding, particularly the mini-production cut. I can only speak for myself, but feel free to contact me with your concerns or say how the changed funding has affected your team. Even if it's anonymous, I want them to understand the impact of their decision. I plan to present my concerns as constructive criticism.

One week later, Robin reported back:

> The meeting with BAT management was helpful. I am hopeful because they say their strategy will include feedback from us and an increased focus on games (despite the budget cut). Yes, seriously! Also, they also said to reach out to BAT directly if Hera can't answer the questions about funding.

Quick Lesson

67. It's not easy to stand up for your beliefs. It's difficult in an organizational setting. The structures protect the organization. People in power want to stay in power. It's especially difficult when there is not a clear societal or moral imperative supporting you (discrimination, injustice). Robin fought alone for additional funding for the video game sector. It was money-as-respect. Robin *knew* they were going to punish her, and she did it anyway. It didn't make things easy for her, but it was who she was.

There are three main takeaways from Robin's rebellion. First, Quarry members were bypassing Hera in order to go directly to BAT. In some ways, the powerplay by the mentor was the first hint of this. In Robin's case, after his appeal to Hera fell on deaf ears, he took her case directly to BAT. It is unlikely that participants would have chosen to circumvent Hera if she was still involved in the Quarry. Second, BAT appeared to quell the rebellion after meeting with Robin. In a later section, we will see the truce was only temporary. Without Hera, BAT did not have a consistent presence in the Quarry. The closest they had was Felix, but his role was just as confusing. Otherwise, participants were directed toward contact with multiple other people or the mentors with their issues. Third, Hera was the intermediary between BAT and the Quarry members. She was a filter or a barrier. There may have been the impression that access would have been smoother without her. While there was uncertainty, there was also a feeling of hope on the horizon.

4.6 Transition

Monday in the Quarry was the first day without Hera. Her desk was still not cleaned off. She even left a beer bottle from Friday there. Valentine, the only other BAT employee most participants knew personally, was on vacation the entire week. Quite the coincidence. No one had told Quarry members. Members messaged back and forth trying to determine the right BAT person to contact for different questions. The answer had once been easy—Hera. Now, it wasn't clear for the time being.

4.6.1 BAT Begins to Solicit Feedback

Hera had predicted, on her last day, "nothing's going to happen until they get a new person in." She was half-right. Quincy had been given most of the responsibility until the new hire started. Felix was playing an active role since Quincy appeared "lost."

Felix:	Quincy wants me to write a report about everything that is wrong with the Digital Quarry. I was planning to go around and ask the teams.
Ethnographer:	You will need to promise them anonymity to get some truth.
Felix:	I read every part of my contract. I know I can't be sacked. I have no problem with the blowback coming onto me.

I sat at my desk and made notes. Nola came up and asked me to talk to Quincy. I had seen Quincy when she had visited the Quarry with other BAT members, but I had never met her. My heart raced. I wondered if this was the end. I wondered what she wanted. I told myself to breathe. I had enough data. Really, I did. I followed Nola out to the north wing foyer. Nola asked me to tell Quincy about my experience in the Quarry. Then Nola walked into the boardroom and left us alone. Well, not alone. The sofas in the entryway seating area were filled with other coworking members. I quickly explained my background and the research. I noted that Hera had granted me access, that the companies were okay with it, and that I did not work for any of them.

Ethnographer:	Ah, what do you want to know?
Quincy:	Is the Digital Quarry meeting its goals?
Ethnographer:	It depends on what the goals are.
Quincy:	I would look at skill development, growing and building the region's games industry.
Ethnographer:	I can give you a preliminary report.
Quincy:	Give me the highlights.

I gave her the highlights: several companies have publishing deals, tons of games were made during the RPP, and many of the companies had grown in size (at least temporarily).

Quincy:	BAT is spending £30,000 per company in the Digital Quarry. It's very unusual for BAT to have approved a physical space outside of the corporate structure. I can't find any documentation on the teams and how they have or have not progressed over the year. There is no way to measure the value for the £30,000. I'm not sure what has been happening since it appears Hera kept it all to herself. Is there is a feedback mechanism?
Ethnographer:	People have asked for one, but there is not one yet.
Quincy:	Are the mentor meetings recorded anywhere and action points made?
Ethnographer:	Maybe some teams do, but not really.
Quincy:	They need more structure. The games industry is where the animation industry was ten years ago. Look how successful it is now.

The conversation lasted about 20 minutes. She seemed to genuinely want to do better in the Quarry. It is difficult to separate Hera leaving from what Hera left behind. Did BAT see Hera leaving as an opportunity to reevaluate the Quarry and make changes? Is this why they solicited feedback? Or did they have no choice because Hera left little documentation for them to analyze? Maybe it does not matter. Hera leaving allowed BAT to partially embrace change. They began to solicit feedback from multiple sources in order to make changes to the Quarry.

Quick Lessons

68. Relying on a single person has benefits and drawbacks. It makes it quicker and easier to manage everyday tasks. It means you can avoid worrying about things in the present. Unfortunately, when they leave, everything not written down goes with them. Hera kept much to herself. No matter how much a person writes down, you cannot directly replace their institutional knowledge and experience. Besides, most people won't read most of it anyway.
69. If someone says they are going to write things down for you, make sure they do it before they leave. (This is just a statement. It is not a judgment on what Hera may or may not have done.)
70. Soliciting feedback is a good idea. It should have been done earlier and more frequently. The first cohort was nearly done before they were asked for feedback. Their statements weren't going to help them personally. This gave them less incentive to provide the best insight, or it freed them to be blunt.
71. Feedback should be received from as many people as possible. BAT did a decent job. They asked the mentors, Felix, the ethnographer, and company directors. They could have asked company employees (in survey form).

4.6.2 The Rebellion Reignites

One week later, it was announced on Basecamp that "BAT has generously offered to meet with companies at the Digital Quarry regarding changes at the Quarry. This will be an opportunity to get your concerns addressed and voice heard." Meeting times were discussed. A week later, BAT abruptly announced the meeting. Unfortunately, I became ill during the week and wasn't able to make the mid-morning meeting. I returned to the Quarry around noon. Aslani immediately pulled me aside. She was sick again, yet in the Quarry, regardless. I knew that I had missed at least one important meeting. I soon discovered it was two separate meetings that became intertwined. First, there was a meeting about a university job fair. Hera had signed the Quarry up for a table but left the details unfinished. Nola arranged the meeting to discuss when and how Quarry members would participate. Company directors were expected to volunteer a few hours at the booth. Second, BAT management held a meeting to discuss issues with teams directly. The BAT meeting took on a different tone after the events in the first. Aslani reported:

> You missed a lot. The meeting with Nola yesterday was bad. Robin was getting emotional. Then this morning, there was a 10am meeting with BAT.[6] I wasn't planning to come in today, but I rushed in when I heard they were coming. Robin was saying that the Quarry companies have been doing a lot of free work for BAT. I don't think Robin was saying it in the best way. But I agreed with his points. Kreiger told me he thought it was fine. I told him he doesn't see a lot of what is going on.

Thorne described the meeting with Nola as "Robin being Robin … Robin is poking his head above the parapet. He wrote to BAT yesterday saying that he felt he was under attack for speaking up. They replied and copied everyone else in the Digital Quarry. They made fun of him." Later, another informant would tell me, "BAT kinda put Robin down in a way. I mean, they did it in a diplomatic way."

I took a break with Felix outside. He brought his dumbbells as usual, but he set them aside. He shook his arms out to loosen them. It didn't help. He was shaking, head and hands, during this entire conversation.

Ethnographer:	Do you want my jacket?
Felix:	I'm shaking because my heart is racing just remembering the Playroom meeting. My heart was racing faster than ever…. That was the most uncomfortable meeting I have ever been in. Everyone was just sitting there being quiet. Robin has some good points, but people can't see beyond his animated gesturing. I was sitting next to Robin on the sofa. Robin was gesturing wildly and rocking the sofa.
Ethnographer:	Like what points?
Felix:	The goal posts do keep changing, but Robin needs to deliver the prototyping work to BAT that everyone else has. He thought he had two years on the Digital Quarry

---

[6] This is the meeting discussed in the prologue story.

program. The second year was automatic. He said he needed two years to grow his business. Then Valentine said by accident that BAT had paid £30,000 for the leadership training that was canceled. Someone else paid the money. In the second meeting, when Robin confronted BAT management about it, they denied they had spent anything and asked him where he had heard it. No one wanted to name Valentine, so Robin just said "you" [as in BAT]. I think Valentine got in trouble for it. The Playroom meeting never accomplished any discussion on the university outreach. Robin accused BAT of trying to use them as free labor. Valentine told me she felt under attack. Collins tried to bring the conversation back to some discussion on dates, but it didn't go anywhere. Now, I have to meet with everyone individually and coordinate it. Most people were onboard. They should be. It's promoting the Digital Quarry.

Back in the Quarry, I heard Mario, Noah, Aslani, and Titus talking across the room. They were discussing "the shit that went down yesterday." I casually walked over. Aslani roped me into the conversation.

Aslani:	You have been observing this entire time, and now you just missed an important point in the narrative. We are going to have to fill you in.
Noah:	Everything we have been told has been wrong but in a good way.
Ethnographer:	How?
Noah:	We were told that everyone needed to get £1 million in funding. That wasn't true. They don't know where it came from. And the pitch funding. We were told we needed this big business plan and everything. Now they literally just want bullet points. For the pitch for the £30,000 funding, the requirements have changed.
Aslani:	They asked me what I thought should be in a pitch. They literally just took my points and wrote them down.
Titus:	You should have added a final slide about why [your company] is great. Anyway, if Sandy and Quincy are the judging panel, they won't deny anything.

Noah:	The new Quarry manager has been hired and is starting next week. She will be here more than Hera.
Ethnographer:	I'm surprised.
Noah:	BAT had 60 days' notice to hire the person.
Ethnographer:	I know, but as of last week, people were saying it could be January.
Thorne:	BAT sent out a survey.
Mario:	Cohort two got one version and Cohort one got a second version. There is a list of trade shows, trainings, and events. I went to some, but the dates didn't match, or the funding was wrong. The questions weren't the best. I had to figure out how to answer them.
Titus:	Kofi and the BAT committee are doing the interviews for staying in Digital Quarry. The third cohort has been abandoned. I don't understand why everyone can't stay since it doesn't cost BAT anything extra…. I'm not sure the Digital Quarry is worth it. After what we have gone through here, I'm not sure being separated is a bad thing.
Aslani:	We will be fine no matter where we are.

In summary, here was the sequence of events:

- Nola held a meeting to organize an event that Hera hadn't finalized.
- Robin hijacked the meeting after a misunderstanding with Valentine on how BAT was spending money.
- BAT held a meeting to clarify things. It reset some expectations. It made other things worse.
- Multiple people described the relationship with BAT as becoming adversarial.
- Oh, and the third cohort was postponed, a new Quarry manager was hired, and they were still trying to figure out the next round of funding as well as the first cohort.

Quick Lessons

72. Rebellions are rarely about one thing. They are usually a series of things that accumulate until the person, or persons cannot abide the status quo anymore. Here are some of Robin's issues:

    - How BAT allocated funding for the games sector. He thought it was disproportionate to sector revenue. BAT would argue games received *more* funding than was appropriate based on revenue.
    - The "free labor" BAT expected. The most obvious example was "working" the university job fair. BAT would argue the "free" perks of Quarry membership more than compensated for occasional unpaid work.
    - The surprise mandatory events. The most obvious example was the proposed leadership workshop. BAT would argue that scheduling was based on the availability of the consultants. In terms of content, BAT would argue that events were based on benefiting most people most of the time. There was not much consultation with participants on this point.

73. One meeting cannot fix systematic issues. BAT thought they had quelled Robin's rebellion with their first meeting. Instead, a marginally involved person misspoke about something seemingly unrelated, and the complaints resurfaced.

74. Expectations are important. BAT never properly communicated their expectations, or evolving expectations, of Quarry companies.

75. If you feel the need to write rules into a contract, then you must enforce them. One reason for the rebellion was the disconnect between explicit requirements in advance and the surprise requirements in practice. Robin told me:

    - "In the original contract with BAT, we were supposed to have biweekly builds and checks. There have been none. Also, you were supposed to notify BAT if you were going to be gone for more than five days. I realized neither was being enforced, so I stopped worrying."

76. If contractual obligations were not required, why should people agree to new responsibilities?

After Hera left, BAT sought to engage in three ways with Quarry companies. First, BAT reached out to the mentors, ethnographer, and QA intern for observational feedback. Based on suggestions, BAT decided to engage directly with companies. Second, individuals took on duties previously done by Hera. For example, Valentine and Nola tried to arrange the university outreach. Third, BAT met directly with company directors for their feedback. The multi-company meeting did not go as planned. It strained the working relationship between BAT and the Quarry companies. The single company feedback meetings went smoother.[7] The feedback meetings might have started by necessity, but BAT used them to reimagine the Quarry.

4.7 After Hera

Three vignettes provide some perspective on Hera and her time running the Digital Quarry.

At a local game industry meetup, I stood with Collins by the pizza. No free beer. Hera came up to us. She was back in town, visiting. She asked Collins about some specs for the Unreal engine.

Collins: Are you planning to make games?

Hera demurred at first, but then admitted that "everyone has dreams" and she wanted to learn Unreal for her own personal benefit.

Hera: I miss the Digital Quarry already. People from the Quarry haven't really been in contact with me. It feels longer than six weeks.

It was a confession and bittersweet.

On a random weekday in the Quarry, Ruby went over to check out Hera's last desk. Hera had left her red appointment notebook with the rest of her stuff.

Ethnographer: I wonder if she wants it back.
Ruby: She doesn't care anymore.

---

[7] I attended Robin's feedback meeting. It was surprisingly civil despite the earlier tension.

Ethnographer: What happened to Hera's final beer bottle?
Ruby: I threw it out. If you saw it there, why didn't you do something about it? People are weird.
Ethnographer: It was a natural experiment to see how long it would last.

Almost two months.

Near the end of the fieldwork, at a regional industry gathering, I jotted down three different reflections on Hera's time managing the Digital Quarry.

- Hera—The best thing I ever did in the Digital Quarry was the rapid prototyping. We pushed people really fast, really hard. I saw dozens of great ideas come out of it.
- Jefferson—Whenever I see Hera, I just remember her going away party. It was Titus, Aslani and me and it went on forever. It just went on forever.
- Monroe—Do you remember when Hera tore into Charlie during the prototyping?

4.8 Conclusion

The Quarry manager quitting was a surprise crux event. BAT reacted by embracing the change as an opportunity to reevaluate the Quarry. A mentor used it as an opportunity to implement changes. A Quarry developer used the departure as a means to question the purpose of the Quarry and complain directly to BAT. There were multiple outcomes. The mentor and developer lost their battles. BAT took the chance to solicit feedback which they used in some ways to make changes. In the end, Hera leaving was a brief distraction in the overall timeline.

4.8.1 Reflections on Practical Lessons

1. The (lack of) announcement of Hera leaving was a mess. The aftermath was a bigger mess. Where does the blame fall?
   (a) Not with the developers. They had no control over any of it.
   (b) Maybe a little with Hera. Did Hera "owe" the Quarry members or BAT anything? Collins said no, but I would argue she had

some responsibility to the Quarry members. She had known some of them for years. The length of time meant something.

(c) Probably with BAT. Communication failed at several steps: the announcement, the transition, the aftermath. They did hold a meeting directly with Quarry members. This caused as much trouble as it solved. Most importantly, BAT were the organizers of the Quarry. It was ultimately their responsibility to ensure it functioned smoothly.

2. BAT had a large remit, so they needed the Quarry to be many things to many people. Kofi wanted something tight and focused. The two visions were incompatible.
3. At the time, the funding cut (from 50,000 to 30,000) was important. Later (see Chaps. 5 and 6), two other changes would be more significant. The overall funds available were reduced from "everyone" to "max of three projects." There was also not a "second round" of another 20,000 as originally suggested.
4. People admired Robin fighting. They were uncomfortable being involved. They thought it was fruitless. There were better uses of their time. They were probably right.

CHAPTER 5

Boss Fight: Changes in Priorities Lead to a Self-Inflicted Crisis

*Drawing by PhDcartoon (illustration used with permission)

5.1 Introduction

In this chapter

- The first cohort is told their options.
- The RPP teams pitch for secondary funding.
- The funding process fails.
- BAT conducts exit interviews.
- Several members of the first cohort leave the Quarry.

5.1.1 Conceptual Development

After the announced departure of the Quarry manager, BAT took a series of missteps. These choices lead to a *self-inflicted crisis* within the Quarry. This crux event has origins in the first two crux events (introduction of new members and changing the rules).

The boundaries are fuzzy around this crux event, the previous one, and the next one. They are like a trilogy. The chapters are thematically grouped, so this means jumping back and forward in time to tell this story. Don't be alarmed. Hera appears in the opening scene.

5.1.2 Practical Lessons

1. Fixed-term contracts may end as scheduled, or they may not. It is a good idea to plan for both eventualities. Prepare for surprises. Get it in writing. The first cohort were on one-year contracts to be in the Quarry. With Hera leaving, might something change?
2. Pitching is a skill. It can make a good game appear bad. Practice will make it easier and more polished. It can even make a mediocre game *appear* good. It cannot *make* the game good.
3. There are multiple sources of video game development funding, even for a small indie studio. The type of funding can make you feel more or less like a "real" or "true" game developer. There is a hierarchy (see end of this chapter).
4. Time is precious for a small indie studio. Should a company invest time in more than one project at once? Advantage: more projects mean more chances for people to get excited. Disadvantage: each

project takes longer to develop; therefore, it takes longer to attract investor attention.

5.2 The Beginning of the End

Both the Quarry manager and the marketing intern departed the Quarry the same week. On her last day, the marketing intern led off back-to-back meetings attended by five companies from the first cohort. Hera introduced her.

Hera: I coerced her to present about what she learned over the last ten weeks. It feels longer than that.[1]

The presentation mainly served to illustrate the lost opportunity of her time in the Quarry. At the close of the presentation, Hera immediately moved on to the second meeting. The topic—what was happening to the first cohort?

Hera: Ultimately the goal here is to support everyone in the process. The Quarry is not for everyone. If you want to drop off, that is fine. We want to see progress toward corporate business and corporate intent. BAT will do due diligence and see that you will not take the money and run off.... There were not enough metrics and KPI that were reviewed quarterly. I have to suffer through KPI. Every business has them. The most important thing is, what do you need from the Digital Quarry? We have been guilty of throwing a lot at you. We want to know that you can get value. It needs to be articulated in some way. There are talks of reviewing the whole thing from April next year.... You may not want to stay here for another year. We want to be responsive to your needs. I think we are guilty of being too top down. We don't want to be in the position to hound people all the time. Some of the feedback we have received is that the mentor sessions have turned into casual conversations. The mentor sessions are to review plans and achieve what you need to do. If we don't have reviewable code, it's hard to check how you are doing. Talking themes and concepts doesn't help us. You need to

---

[1] *It was actually 12 weeks.*

	map that out and then in the business plan you need to articulate those things. BAT needs to see that progress is being made. It's not up to us to tell you what that progress is. It's up to you to tell us and how you will achieve that by being in the program again.
Aslani:	So, do you know the capacity, how many companies?
Hera:	We are limited by the seats. Technically we can have 42 people.
Vincent:	What is the make-up of the groups? Are you taking on new startup companies?
Hera:	Yes. Once a decision has been made and accepted, any new companies will go through a boot camp like the prototyping. You are more than welcome to attend that. [Everyone laughed.]
Aslani:	Is there anyone here not going to reapply and comfortable saying it?
Mario:	I'm probably not going to reapply.[2]
Collins:	Can you still take part without being in the Digital Quarry?
Hera:	You can still ask for BAT funding, mentor support. The space is an investment, but we are not trying to cut anyone off. It's not as 'on tap'. If you are in here, you have more access to it.
Collins:	I have a feeling I won't be applying for the second stage.
Aslani:	Are there any alternate arrangements for those that don't get in?
Hera:	We are asking for a graduate rate, but they haven't got back to us yet. There is also another building, but we haven't figured it out yet.
Aslani:	How many companies will apply for the next stage?
Hera:	The plan is that there will be two calls a year, five companies each time.
Collins:	These two calls, what if in six months we want to come back?
Hera:	I don't see a problem with that. This isn't the end.
Valentine:	I keep on thinking of divorce.
Hera:	No one wants you to fail. Everyone wants you to succeed.
Aslani:	This is in parallel….
Hera:	To the production funding. Yes, you can do both or neither.
Aslani:	So you're telling us that if we don't get money, we can stay. [Laughs.]

---

[2] *An informant would tell me: "Mario never expected to get into the Digital Quarry in the first place. I think he always saw it as just a desk."*

Later, I spoke with one of the missing companies. Vonn was recovering from a car accident. The concussion was not bad. I confirmed that he was the only one not applying for the mini-production funding. He chose not to go for the 30k "at this time. We might consider it later if it's still available.... BAT promised one thing and then delivered something else.... None of the games are going to be great at this stage." Besides, he already had separate funding for a project, and he didn't want to overcommit to either BAT or his other funder. Vonn continued, "BAT doesn't want to hear it, but office space and funding are the two important things. I can't afford to stay in the region without Digital Quarry funding." However, he had an issue if his company couldn't stay in the Quarry. His partner was on a visa that allowed him to stay in the region. Vonn could go anywhere, but his partner might have to return to India, which would hurt the plans for the game.

Quick Lessons

77. Each new cohort is a chance to refine the program. Feedback should be incorporated in a virtuous cycle of perpetual improvement. In this round, BAT decided the main changes should be cohort makeup (consistently in size and start dates), application process (interviews instead of business plans), and motivation (what can the Digital Quarry do for you).
78. Marketing is necessary. The Quarry companies did not think so. The marketing intern was wasted, but at least she got some practical experience.

There are several important things to note. BAT viewed the first cohort as failing to meet key performance indicators without discussing directly what those were. The Quarry was not a perpetual program. First cohort teams would have to leave. Some teams were ready to leave. Others were worried about the consequences. There were not ready replacements teams on tap. BAT did not know which companies were ready and available. Intending to remove 70% of Quarry participants without replacements combined with what happened in the RPP pitching led to the self-inflicted crisis.

5.3 Pitching

Six companies pitched games to BAT for additional funding. Most assumed the funding was a mere formality. Only two games were funded, both from the original cohort. By not funding any of the newer companies from cohort two, BAT was essentially killing the fledgling companies.

Monday afternoon—1:30pm.

I was waiting for Yohan when he arrived back from his presentation for the mini-production funding at the BAT office. Felix had gone over at noon to discuss the games with Buzz (one of the mentors) and Riley (BAT finance person). Originally the pitch was scheduled for a ten-minute presentation and ten-minute Q&A, but they upped the presentation to 20 minutes a couple days ago.

Yohan:	I had 18 slides. I didn't think I would fill the whole time, but I did.
Ethnographer:	What about the questions?
Yohan:	I don't know how long the questions lasted, but I think it was about ten minutes. Felix is the only one that has played the games, but he didn't ask any questions. Buzz mostly asked about the gameplay. Riley asked about ROI and where I got my numbers.
Ethnographer:	What did you say?
Yohan:	Research. Lots of research. It's hard to find revenue on mobile games. I offered to share them with her, but she declined. You can't expect your first game to make a million pounds.[3]

Sawyer came over to us and joined the conversation.

Yohan:	When are you doing your presentation?
Sawyer:	2:30pm. I have 22 slides including a title and thank you slide.
Yohan:	You actually have a chart so that is more impressive. I just had a table.

---

[3] *Holly and Celeste were in the pitch meeting too. Yohan wanted to show that he had a real team of people even if they weren't being paid by him at that moment. Holly was now looking for another job.*

5 BOSS FIGHT: CHANGES IN PRIORITIES LEAD TO A SELF-INFLICTED CRISIS

Sawyer:	I had a table for a long time. I assumed that Quincy would be there.
Yohan:	She is HR only.
Ethnographer:	Which prototype are you pitching?
Sawyer:	I'm pitching my week four "Lost at Sea" game.[4] I have three big publishers interested in it. Go with your strongest. I have two smaller publishers interested in week one game. Hera told me that once the money is mine, I can do what I want with it. I plan to work on both week one and week four games with the money. There is a lot of overlap. The week four game only includes one feature that couldn't be used in week one game. It would take two weeks to do.
Yohan:	Two days before the application deadline, BAT committee said we could deliver a vertical slice instead of a complete game. I told Buzz my week six game was the best, but I was unable to apply with it.[5]

Capone arrived and joined the conversation.

Capone:	You do your pitch yet?
Yohan:	Yes. I was glad there were game literate people there.
Capone:	Any probing questions?
Yohan:	Just where I got my numbers. The gameplay. Nothing I was caught up on. If you followed the guidelines 100%, you will be fine.
Capone:	Did they give you any indication when they were giving you an answer?
Yohan:	Sometime after the 29th.
Capone:	Oh man. That's a long time.
Yohan:	They said it's just like any other BAT thing. It has to go to committee.[6]

[4] *Someone said about Sawyer's week 4 game—"I thought he was doing a game he didn't want to do."*

[5] *Holly echoed the thought: "I was surprised he was pitching the week three game. I thought the week six game had a clearer way to make money."*

[6] *The second committee was a four-person panel with "the usual suspects and one board member." It doesn't list the board member, but Yohan said that unless it was legendary game developer, none of them really knew game development.*

Sawyer packed up his gear and departed for the pitch. Capone and Yohan continued talking.

Capone: There are no mentor meetings this week?
Yohan: I haven't seen any on Basecamp. Maybe because he is doing this. I'm fine with it honestly. Did you have the feedback meeting with BAT?
Capone: Yeah. It was very good. It was booked for half an hour, but it went on for an hour. Quincy canceled one of her other meetings. For me it's just communication. Communicate things better. Ask for our feedback once in a while.

Sawyer returned from his pitch. Capone immediately wanted to know about the questions.

Sawyer: Buzz wanted to know what I might screw up on. They were mostly gameplay-based questions. Riley only asked if I could get a local programmer. I told her that using local talent would cost 2–3 weeks of time and money in lost efficiency.
Capone: Where are you getting the programmer? Did you use that freelance online service I showed you where the person could be in Lithuania or Brazil or Spain?
Sawyer: I might. I told them I had a programmer in London, but I classified this as local-spend. I calculated that 84% of the £60,000 budget was local spend. BAT wanted 90% local-spend because it's a Quarry-only program.
Ethnographer: I thought the budget was only £30,000. Where did you get the other £30,000?
Sawyer: The application makes clear that the total budget can be up to £60,000, but that only £30,000 would be coming from BAT funding. The rest can be "in-kind" contributions. I listed myself for four roles within the project. Three of them pay me £10,000 each for the project. That becomes the in-kind contribution. I won't take any of that money until I make a profit. The fourth role pays me my "real" salary [at least until the game makes money] which is out of the £30,000. I could use the video game tax relief rebate cash to draw down on the money that the company will owe me after the project. You have to be dishonest.

Capone: I will do a version of that. Everyone will, but if they have more people in the company, they have flexibility. You feel good about it?

Sawyer: I feel fine. I had an answer and reason for every question. If I don't get it, I know it wasn't me.

Titus stopped me as I was about to leave for the day.

Ethnographer: Which game did you pitch?
Titus: Patterns.
Ethnographer: I'm surprised. That is not what I expected.[7]
Titus: We went around and asked what everyone's favorite was. It wasn't anyone's favorite.
Ethnographer: Interesting strategy.
Titus: We have a third meeting with [publisher] and a second meeting with [publisher]. We could come away with a big contract for our main game. If we get it, we might just have to crunch for a week to get stuff done on the week five game and keep BAT happy.... We said these similar games have made a lot of money. Hopefully our game will make the same. We have talked to some mobile publishers, and they would be interested if we made the game. We didn't want to pitch something that would take a year of our time. We wanted to get it out quick. I think we said the timeline is five months. So, it would come out in March. We can do it for £30,000. We probably would have done week three game, but I think it's a 100,000 quid game.

The Quarry was quiet with many people away at EGX. I sat alone at the back wall. Felix came over to me. I asked about the pitches. Felix:

It was unexpected. I just thought I was going to go there and talk to them about the games. I didn't realize I was going to stay all day. I didn't know my role there. I didn't know if I could ask questions or what I should say. I was told to evaluate them as if I was seeing them for the first time. It was weird since I thought they wanted me there because I had played all the

---

[7] *I didn't remember the prototype (without my field notes).*

games. By the third one, I got into it. I know that some teams went in with their second-choice game. I was surprised by some of the games people chose. I had to keep my mouth shut and not say if the company had a better game they didn't present. Buzz said that some of them were taking the easy route. I had to tell him that I have seen their community, and I think they can do it. They chose the game based on the budget.... Buzz said he talked to Capone two months ago about it, and Capone said he wasn't even sure he was going to be here in the Quarry.... It was surprisingly stressful.

The key takeaways from the pitching were as follows. Participants felt generally positive about the pitches. There continued to be confusion around the available funding and the deliverable requirements. Similar to the week 7 prototyping commercial presentations, participants guessed or fudged financial numbers to make the math work. Several companies did not choose their strongest offering. BAT blunted Felix as an asset by ignoring his feedback on playing the games.

Quick Lessons

79. Lying is required to get funding. At the very least, every team fudged, stretched, omitted, or bent the 'truth' to fit within the funding requirements. Then again, who really knows how much it will cost, how long it will take, or how much it will make?
80. Pitch the best game. What was the point of the prototyping if not that?
81. Utilize pre-existing knowledge. BAT probably thought they were being "objective" or "fair" by only considering the proposal in front of them. Felix had played the actual games! Why couldn't he use that knowledge in evaluating the projects? The games didn't lie. Based on his experience with the companies, he knew that talk and action may be two different things. Buzz had mentored the companies for months. He knew their capabilities, their weaknesses, and their chance of delivering. He knew it better than anyone else involved in the funding decision. Why not use this knowledge?

5.4 Aftermath of the First Cohort Exit Interviews

Members of the first cohort had exit interviews at BAT headquarters on Victoria Street. Several people from BAT along with Kofi and Felix were in the interview. The interviews progressed differently partly depending on Kofi's impression on companies' progress.

5.4.1 Challenging Power

While hanging out, I overheard about the exit interview for Aslani and Titus. Felix thought Kofi was in a bad mood from the start. Felix thought that Kofi didn't like them. Aslani agreed. Kofi wanted to give them a three-month business course. Aslani refused. He accused Aslani of "working *in* the business instead of *on* the business" with the emphasis on the 'in' and 'on'. Kofi tried to say that by giving her a spot, she was taking it from someone else. He talked about his responsibilities to the man on the street. She turned to BAT management and said that he had shared that there will not be a new cohort. Kofi fumed. Aslani offered to make an anonymous feedback form (Hera hadn't wanted one). Quincy argued that they couldn't bring in new companies until they fixed the problems. Aslani reflected, "If we didn't get back in, at least we wouldn't have to work with BAT ever again."

Another participant (Chiyo) provided additional context:

> Aslani and Titus took advice from Kofi and got screwed over. Kofi gave us advice multiple times and we just said 'yeah, we're not going to do that.' I think they had a problem because they didn't have a plan for the full year. I don't even know if Kofi will be back.... Sometimes he just disappears.

Aslani's exit interview illustrated the self-inflicted nature of the crisis. Kofi accused Aslani of not doing enough in the Quarry while concurrently faulting her for trying to get as much as she could from it. Despite her success in the Quarry, there were bitter feelings toward BAT.

5.4.2 Vonn Reverses His Decision

Vonn discussed strategy with his partner (Rocky).[8]

Vonn: So I talked to BAT. We are going to be here until the end of March. Afterward, do you want to pay for it?

Rocky: How much is it? Worse-case scenario, we can get a bigger house. Is it possible to share a working space with other people?

Vonn: That is what I am trying to figure out. Do you want to stay in the city?

Rocky: Yes, the city is good. We don't have to stay in this area of the city.

Vonn: If we are going to share office space, it will be in the city. Back home in my parents' house, I do have a space, if you want to go completely free.

Rocky: Or we can just rent a studio or a house here.

Vonn: We can't register the office to a house. If we are renting a place, a lot of the letting agencies will have a clause that you can't do that.

Rocky: If we just need a registered office, we can use the Gymnasium.

Vonn: Ok. I will look for a place here.

A week later, Vonn came back from his mentor meeting with Kofi. He stopped in the corner, breathing hard. He seemed on the verge of a panic attack. This would become a turning point for Vonn. Before this, Aslani had told me that Vonn was staying. Later, I heard from another team that Vonn was leaving. Collins speculated: "He has outside financing. Maybe BAT doesn't like it since it is not match-funding through them."

In the end, Vonn decided to join Collins and Mario in leaving the Quarry after one year. All three companies slipped out under the proverbial cover of darkness. There was no fanfare. They left on different Mondays, but the pattern was the same. They worked normally then one morning their equipment was gone.

The remaining teams fought and received a six-month extension. The original BAT plan for a third cohort was canceled. BAT reversed its decision to expel the first cohort, but the damage had already been done. The threat raised questions, again, about the philosophical purpose of the Quarry.

---

[8] As a reference point, the cost of an office for a larger team (up to ten people) was £12,000 per year. This was the equivalent of an employee for six months or more. For some teams, this was reason enough to stay in the Quarry.

Quick Lessons

82. If you want the money, you need to jump through hoops (Aslani and Titus) or be good enough to not need it (Chiyo).
83. Alienating your passionate supporters does not help. Aslani and Titus were probably the most emotionally invested of the Quarry companies. Many other companies either treated it as a "free desk" (Vonn and others) or a "nice to have" (Chiyo). Asking them to leave was one thing, but sullying the relationship was counterproductive.
84. Indie game development means saving money wherever possible. In terms of workspace, the teams were considering everything from their parents' basement to full offices. Advanced planning would have helped. Some teams did not fully appreciate that their time in the Quarry might end at the one-year mark. This left them scrambling for alternative options.

5.5 Funding Results

Capone was told the mini-production funding results would come back on the 29th. On Wednesday morning, the 30th, Sawyer emailed Riley to ask. She said they would all get answers by the end of the week. Collins admitted, "I had forgotten about it. There is no point sitting around waiting for an email.... Maybe they are thinking about giving some people part of the money, like £10,000 and instead saying 'screw them all.'" He was almost right.

5.5.1 The Other 10%

I talked with Aslani and Chiyo in the kitchen.

Aslani:	Have you heard back on the mini-production funding?
Chiyo:	No, but I'm 90% sure that we're both getting the funding.
Ethnographer:	What's the other 10%?
Chiyo:	BAT.
Aslani:	What do you think are the chances that we never hear about it again?

Ethnographer:	10%.
Chiyo:	Funny.
Aslani:	We have people interested in some of the prototypes. One publisher asked for a build of the week three game. We don't have a working build. Another wanted us to send over week six game. That was before EGX. I still haven't done it.
Chiyo:	Was there any commitment?
Aslani:	No. They just asked for the build.
Chiyo:	They say just send over a build like it is no big deal. It's only a week-old game.
Aslani:	We're a small team. I don't have fucking time.
Chiyo:	We've been turned down by one publisher so far. I have a couple more that I am waiting to hear back from.
Aslani [looking at her phone]:	We will know by the end of the week. BAT will send out an email.

> **Quick Lessons**
>
> 85. Money is given to teams, not games. Aslani was waiting for 90%-likely-to-be-successful funding results on one prototype. Meanwhile, publishers were asking for builds on two other prototypes, neither of which was available. Maybe the prototypes were that good, but more likely, the people with money felt confident in her team.
> 86. Getting publisher interest is not the same as getting publisher money. You can get interest based on a concept or prototype. Then they will want to see a build, and another build, until they have basically seen the final game. It's no big deal for them to ask. The developer is the one that has to invest the time and the money with no guarantee of success.

5.5.2 *Finding Out the Results*

The results of the funding traveled fast. Almost everyone seemed to know even if some of them haven't been in the Quarry. I found out that the second cohort had a Basecamp group: "We need a place to bitch about some things…. They must have sent all the emails at the same time." Sawyer posted first that he didn't get the money, then Yohan, then Capone, before Chiyo, then Aslani added that they were funded.

As a reminder, Hera originally said that there was money for all teams. They would be competing against an idea or the marketplace. Instead, unbeknownst to them, they began competing against each other. Collins came up to me.

Collins:	I didn't get the mini-production money. No one on the back wall did…. They attached an appeal form. I have failed to get funding before, but I don't remember them attaching the appeal form before. They said that more feedback will be coming this week…. I'm surprised they didn't give it to any of the new companies.
Ethnographer:	Do you plan to appeal?
Collins:	I don't know. Monetization is not even a word you use with premium games. You have a price…. They said there were three pots, but one team got development funding and one got production funding. They changed the wording on it to 'development or production' funding. I've never seen that before. They said development means creating a minimum viable something…
Ethnographer:	Product.
Collins:	No, not product. Material that can secure a publishing deal. Production requires you to release something…. I'm not bitter. I'm not even really bothered…. It was idiotic. Maybe that is too strong a word. It was idiotic to think that we could get any real interest at Gamescom for games we built in a week. Everyone at Gamescom says the idea sounds good and send me a build after you spend 50,000 quid on it…. I'm going to wait to see what Juno [the new Quarry manager] says after she talks to them…. I'm not even sure I want the money. This way I can just wipe my hands clean of this last year. I won't have to worry about paying back a loan. We'll close all the prototypes. We'll change the title and start on the week six idea again…. Am I leaving 30,000 pounds just sitting there because I don't want to deal with it?

After I heard the news from Collins, I went up to Aslani and Titus when they arrived back from lunch.

Ethnographer: Congratulations.
Aslani: Yes. I feel bad for the second cohort.... I don't know if I should be celebrating. It feels like I am rubbing it in their face.
Titus: I feel bad, but at least we got it. They didn't make it out to be so competitive. I thought that it was earmarked for us.
Aslani: How do they expect to derisk the new companies if they don't give them funding to do it?

Initially, the funding results created conflicted ambiguous feelings in the teams. Some looked back at the pitch and choice of game and wondered if something could have been done differently. Some felt almost guilty because they knew what it meant for the other teams to go unfunded. There was a feeling of wanting to share the information and experience with others. They needed to process what it meant.

Quick Lessons

87. Walking away from potential funding can be the right choice. It's difficult to ignore the sunk cost (what you have already invested in a game—money, time, belief). Unless you already have a deal or are minutes from the finish line, there will be a lot more cost to keep going. Base the decision on what is left to be done.

88. Collins made the right choice for multiple reasons:
    - It was a *chance* for 30,000 GBP. There were potentially three other competitors. But wasn't his pitch regarded as the best unfunded one? Sure, but they weren't pitching. They were appealing. It was about the process. The prototype didn't matter.
    - The funding was 20,000 GBP short. Collins knew he needed 50,000 to pique publisher interest. Unless BAT was going to fund the prototype a third time, he had enough money for half a vertical slice.

(continued)

> (continued)
> - The funding was technically a loan. It was only repayable if he made money, but it added another layer of administration.
> - There was an idea that excited him more. He had put it on hold for the prototyping, but it better fit his company ethos.
>
> 89. It's okay to feel multiple conflicting things. You can feel happy for yourself and sad for someone else. You can feel you deserved the money and that the process was unfair.

5.5.3 Disorienting

Capone showed up for his mentor meeting with Buzz. It had been a few months since the two had talked.

Buzz:	I heard from our friend here [the ethnographer] that you didn't get funding. No one tells me anything.
Capone:	Were you surprised by that in my case?
Buzz:	I was a bit. It was physically disorienting. I think the big problem was that you hadn't figured out how the main gameplay feature worked.
Capone:	I had two weeks before Gamescom. Then I had two weeks for the panel. That's all I've spent on it. I tried to get it across to the panel.
Buzz:	It was close. Ultimately, we were choosing three teams.
Capone:	Winners?
Buzz:	Only so many people were going to get funded. There was only funding for three projects. It wasn't solely judged on its merits. It wasn't a wholesale rejection.
Capone:	That's how it felt.
Buzz:	If you had a team of four in there working away, you would have been in a stronger position. Realistically, you weren't in that position.
Capone:	I don't know where to go from here. The most established teams got funded. It was rather cynical. I know what projects they pitched. They were safer. I went with the one I thought was the coolest. It was different. It creates doubts.
Buzz:	If you are funding based on the likelihood of delivering, then you look at the teams.

Capone: The teams that got the money, they have other projects. They have other priorities. I was really disappointed that neither of the three of us got funded. Firstly, there was the thought for myself. I knew I had a weird idea. I hadn't figured out how to pitch it. Then the three of us got declined. And two first cohort companies got funded. What is your feedback to me?

Buzz: It needs a little refining.

Capone: I made an honest presentation. I put all my cards on the table. I know I am not there yet, but I am making steps in the right direction.

Buzz: For what it's worth, I thought it was one of the top three.

Capone: You don't know how the committee went?

Buzz: No, I just sent my recommendation. There was a lot of debate.

Capone: I feel that sends a bad message. I feel like they could have funded one of the three from the second cohort. It's like they're saying, you come in here, and we don't have confidence in any of you three. It's very damning. There's money still on the table. They couldn't have given us like 10 or 15,000? I could have used that until January.

Buzz: I don't think it's the end of the road for you.

Capone: It feels like ... the thought has crossed my mind. My objective was to make a game. I have doubts. I had been feeling more confident about it.... For me, what I have, I am less worried. I have this other job. I can self-fund to a point. Not getting the vmoney, it was a real gut punch.... I got feedback from friends. I'm not a visual person. I only made the changes I had time for. I am going to explore the possibility if I can resubmit later.

Buzz: I don't know. I am going to sit down with Juno later on. All the mentors are meeting next week over on Victoria Street. Hopefully we will find out more then.

Capone: They only funded two of three. That makes you think.

Buzz: I don't know how BAT funding works. They have invested a lot in this place. Vincent hasn't got his project out. Mario hasn't got his project out. They don't have any money coming back in.

Capone: If the feedback is kinda what you said. What is the appetite to resubmit with the tweaks? The three of us are kinda stuck.

Buzz: It's a blessing and a curse. It takes up a lot of your time.

After the meeting, I spoke with Capone over a mug of tea. I asked how he was feeling. Capone commented:

Bittersweet. I really thought more of us would get the money. I got the email late afternoon. I just couldn't work after I read it. I wasn't sure if I was going to continue in the Digital Quarry. I was asking what is the point? If you had asked me yesterday, I would have said I wasn't going to continue. But today I had two good meetings. First with Juno and then with Buzz. I think BAT got lucky. I need to leave a few days for this to settle. I will get back to work tomorrow. I can see why some people didn't want to stay.... I might consider paying someone out of my own pocket if they give me another chance. If they say, do a new build and submit it in a month and Felix and Buzz will evaluate it, I will have to make something.

For Capone, the funding results led to an existential crisis. Did he want to continue in the Digital Quarry? Did he want to continue as a video game developer? Capone brought up two important points. First, none of the second cohort companies received funding, and they were the teams that needed it the most. Second, the timing of everything worked against success. The teams didn't have enough time to produce a quality product while at the same time, BAT took a long time to reply with the results. The teams went from one limbo to another.

Quick Lessons

90. Rejection sucks, but it is inevitable. The problem for Capone was twofold. The timing was unfavorable. He had invested his pre- and post-Gamescom time into the project, and then waited a long time for the answer. It was a drawn-out death, and the option to appeal suggested it would continue. Additionally, he identified with the second cohort. He felt the rejection of the other teams. It felt personal.

    - Buzz reflected, "I have been applying for jobs. Some I don't even want, and it still hurts when I don't get it."

91. Mentors can be useful as judges, but it puts them in an uncomfortable position. The meeting with Capone wasn't too awkward. Buzz could truthfully say that he recommended funding Capone's project. It also meant he had voted against other mentees.

    - In contrast to Kofi, Buzz seemed to effectively balance being both mentor and judge in this instance.

5.5.4 Never Do or Die

Buzz next met with Collins, another of the unfunded.

Collins: The mini-production funding didn't come through. I felt that what I presented wasn't what they expected.... What did the ones that did get it have that we didn't? Maybe I stayed too true to the concept of the period. It was supposed to be a small project. That's how we pitched it.

Buzz: Specifically in your case, I don't know why they didn't go for it. I would be interested in knowing.

Collins: The mini-production thing was never do or die for us. We will continue on with it. We can make it small and make it in a year. We have these publishers that are interested. They weren't going to be interested right now. If we work on it and get something for January, we can see if they will give us money. Then we can get BAT to invest in a different way.

For Collins, the funding results were disappointing yet symbolic of the Quarry as a whole. The rapid prototyping and mini-production funding promised great things. In the end, they did not deliver, and if a team wanted to make them work, they had to go it alone. Collins took it all in stride. The negative funding results essentially ended his involvement in the Quarry. He would leave the Quarry and seek future funding elsewhere.

> **Quick Lessons**
>
> 92. Perceived funding boundaries can impact creativity. Collins believed he was rejected for two general reasons. First, he pitched the project within the funding boundaries—small and quick. He was punished for lack of ambition rather than rewarded for a tightly scoped project. Second, he wanted something inventive—not a Zelda knockoff. This was hard to make and harder to pitch.

(continued)

(continued)

93. Each funding opportunity is simply one opportunity. For Collins, the second round of funding would have been nice. At a 50,000 budget, it was the chance to make a small, nice game that might attract publisher interest. At a 30,000 budget, it was the chance to make a quick, small game and self-publish it. The alternative was contract work or restarting the (on hold) main game. BAT pushing contract work in the first six months of cohort one helped Collins (and others) to have alternatives to BAT funding. The second cohort went immediately into rapid prototyping. It was all they had.

5.5.5 A Mentor Reacts

Collins left, and I stayed on to talk more with Buzz.

Buzz:	It seemed like it was universally agreed that Collins and Chiyo had the best games. Others preferred Aslani's game. It was too simplistic for me. I preferred Capone's game. Sawyer and Yohan had no chance. They weren't at the same level. But I agree with Yohan that his week six game was better, but he chose to pitch based on what he could get done with the money. Capone did the same. I preferred his week three game, but it couldn't be done within the budget.
Ethnographer:	It was tough when the funding dropped.
Buzz:	I think it made everyone mad.
Ethnographer:	How would you rank the games?
Buzz:	Personally, I put (1) Chiyo, (2) Capone, (3) Collins, (4) Aslani, and Yohan/Sawyer in back. I think collectively it must have been (1) Chiyo, (2) Aslani, (3) Collins, (4) Capone, and Yohan/Sawyer in back. I'm going to ask Riley why Collins was not funded. I thought there was a feeling toward wanting to give Collins the money.
Ethnographer:	What about the second cohort?
Buzz:	I'm disappointed that one of the new teams didn't get any money.
Ethnographer:	Did you see any of Vonn's games?

Buzz: I didn't even know he did the RPP.... Something needs to change about the Digital Quarry. All the new teams are in trouble. Capone is probably in the best position because he has flexibility with his part time high paying job. I'm meeting next week with BAT.... There's a place in the southwest. It's like an incubator that has a combination of mature companies and start-ups. They are paid like £14,000 per year to be there.

Quick Lessons

94. Committees choose the least uncomfortable options. According to Buzz, the top projects and the two bottom projects were clear. This left three teams fighting for "two" funding spots. Different members must have had different issues with the different projects. Buzz liked Capone's game, but he was likely a minority of one (plus, Capone was second cohort). Buzz thought Aslani's game was too simple, but she had the most reliable team. Collins was known for experimental games, so someone was probably worried about the commercial potential of the finished product.

    - As Chiyo mentioned earlier, his team tended to do what they wanted even if it didn't follow the rules exactly (they were that good). He pitched a project that couldn't be completed for 50,000, let alone 30,000. Lucky for them, BAT made a last-minute change to allow developing a "vertical slice." Hence, Chiyo received "development" funding rather than "production" funding.

95. The best games don't always get funded. According to Buzz, it seemed people agreed Collins had the second-best game (although he personally put it third). Therefore, his failure to secure funding was based on non-game factors.

96. Indirect investing leads to vulnerability. BAT did not invest directly in the companies. Even the prototyping and second funding were project based. This made the teams vulnerable and the Quarry vulnerable. Many accelerators take an ownership stake (Cohen, 2013). BAT did not want to enter video game management. Their outsized role in the region meant this choice carried additional consequences.

Like others, Buzz felt that not funding any of the newer teams risked letting them fail. He tied the results directly to potential problems with the Quarry as a program. BAT had picked winners with the funding (Baum & Silverman, 2004). The alternative would have been to support some of the smaller companies in the hope of moving from start-up to more mature companies. It was a philosophical choice—one Buzz did not entirely support. He suggested a need to re-envision the Quarry.

5.5.6 Congratulations

The next day brought more mentor meetings discussing the fallout to the funding. Aslani was in an enviable position. In the same week, her team had secured funding twice. Her week five prototype received BAT mini-production funding. Next, another game received a second round of funding from a national agency. She also had a third project in development (although it was unfunded). Her team was currently five people.

Aslani: We got the funding, but I'm sure you heard about that.
Buzz: I heard it secondhand. There was a possibility of three teams. I think some teams just thought if you had a good idea-
Aslani: I literally thought it was a formality. I'm glad that I thought that.
Buzz: So you have £30,000 of funding for that. That is for what?
Aslani: That is for soft launch with day one and day seven retention statistics and then shop it around.
Buzz: Congratulations on your main game.
Aslani: Thank you. The people that are interested in that type of game were really into it. The Twitter feed has been blowing up.... I went to bed last night, not stressed for the first time in ages.
Buzz: What is the production timeline for week five game?
Aslani: It's scheduled between now and March.
Buzz: So you are out of here in April?
Aslani: Pretty much everyone is looking for a place together.

For Aslani, the mini-production funding was good news. One of her company's other projects had also secured the next round of funding. The two sources of funding would buy her another six months of operations. It should have validated her time in the Quarry. Her company should have been considered a Quarry success story, but as illustrated earlier with her exit interview, that was not the case. Even funding a team did not lead to hope or inspiration. Later, she said, "Thinking back to the rapid prototyping, there was no good reason why those new teams should have been competing with us for the same pot of funding. They were too new. They were not on the same track. We are three years old and have five people. It was really messed up."

> **Quick Lesson**
>
> 97. Running an indie video game development company is stressful. It took not one but two successful funding bids in one week for Aslani to not feel stressed. The respite was only temporary. She was already thinking about what would come after the next six months.

5.5.7 Confused and Frustrated

I waited in the boardroom for the next mentor meeting. It was more intense than usual. Yohan spoke loudly during most of the meeting. He was visibly upset. His voice quivered during various moments. He apologized several times for being emotional.

Buzz: How are you doing?
Yohan: A little confused. I got the feedback. It looked like it was cobbled together by someone that wasn't there.
Buzz: I haven't seen the feedback. I saw Collins' feedback. Honestly, I didn't understand it.
Yohan: The committee noted that 'without a defined art style it is difficult to tell the target audience.' Not true. It's in the pitch deck. I also had target slices. It's not unheard-of thing to say this is an all-ages thing. It's just an old form of marketing. That is stuff we have been told throughout the process. 'The project intends to change rules throughout gameplay that could lead to frustration for the player if not handled well.' We developed that because the theme was gaslighting. 'The monetization is based on buying items for your character which is costly.' That is like one of the least costly things. A lot of us thought it was a formality. It felt like it was decided before we even did the pitch.

	It didn't feel like it was in the right faith. Looking at this feedback, it makes me feel worse. At first, I thought I should appeal, but I'm so frustrated with BAT that I don't think that I should. I have lost trust in the institution. That is why I am never here. When talking to BAT management, they kept talking about the Digital Quarry as real estate instead of an accelerator.... They keep changing the rules. Hera told us directly that each team was earmarked 50,000 which was obviously not true. I have lost trust in BAT.
Buzz:	The whole second cohort is in the same position.... So, you are in position now where you have no funding, and you don't have a viable product, presumably.
Yohan:	I've said this whole time, if they had been consistent on their deliverables, I would have chosen a stronger product. I do have interest from other companies. The amount of frustration I have felt here is not worth it. I feel bad for my team.... I don't work for BAT. I work for my company. I work for my team. I was forced to go against my own values with the 'crunch' stuff, but I did it for BAT. I've participated in some of their events. They seem to want us to be shinny dancing puppets to show how nice the region is.
Buzz:	It was a mismatch of expectations.
Yohan:	They gave us that expectation numerous times.
Buzz:	I honestly don't believe there is bad faith.
Yohan:	Some of this probably has to do with Hera leaving.
Buzz:	Hopefully, having Juno on the ground will help.
Yohan:	I'm just worried because she is a business developer.
Buzz:	A lot of the funding they have done has not come out. They don't know the returns yet.... The three new companies are at a dead-end.
Yohan:	A vote of no confidence. A late vote of no confidence because we got into the Quarry in the first place, so they must have seen some commercial potential.
Buzz:	There was no debate about your company getting in. Everyone was confident. You have been unsuccessful in this application, but it doesn't mean that everything you are doing is wrong.
Yohan:	I know that. Rejection is part of the process. I'm used to it. I just don't know if I can trust BAT to have the capacity to understand the pitch I submitted.

Buzz: The first cohort leaving, the whole Hera leaving, it's a chance to look at it and do it differently.

Yohan: They keep telling us that we are not meeting KPI, but they won't tell us what they are.... I've mostly avoided coming in because I've gotten bad vibes here.

> **Quick Lessons**
>
> 98. Feedback can make things worse. Misunderstanding and injustice are especially problematic. For Yohan, he felt his game was misunderstood. He blamed it on non-gaming people making the decisions (while ignoring Buzz and Felix). They disagreed on facts (did the pitch deck include something) and method (how to market the game). Feelings of injustice arose from multiple places—the funding cut, the last-minute change on what could be pitched, and detriment of adhering to the prototyping week's theme. This type of feedback, although perhaps unbeknownst to BAT, made Yohan angrier than a generic form letter of rejection.
> 99. Sometimes life imitates art. Yohan pitched a game where the rules keep changing. The committee thought it would frustrate the player if not done well. That is exactly how Yohan (the player) felt about BAT and the Quarry (the game).

For Yohan, the funding results were just another mistake in a long line of mistakes perpetuated by BAT. He connected Hera leaving, the change in available funding, and the limited feedback on the pitches. They were all symptoms of how BAT viewed the Digital Quarry—in his words, quoting BAT, as "real estate instead of an accelerator." This was a philosophical view on the Quarry—what it was and what it should be. For Yohan, the fundamental issue was that Quarry participants and BAT did not agree on the point of the Quarry and therefore, how it should run.

5.5.8 A Part-Time Job

The next day, the mentor meetings continued. Buzz had a video call with Sawyer. He reported that Sawyer was "devastated" about the lack of funding. He might need to get a "part-time job." I managed to sit in on the following week's mentor meeting. Kwame asked if he was "in stasis." Sawyer replied:

> Even after the pitch, I kind of was in a holding pattern. I haven't known what to do, especially since I found out that I didn't get the funding. I'm going to have to go find something else to do that will pay me to be in the Digital Quarry part time. I was talking to Juno, and she said that the £30,000 pot is still there. We could divide it among the four teams that didn't get it. But we won't find out about that until 9th of December at the earliest. Instead of spinning my wheels, that will give me something to do…. The feedback I got on the mini-production fund was one paragraph. I didn't have concept art, so they couldn't judge it. Was that all that was wrong? They didn't tell me anything else. It wasn't valuable feedback. I was also at a disadvantage because I had to go into the monetization a lot … where I got my numbers. I spent half of the time pitching, explaining that. Still the mini-production funding would have been nice.

> **Quick Lesson**
>
> 100. Pitch the game, not the money. People are not inspired by spreadsheet figures of all the money they can make. They are excited by ideas, stories, and art. Get them invested in the concept, then prove it's not commercially dead.

All second cohort company directors would eventually seek part-time employment. They lost most of their employees as well. Companies invested two months in the rapid prototyping (for which they were paid for six weeks) and another two months afterward (unpaid). In the end, it appeared that most had little to show for it. By funding only two of the seven rapid prototyping teams, BAT was wiping out four months of effort by five teams.

5.6 Conclusion

BAT self-inflicted a crisis in the Digital Quarry via two intertwined crux events. First, BAT blew up the mini-production funding for rapid prototyping teams. They reduced the funding amount available per team, reduced the number of funding pots available, and failed to fund any of the second cohort. Together this threatened the viability of several companies in the Quarry. Second, BAT fumbled the one-year anniversary of the first cohort. They tried to expel the first cohort, reversed their decision, canceled the third cohort, and ended up losing three companies anyway. All this created general and unnecessary animosity and set back the development of the Quarry, and Quarry companies, by six months.

The self-inflicted crisis was not solely the failure to fund the teams (although that didn't help either), it was the lack of communication and transparency in the decision making—specifically around reducing the funding and then only funding some projects. The same issues also appeared in the decision to extend the first cohort. It was nebulous and changing and somewhat preventable. It appeared that after BAT had made the decisions, they knew there would be consequences. They waited to deliver the decisions until Juno was available, so she could clean up the mess.

5.6.1 Reflections on Practical Lessons

1. BAT did not have a plan for the third cohort. They probably expected Hera to have the plan, but once she decided to leave, she did nothing about it. Most of the first cohort did not have a plan for what would happen at the end of their one year. Mario had made his decision around the time the rapid prototyping disrupted the working space. He had already received what he needed from the Quarry (help securing a commercial publishing deal). Collins waited to see what more was on offer from the Quarry before deciding to leave. The rest of the first cohort were motivated by a desire to delay decision-making. In the end, BAT likely delayed the third cohort because they needed a Quarry manager to manage it all.
2. Money changes everything. It can send you to the moon, or it can bury you in the ground.
3. Should small indie game studios work on multiple projects at the same time? The results of the mini production funding reveal insights but not a clear answer. In the case of the second cohort, all three studios abandoned their main game in favor of going "all in" on the rapid prototyping and mini production funding application. When none of them received funding, it was crippling to their studios. In contrast, two of the first cohort studios continued to work on their main games at the same time as pitching for the mini pro-

duction funding. Yes, they both secured the funding, but because they had other games in production, the result mattered less to them. A further perspective is provided by Collins and Vonn. In both cases after not securing funding from BAT, both directors chose to abandon the prototypes in favor of existing games. For the three non-participating studios, they were all working on a single game and had been for a long time.

4. Here is the hierarchy for indie game studio funding:

   (a) Commercial publishers
   (b) Royalties:

   - From previous games
   - From early access
   - Other (e.g. licensing—very unlikely)

   (c) Semi-public creative funds
   (d) Online fundraising (e.g. Kickstarter, GoFundMe)
   (e) Subcontracting:

   - Building a full game
   - Building a partial game
   - Building a prototype

   (f) Client work

   - Private games (e.g. educational game for private company)
   - Making assets
   - Gamification

   (g) Family and friends
   (h) Side hustles:

   - Teaching games
   - Semi-creative gig work
   - Everything else (e.g. self-financing from non-games jobs)

References

Baum, J. A., & Silverman, B. S. (2004). Picking winners or building them? Alliance, intellectual, and human capital as selection criteria in venture financing and performance of biotechnology startups. *Journal of Business Venturing, 19*(3), 411–436.

Cohen, S. (2013). What do accelerators do? Insights from incubators and angels. *Innovations: Technology, Governance, Globalization, 8*(3–4), 19–25.

CHAPTER 6

Extra Life: New Power Leads to a Change of Direction

6.1 Introduction

In this chapter

- A new Quarry manager begins.
- Some members of the first cohort leave without a trace.
- The second cohort is given some funding.
- A new hybrid space is proposed.
- A global pandemic shuts down the Quarry.

6.1.1 Conceptual Development

Chapter 2 (new cohort entering) and Chap. 4 (powerful social actor surprise departure) established entries and exits as crux events. As a complement, the *introduction of a new powerful social actor* and *departure of some original cohort members* is a crux event. BAT installed a new manager one month after the previous one left. The new manager (Juno) was faced immediately with the self-inflicted crisis and the impending departure of some original Quarry members. Additionally, she discovered a lack of documentation from her predecessor, an underutilized QA trainee, and

© The Author(s), under exclusive license to Springer Nature Switzerland AG 2025
D. Gidley, *Innovation and Entrepreneurship in the Indie Video Game Industry*, https://doi.org/10.1007/978-3-031-80877-7_6

unused feedback from Quarry companies. Once again, we must return to the past to tell the thematic story. Chronologically, this partly overlaps with the previous chapter's events.

6.1.2 Practical Lessons

1. Programs like the Quarry need an active everyday manager. If there are specific goals, which there always are, participants cannot be allowed to roam free-range.
2. Accelerators and incubators require participants. Without them, there is no purpose to the program. Coworking spaces only require paying members. It does not matter if those members show up to use the space.
3. If you have an underutilized asset (e.g. interns), there are a couple of options. First, you could offload the asset (e.g. fire the person). You can modify the asset to make it more useful (e.g. have the intern do something else). Or you can modify the structure to make the asset needed (e.g. intern as compliance officer).
4. There are no set rules on how an innovation space should be run.

6.2 A New Quarry Manager Begins

The expectations for the new Quarry manager differed depending on perspective. One Quarry member observed that the QA intern was taking a more active management role: "I think Juno has been on Felix to whip us into shape." In some ways that fit with one mentor's prediction: "I think there will be a division of labor. Felix will be doing the dirty work and that will free Juno up to work on higher level stuff." And yet, her first Basecamp post: "Hi everyone, regarding stuff not working, I'm working on it. Please bear with me." She meant some technical equipment, but it could also be read organizationally.

6.2.1 First Impressions

I had met Juno once before, but when she made her first official appearance in the Quarry, I didn't recognize her. Her business attire didn't disguise her habit of running half-marathons on the weekend. She wore her hair in a ponytail and walked silently in high-performance running shoes.

She came up to Collins and me. She shook my hand, and asked Collins how he was doing. We said fine.

Collins: Will you be based out of the Quarry?
Juno: I will be here and there. I think you would get tired of my face if I was here all the time. You don't need me here all the time. Right now, I am reading up on four years of information.

After a few minutes, she left. Juno had this certain abruptness about her that gave the impression she was 'short' with people. I didn't really think he meant it, but it was difficult to tell in the early days.

Ethnographer: Do you think Juno knows you're leaving?
Collins: I don't think so.
Ethnographer: Maybe she will ask you to stay.

As I left a mentor meeting, Juno invited me to join her in the Playroom for a chat. She said that she had just wanted to meet with people for 15–20 minutes each. She asked me about my project. I explained what I had been doing and how long I planned to stay.

Juno: It's not quite clear to me your role.
Ethnographer: Well…[1]
Juno: Are you here every day?
Ethnographer: Most days.
Juno: I have to answer to my bosses back at BAT. I have to protect the privacy of the people in the Quarry.
Ethnographer: Of course.[2]

Probably, Juno was simply trying to figure out all the social actors in the Quarry. At the same time, it established the tone that she would be different than Hera. People would have a different relationship with her. On a personal note, I would never develop the easy relationship with Juno that I had with Hera. Professionally, we had no issues. I think she was happy (or relieved) to see me depart the Quarry although that might also have applied to all the members in the liminal space.

[1] *What was I going to say—neither is anyone else?*
[2] *I wondered if BAT had warned her about me (see the prologue).*

> **Quick Lesson**
>
> 101. Seek to understand structure and practice. One tells you how things are supposed to work, and one tells you how they actually do. To her credit, Juno immediately sought to understand the Quarry and its members. She read documentation, and she talked to people. If something didn't make sense, like my role, she kept watch on it.

6.2.2 How Juno Initially Views the Digital Quarry

Juno led an international trade delegation on a tour of the Quarry. A ten-minute introduction summarized her view of the Quarry. Juno:

> I'm a program manager at BAT. The Quarry is effectively an incubator slash accelerator for the video game industry in the region. It's a space where they can collaborate with other game companies. They get space. They get access to mentors. They get access to workshops. Our goal is to give these companies the opportunity to grow as a company. Some came in as one or two people and will leave in March as five or six. They also have the opportunity to pitch for funding. BAT supports a lot of interactive development. Predominantly, the industry in the region is all local. By nature, it is very collegiate. There is a lot of work done between the team in supporting each other and helping. Everyone in the region kind of knows each other. They share in each other's successes. The companies sort themselves.... This [the Digital Quarry] is part of our commitment at BAT for four years. Hopefully, it's a space where they can feel comfortable. The Gymnasium [as building host] is being recognized in the UK as a space for innovation. It's a testament to what they have been doing. Currently, we have seven from the first cohort and three from the second. Several have left, but we are sitting at six to eight for the moment. The next cohort will start in March/April 2020. They can apply for funds throughout the year.... I am kind of doing a lot of research into incubators at the minute. In the UK, there is a lot of balance between tech and gaming. We were lucky to set up here because of the immersive lab as well.

Juno touched on all the main points of the Quarry in her speech: incubator-accelerator, growth, BAT's commitment, congeniality, and a new cohort. It was the old Quarry, the one she had joined. Her vision would be different, but at this point, she had implemented nothing new. She was just another social actor in the Quarry. She may have had the title of Quarry Manager, but she had not yet become the *powerful* institutional actor that her position allowed.

> **Quick Lesson**
>
> 102. People pitch the good things. It's the ideal. It's not always like that. It's certainly not like that for everyone. The Quarry was a place where people had "access" to mentors and workshop, but it didn't mean they used them. In a moment of confession, Juno acknowledged that the ten Quarry companies were currently more like "six to eight." She didn't pitch it as a place where the manager didn't know the current count of members. It just came out.

6.2.3 Quality Assurance Reset

I asked Felix how things were going.

Felix:	It looks like Juno is getting things together. We are going to start using a QA sheet next week. That will be good.
Ethnographer:	Did your role get sorted?
Felix:	Somewhat. I have been given a list of business development contacts. I'm supposed to go through them and find one for each company. It has really helped having Juno here. She is doing a lot. Juno is pushing for me to get an extension on my training.
Ethnographer:	Do you want an extension?
Felix:	Yes. They owe me. They left me sitting around for five months. Juno agrees.
Ethnographer:	Would the extension fulfill some of the things you were supposed to get the first time?
Felix:	I didn't know what I wanted when I first got here. I knew getting some experience would show me.

Juno began by addressing the QA role. It made sense. Felix was her one direct report. BAT had been liaising with Felix in the absence of a Quarry manager. With the limited documentation left by Hera, the institutional knowledge kept by Felix became more valuable. He had insider knowledge and opinions on how to change things. Eventually, it would seem like he was marginalized, but for now, he helped Juno to overcome her knowledge deficit.

> **Quick Lesson**
>
> 103. Without power, you are on the whims of others. Felix experienced a brief period where he was valued by BAT and others. It was his position within the Quarry. First, BAT used him as a surrogate in between Quarry managers. Second, Juno used him as a knowledge bank while she onboarded with the Quarry. Felix was rewarded with an extension on his role, but it wasn't clear if he ever received what he wanted from the job.

6.3 Cohort One Shrinks

I walked up to Collins talking to Ruby.

Collins:	I am moving my equipment this weekend.
Ruby:	Oh, shit. Vincent said you were going to be here until the end of November.
Collins:	No, I had to be out by the 17th. This just works out better.

I went over to my area. It was empty. No one sat in the back row. It felt lonely without Collins.

I heard Vonn had left the Quarry from another participant.

Dante:	He says it's easier to work from home. He doesn't have a reason to be here. None of the three teams do. Luigi and I worked from home for the first year. Maybe somebody needs the space to come in and work, but it's easier to work from home.
Ethnographer:	What about Rocky?
Dante:	He said something like it's broken apart. I don't know. I didn't think it was a great idea to ask him at that

moment.... I think it was the car accident. He hasn't been the same since then.

Others hadn't been the same recently either.

Thorne: I haven't been in because I didn't want to depress people.
Ruby: I don't think anyone is paying attention to what you are doing at your desk.
Thorne: They would if the sound of Super Mario is coming from there.

As mentioned in the last chapter, several of the first cohort disappeared from the Quarry without fanfare. Juno did not try to retain the departing first cohort members. In the case of the second cohort, some disappeared temporarily. There were no consequences for not being in the Quarry. Juno made no effort to change Hera's practice of non-enforcement of the attendance policy.

Quick Lessons

104. If space is a big seller, then it has to be sold to people that value it or made valuable to those that don't want it. Video game development can be done anywhere with a laptop (assuming you don't need access to proprietary kits from console manufacturers). Krieger told me about working on the steps of city hall on sunny summer mornings. Others preferred the short commute of working from home. Probably half the companies in the Quarry did not value the office space, yet it was a big selling point for BAT. There are two ways to meet the goal. Find companies that value the space, or make the space valuable for the companies in it.
105. Coworking neighbors impact each other. A lot has been written about certain aspects of coworking spaces—the community, the distractions, the flexibility (Garrett et al., 2017). Less attention has been paid to how fellow coworkers may impact a person's emotional state. I felt melancholy when Collins left. I hadn't felt that with any other departures. Others talked about feeling depressed after missing out on funding, but Thorne was worried about infecting others. In neutral times, no one would pay attention to what he was doing, but highs or lows rippled out to the rest of the space.

6.4 Saving the Second Cohort

Hector arrived as the week's mentor. It was short notice. Yohan said as much at the start.

Hector: Valentine was quite apologetic. How is our week three game?
Yohan: I have effectively lost most of my team. Holly is looking for another job. I don't blame them. I don't think BAT has handled it very well.... I may have mentioned this, but [a big American company] has shown an interest. They literally said, 'we are really keen on this'. Bolded. Underlined. That was one of the original things to get out of the rapid prototyping program. The talk I had with Juno today was encouraging.
Hector: I think Juno is good.
Yohan: I think she is earnest. I just hope she doesn't get burned out. I think that happened to Hera a bit. There are always problems with staff transition.
Hector: The timing wasn't great.
Yohan: I have been doing a lot of work. It just hasn't been in the Quarry. Frankly, it's been giving me bad vibes for a while.
Hector: I'm thankfully out of the politics. The joy of being a freelancer.
Yohan: I'm feeling a little bit better in the Quarry. For a while there, I was like, is it even worth it?
Hector: I don't think they will run the next year like this year.
Yohan: I get it that we were the guinea pigs and stuff.
Hector: I really like your week six game. It's such an addressable audience. I think it is smart going after that market.
Yohan: I think it would be a cool story and fun to play. Do you think it is the strongest of the prototypes?
Hector: I think so. What were the others? [Yohan goes through each of his prototype games.] Yeah, I still think it's the strongest.[3]
Yohan: The rapid prototyping thing was difficult but successful. I'm looking for a soft reset of the BAT relationship with Juno. I hope she doesn't get burned out. I think they should have another person on for interactive. Hera was doing the jobs of two people.

---

[3] Yohan pitched a different game since the week six could not be made and released for the low budget.

To some Quarry members, Juno offered hope. She did that by dangling a small amount of funding (see next section) and her presence (a "soft reset"). Hector believed that Juno would change things; however, for the mentors, it made little difference. They showed up. They were paid. They helped when people asked, and (generally) did not force their mentorship on participants. After a couple months, Juno would begin filling empty mentor hours with companies from outside the Quarry. It was difficult to assess the impact.

> **Quick Lesson**
>
> 106. Indie video game development can feel like a collection or series of contradictions. Yohan knew his best prototype (week six) but didn't feel he could pitch it to BAT. He lost his team and further funding while receiving **positive** feedback from a very large publisher. He had hope Juno would change things in the Quarry while expecting she would mostly likely fall into the same traps as Hera.

6.4.1 *The Dredges*

I sat with Thorne in the kitchen. We drank English breakfast tea with milk and sugar. It was the afternoon.

Thorne:	Juno was saying not to tell anyone, but you're not really part of this so. They are going to split the £30,000 amongst the teams that didn't get funded. £7,500 each.
Ethnographer:	Did you know how much money was available?
Thorne:	I didn't know there was only three pots of £30,000. I found out later. There was only ever two when it was £50,000.[4]
Ethnographer:	What did Hera tell you?
Thorne:	I asked Hera directly. She told me there was possible money for everyone.

---

[4] I never had this confirmed, nor did I find out the behind-the-scenes reasons for the drop in funding. I could imagine Hera arguing for three teams at 30,000 over two teams at 50,000.

Ethnographer:	What are they calling the extra funding?
Thorne:	I'm calling it 'residual.' Other people are calling it 'the dredges.'
Ethnographer:	What game are you doing?
Thorne:	I'm trying to do both games.
Ethnographer:	I knew you were going to say that. Thorne always trying to do twice as much with a quarter of the money.

As a reminder, the second cohort company directors lost all their employees and took part-time paid employment in the wake of the funding results. The £7,500 represented an even split on the remaining £30,000 originally allocated for one team. It was framed by participants as Juno advocating for them. Practically, the funding served to keep the second cohort nominally attached to the Quarry for another few months. For that reason, it was primarily symbolic. Like allowing the first cohort to stay until March, the funding would allow the second cohort to stay in the Quarry until the new fiscal year. At that point, Juno could fully implement her new vision of the Quarry.

> **Quick Lesson**
>
> 107. Does a month or three make a difference? With the second cohort losing most employees, the extra funding bought the directors another few months of bill payments. For Collins and his partner, it would have been a month. They declined the residual funding. They couldn't produce a vertical slice in time. It was doubtful the second cohort could either. The most likely motivation was to keep them in the Quarry until the end of the one-year contract.

6.5 A Hybrid Space

Juno had only been in the Quarry for a couple weeks. Hector and Thorne met in a mentor meeting.

Hector:	You're the second cohort?
Thorne:	I have until the end of March. I asked Juno what will happen. Would it become hot desking? Would we stay here? She didn't

	give much away. I don't know if she didn't know, or she didn't want to tell me. I guess we'll find out. It's a huge advantage to be in here. Having access to the mentors and the reputation when I talk to publishers. Even if the structure in here changed and I had to pay for it, it would still be an attractive option.
Hector:	Talking to Juno, we were talking about how anybody in the region would have access to the mentors. That's the way it used to be. In theory, that is the case. That is why I went to [non-Digital Quarry company] yesterday. She wanted to kind of bring that back in.... I think the plan is the Digital Quarry is still happening, being supported.

A couple months later, Thorne explained that he had talked with the Gymnasium manager about staying in the Gymnasium after March. But later, he talked to Juno and found out that BAT was giving the second cohort another six months in the Quarry. Companies from the first cohort could return but only after leaving for six months first.

Around the same time, the plan for reshaping the Quarry was revealed. It emerged from a behind-the-scenes power struggle between a mentor, the companies, and the new Quarry manager. The new Quarry structure would split members into two groups: accelerator participants and everyone else. Some companies (three at the start) would join an accelerator program called Moonshot. BAT would fund the teams for one year. The program began with rapid prototyping, borrowing the idea of the six games in six weeks. Next, participants (with BAT guiding) would work to turn one prototype into a released game. The program made explicit and funded several aspects of the original rapid prototyping concept. It intended to address some of the shortcomings of the original program. The rest of the Quarry would lean into the coworking space concept. Hot desking was introduced. The idea was to make the Quarry a hub for interactive developers in the region. The Quarry would no longer be the exclusive domain of video game developers.

Juno decided to wait several months to implement the changes—allowing the remaining original cohort, two mentors, and the ethnographer to almost leave the Quarry before commencing the changes. The wait would allow two things: time to recruit a new cohort, and time for existing entrenched members to depart. Some Quarry members suggested that the wait also had to do with funding. Dante speculated, "BAT have run out of funding this year. There is no more funding.... People are messaging me and saying, 'I heard the Digital Quarry ran out of money. Are you okay? Have you run out of money?' I have to tell them we are fine."

I asked Noah privately for more information.

> There's barely anyone left who hasn't been in the Quarry that would want to be. It will just be kids out of uni. The only way we were able to keep people on was because they had just graduated. We used the graduate placement scheme and BAT paid for half their salaries [applies to both programming and art graduate]. We have another programmer starting next week.... I wonder if they are just going to cram it full of desks. I know how much BAT are paying the Gymnasium for the space. Maybe they will want to maximize the output.

Quick Lesson

108. Accept feedback and make changes. Juno and BAT did this with the modifications to the Quarry. The hybrid space kept some of the first-year successes while making structural and cultural changes. The rapid prototyping was considered a success, so the structure (six-in-six) was retained. The second round of funding (obviously) didn't work. They removed the second round and incorporated it into the prototyping. A cultural shift was coming, whether BAT knew it or not. Noah predicted more young recent graduates without experience. They would need a long runway. They were not going to immediately grow to the next level. Additionally, Juno meant to introduce "hot desking" as a response to dichotomous feelings on the Quarry as office space. Those that valued the desk, or association with the Quarry, could pay for the space. This would likely mean more freelancers and temporary visitors. Finally, Juno didn't have any special feelings for gamers. She planned to open membership to non-video game developers. This would shift the Quarry culturally away from indie video game development toward a more generalized coworking space.

6.5.1 An Alternative Quarry

While Juno was potentially opening the Quarry up to a larger membership, the first cohort companies were scrambling to find their next working space (after their six-month Quarry extension). Dante and Noah were in contact with a business development rep at ZZZ Bank about funding a variation on the Quarry—possibly even in the same building!

Dante: Do you think they will give us office space? ZZZ Bank?
Noah: I don't know. I know they are trying to get us free kit to offset costs.
Dante: I emailed him a list. In bold, here is what we need.
Noah: I am going to send him what our company needs for hardware, software, office space.
Vincent: Sometimes you just want to try things out for a project, but you don't need it for a full year.

A similar conversation unfolded on Basecamp. An informant explained some of the history (on Basecamp) behind the ZZZ Bank idea:

> We tried this earlier in the year, but nothing happened. ZZZ Bank has a gaming consultant visiting today and tomorrow. They said they would send an enterprise vendor list so we can get discounts on supplies. They are also looking to provide relevant license to Hawk hotspots in areas they want to create a 'gaming emphasis.' No promise or guarantees or anything. I'm updating it to send to the ZZZ Bank guy in case he can make something happen.

Despite ZZZ Bank's creating a potential competitor to the Quarry, Juno did not object. She said, "ZZZ Bank seems interested in helping where they can. I'll need to figure out how the Digital Quarry as an organization works with ZZZ Bank. However, you are free to deal directly with him, either as individual companies or as a collective. If they have equipment or software, please take advantage."

Quick Lessons

109. Take free stuff (if it's relevant). Obviously, ZZZ Bank was trying to establish itself as the bank for game developers. If they were willing to provide access to expensive equipment, sitting down for a sales pitch on bank accounts may be worth it.
110. People change cultures. The ZZZ Bank discussions were another example of Juno moving the Quarry away from indie gamers. She had no objection to a quasi-competitor ("gaming emphasis") setting up in the same building. She wasn't concerned with cornering the gaming market in the region.
111. Don't encourage your customers to go to the competitor. Juno had the right sentiment ("please take advantage"), but she should have become involved immediately, if only informally.

6.5.2 QA Revamp

Juno took a few weeks to revamp the QA process. He communicated with Quarry members about the changes:

> Regarding QA, I've worked with the mentors and BAT to review our QA process at the Digital Quarry. QA is an important aspect of the development process, and I want to encourage companies to use and adopt it at all development stages. I also would like to see a lot more of your games and builds. That being said, here is how QA will be run: Starting next Friday, you will receive an email asking for builds of games to QA test. You will receive a QA form where you can select parts to be tested. I understand that the date might be in the middle of a sprint. For those companies, you can tell us when your current sprint ends. We can stagger projects, so QA can be done and feedback returned to you. I appreciate that some companies are in pre-production stage or working on concepts. Please indicate that on the form. We can accept concept artwork or game design documents or anything else you can share. If you require additional QA work (ongoing or as needed), please contact him directly to arrange a meeting. This isn't a test or evaluation. It is meant to be a process to help with developing games and addressing technical issues before it becomes too late or too difficult to fix. It is also free! Free stuff is great.

Juno initially relied on the QA intern for institutional knowledge, interfacing with Quarry members, and general management help. After a couple months, she revived the quality assurance aspect. In contrast to Hera, there would be a more systemic method to QA. At least that was the plan.

> **Quick Lessons**
>
> 112. Set clear expectations. Juno communicated a QA process to the companies and the QA intern. Previously, there had been no structure. Now, everyone was clear on their roles and responsibilities (although punishments were left unsaid).
> 113. Sell the benefits. It's not enough to say, "free stuff is great." Quarry members had already shown that being free, like a desk or mentor session, was not enough to justify using it. The benefits of QA should be easy—better games and less work (since fixing things is easier in the beginning). It just needed to be said.
> 114. Follow through. Getting people to follow the structure was one of Hera's biggest challenges. This would not change unless Juno did something differently.

6.5.3 Moonshot and a Third Cohort

The deadline for Moonshot was late February. It would be the new accelerator part of the Quarry. Companies looking to join the Quarry to use the space in the old way would have to apply elsewhere. I talked to a mentor (Evans) when Dante and Vincent walked up to us.

Dante:	Evans, do you know about the new cohort?
Evans:	Don't even finish that sentence. I don't know anything after March. I haven't talked to Juno since November. We don't know who is going to be in the Digital Quarry.
Dante:	There is a new Digital Quarry application online. It just went up on Facebook. It says it's going to be on a first come first serve basis. Felix is supposed to be coordinating it, but he doesn't know anything.

Vincent: Juno told me that she needs to talk to everybody because there is a lot of misinformation going around. I think they are going to allow three teams of three in as the new cohort. Then turn the rest of it into coworking desks.

Ethnographer: What's going to happen with the second cohort?

Dante: I don't know. Juno said it was between Noah and us. I don't know where Capone is. I don't think Larissa would want to stay. Thorne is away at Pocketgamer right now. Maybe he would want to stay if it was available. We just interviewed with AB accelerator this month, so we won't find out until the end of next month. It's just a matter of seeing which egg hatches first.

Later that day, the speculation continued. Evans and Vincent went into a mentor meeting. A minute later, Juno stopped by to talk to Dante for a minute before leaving for her other office.

Dante: Is there any chance we can stay on [after April]?

Juno: If you are first in, you are first out. If the new people need the space, they are first.... We don't want to have to play favorites. We want people to move on.

Dante: We should hear back from the AB accelerator by the end of the month.

Juno: I would rather the [Quarry] space be used than not used.

Juno left. Dante looked over in my direction. She came over to talk with Noah for 30 seconds.

Dante: It's still going to be free. It's going to be first come first served for newcomers. If five new teams want to use the space, it will fill up. If there is space, we can still stay. She said she wanted to avoid favoritism. So you know as much as I do. [She looked at Felix].

Felix: I heard that we were going to keep people in for a maximum of two years.

Dante: That seems standard.

Noah: If you can't do something in two years, you need to go.

Felix: I don't want any of you to go.

6 EXTRA LIFE: NEW POWER LEADS TO A CHANGE OF DIRECTION

Noah: Maybe one of us will hire you.
Felix: I'm stuck here until March 2021.

The information wasn't any clearer to the rest of the Quarry members. The following exchange occurred over Basecamp.

Developer: Any additional information on the Moonshot accelerator? Friends are asking about my experience in the DQ. Based on the second cohort treatment (the issues with the rapid prototyping management, the preventable leadership void after Hera's exit, to none of the second cohort being listed as members on the Digital Quarry website), I doubt I can recommend the program. Unless BAT assures us they have dealt with their obvious issues and made it right with current Quarry members.

BAT: They can visit our website for info on Moonshot, or they can read the news story in the local paper. They can contact me directly about Moonshot, so you can give out my contact details.

The announcement of the Moonshot program represented an interesting perspective on the new Quarry. First, existing Quarry members would be impacted by it, but they did not understand how or when. The "first in, first out" statement appeared to be bureaucratic speak to obfuscate the situation. There were four original cohort teams still remaining in the Quarry. They had all started at the same time. If there was only room for three to stay on, which three would it be? The "first in, first out" statement provided no clarification. There was also the unknown surrounding the second cohort. Would they be extended another six months like the first cohort? Would they have to shift to hot desking? Would they even survive as companies after spending the small residual funding from BAT?

Second, none of the Quarry members were eligible for Moonshot. This is probably the reason why Juno did not share information about it with them in advance. There were two consequences to this. The second cohort still had several months remaining in the Quarry, but it felt as if they were being ignored in favor of the next cohort. Additionally, members were well connected to the local industry. As shown above, multiple members received inquiries from developers interested in joining. Juno appeared to be moving on from the existing Quarry members in multiple ways; however, the local industry was small enough that this was not easily done.

> **Quick Lessons**
>
> 115. If official information is not communicated to all stakeholders, then gossip and rumor will spread in its place. BAT did not share the full plan with anyone; therefore, people resorted to asking others for information. Rumors did not help in promoting the Quarry to potential new members.
> 116. If you have an everyday relationship with someone, you should not expect them to receive relevant news from your website or press release. Not informing Quarry members or mentors about Moonshot was shortsighted. They may not have been eligible, but they were still stakeholders in the regional community that BAT was trying to build.

A new Quarry manager beginning was a crux event. There was the potential to significantly affect the organization. Juno did that. If the Quarry had been more developed, the likelihood of significant change would have been lower. After finding her feet, Juno did three main things:

1. She saved the second cohort for a few months.
2. She let some members of the first cohort leave and left the rest to their own activities.
3. She reinvented the Quarry as a hybrid space. This last one had the longest-lasting impact.

6.6 Game Over: People Abandon the Digital Quarry

In this section

– Participants wait for the next thing—

In Juno's vision of the Quarry.
What lies beyond the Quarry.

– COVID-19 lockdown shuts down the Quarry with no fanfare.

6.6.1 Conceptual Development

An *external crisis* is identified as a crux event. The external crisis in this case was the COVID-19 global pandemic. As such, this chapter ends abruptly. In contrast to the self-inflicted crisis, there was no preventing or controlling this crisis. Participants had little warning—at most a couple weeks—that a major disruption was imminent. On November 25th, one Quarry member was sick and told me that people wearing surgical masks around town were for fashion reasons not practicality. On March 5, I attended an event in the Gymnasium where I sanitized everything and hesitated before taking the leftover pizza home. Two weeks later, lockdown closed the Quarry.

6.6.2 Practical Lessons

1. It is interesting to see which things change with a new manager and which ones do not. The structure was reshaped, but communication was still last minute.
2. A crisis can challenge the fundamental nature of an organization. Oftentimes it affects one aspect. Stakeholders are then faced with the question: is this essential to the organization? In the case of the COVID-19 lockdowns, how important was the physical space to the Quarry as a concept?

6.7 WAITING

6.7.1 Meeting a Third Cohort Member

At an industry event, I talked with Kirby, a developer. He was joining Moonshot, the new accelerated Quarry program, in April.

Kirby:	I want to release a game a month and build an audience.
Ethnographer:	Have you run that by Juno yet?
Kirby:	Not yet. I don't see much difference between my team and everyone else in the Digital Quarry. Last year, they were all struggling and trying to get money and being turned down from publishers. They all still are.[5]

---

[5] *Aside—He made a good point.*

Quick Lesson

> 117. This was a clear case of misaligned expectations. Kirby wanted to use rapid prototyping as a marketing device. I doubted he would be allowed to do it. The strategy document made clear that Moonshot would involve a repeat of six games in six weeks. BAT would then support teams for another ten months with the goal of releasing the game after a year. It was basically Hera's original idea with additional carrots and sticks to push and pull the teams forward. Juno certainly intended it as strict.
>
> - Aside—Kirby did release a free prototype game that received around 10,000 downloads. It received some press attention because of its theme. That is an impressive return for a one-week prototype, even if it was a free download. The hosting website allowed people to donate to the developer. It made about 600 GBP.

6.7.2 Planning to Attend the Game Developers Conference (GDC)

BAT was sending Felix along with Juno to GDC. He guessed it was a reward for doing something right over the last six months. He was excited. He had never visited America.

Felix: Juno got GDC all sorted. I think BAT forgot about it. They wouldn't have done it if she hadn't reminded them.... I don't know who all is going. I know [Imani and Noah company] are going. And Juno.

Felix turned to Imani.

Felix: I need a one-sheet from you, so I know what to say if people visit the booth. Are you bringing your week one game?
Imani: We're bringing both.
Felix: Oh both. That's great.
Imani: We have a meeting with a publisher. They are interested in our main game.

Felix: If there is anything I can do—
Imani: It's a big help, having someone there.
Felix: If there is anything I can do to help. Like filling in forms.
Imani: We are working like crazy mad to get new builds before then. We're just working on polishing and introduction quality.

GDC was canceled. Felix did not visit America.

Quick Lessons

118. An opportunity for change is the beginning. The next steps are to implement change and maintain change. BAT became more involved with the Quarry during the manager void, but they stepped back quickly. They did not maintain the change. Forgetting about GDC reinforced the point. It also meant repeating the same mistakes. They were leaving everything to the manager (Juno, Hera, whoever).
119. A warm body is not "big help." Once again, Felix offered to help—in any way he could, or people wanted. Disappointingly, "help" meant standing there in case someone visited the booth. It was one step removed from being a "booth babe" (Taylor et al., 2009). People ignored not only his role (improving games) but also his passion. The help people wanted rarely matched the level he was willing to give.

    - Felix told me later, "If they would continue to pay me to do this, I would do it forever. I would be the crazy old guy playing games.... Maybe I'll start my own Digital Quarry."

6.7.3   *A New Company Joins the Quarry*

On a random morning in February with no preamble, the following post went up on Basecamp:

> FYI—next Monday a new team will be moving into the Digital Quarry. They are [name]. They are currently working in the East wing of the Gymnasium, so you may already know them. They make XR simulations for

sports teams. Later this week, I will take them around and introduce them to you all.

The announcement echoed the arrival of the second cohort—unexpected, abrupt, and immediate. The main difference was that the new company would not be part of a cohort. They were joining as a residence company. They were not part of Moonshot. They were not hot desking. This was an indication that Juno was flexible on hybridity.

> **Quick Lessons**
>
> 120. Forgotten lessons will be repeated. Juno surprised the Quarry in the same way Hera did with the second cohort—on short notice with no explanation. It gave the Quarry this unsettled, unpredictable feeling. Members had not yet experienced the Moonshot / hotdesk version of the Quarry and already Juno was introducing something new.
> 121. This might have been the best example of the Quarry as real estate. The new company had seats in the Gymnasium coworking space. The Quarry had open seats (with many more to open in a month). It was a mutually beneficial, quick, and easy agreement.
>
> - They were also not indie video game developers. It wasn't even gamification. Corporate training or industrial simulation might have been the best description. Either way, it was video game adjacent.

6.8 Beyond the Quarry

Everyone else was scrambling for the next thing beyond the Quarry. In late February, the Quarry Manager scheduled a "moving out lunch" for March 30th at 12:30pm–2:30pm.

6.8.1 A Mentor Says Goodbye

The Quarry began with four mentors. After 18 months, three of the mentors moved on. One posted a final message on Basecamp:

> Alas, we have reached the end of my time as a mentor. It has been an honor and a privilege working with you. I will miss it very much. I may be sad to be done, but it's good to see the buzz of game development in the region. I know the future is bright. Several people asked if I had any parting seed of wisdom. If I had been faster on my feet (but I wasn't, of course), I would have said this: just keep going. Making games is hard, making money from them even more so. Just remember that all the developers you admire went through something similar. They made plenty of mistakes on the journey. They got there and so can you. I hope to see many of you in the future. I'll be looking for you.

Several mentors leaving at the same time as the remaining first cohort signaled an end to the original Quarry.

Quick Lesson

122. Just keep going. It was worth repeating. There has been much talk of "resilience" since the start of the pandemic (Montgomery, 2020; Paul et al., 2022). In business, a more important quality is persistence.

6.8.2 Decisions on the Future

Both Noah and Dante committed to the AB accelerator for six months. Noah said, "We are waiting on three things right now. We just need one of them to drop…. The rapid prototyping was the single biggest thing to come out of being in the Digital Quarry." For both companies, the AB accelerator was *not* the Digital Quarry. It was an office space despite being called an accelerator.

Vincent was in the middle of five weeks off. Thorne speculated that Vincent finally finished up the final few things on his game. When Vincent returned, I asked him about his plans after March. He hadn't thought about it yet. With the game complete, his team was small. They had some proposals out that they hoped to hear about in April, and then they would decide what to do. He planned to talk with Juno about the possibility of staying in the Quarry. I didn't tell him that I heard he could reapply in six months—things changed too much and too quickly in the Quarry for that to be set in stone. For Vincent, there was convergence in finishing his game (years in development) and leaving the Quarry (after a year and a half). It made it easier. He had none of the stress of the other first cohort companies being forced out in March.

Capone showed up for the first time in what felt like months. He took a seat across from me. He had lost his usual seat. He admitted, "I'm never here." He was leaving the Digital Quarry at the end of March. His team was remote now. He was headed to Japan soon (for five days) to check out a possible job offer. He would take the job if the trip went well. Of the six companies left in the Quarry, Capone was unique in voluntarily leaving. In this way, he was more similar to Collins from the first cohort. He accepted that the Quarry was not going to propel his video game development forward. Since he had lost his team with the failure of the development funding, he also didn't covet the office space like the larger first cohort teams.

Jabari did not scramble for free office space. His team was large enough that other accelerators and coworking spaces were not an option. Krieger told me that Jabari had left the decision until the last minute. They secured a low-quality office for a few months until they could figure out if more money was coming in. Krieger said that paying for an adequately sized office space "becomes the equivalent of another employee." They were planning to move the whole team out of the Quarry in two weeks. They wanted to do it next week, but they hadn't signed the next contract yet. The office needed a fresh carpet and paint. He negotiated some money off the rent.

Jabari hired an agent to find them a publisher. It didn't sound like early access was happening after all. They also signed a six-month deal to do some contract work. If it went well, it would turn into three years of work. Jabari said, "So it's going well. Knock on wood. It's about keeping the guys working."

On one of my final days in the Quarry, a developer posted on Basecamp:

> Has anyone thought about staying in communication with the departing cohort? Do they lose access to Basecamp? It would suck for the Digital Quarry to lose all that valuable institutional knowledge. Also, there is interest, I will gladly coordinate something, probably on some platform like slack or telegram.

I had been wondering the same thing. In hindsight, it seemed that Juno had gathered all the institutional knowledge she required, and now preferred to make changes rather than keep it around. Established actors and institutional knowledge were a hindrance for the future. It was easier to bring in the new hybrid space without people holding on to the past. As far as Basecamp, Hera had introduced it, but no one liked it. Despite posting sometimes, Juno had shown a preference for email as a form of communication.

In an ominous coincidence, another developer replied: "My company is working from home for the foreseeable future, just keeping everyone in the loop."

> **Quick Lessons**
>
> 123. Temporary homes end. Accelerators, and to some extent incubators, are temporary by definition. Afterward, companies had to find the next thing. Most went back to what they were doing before—to other accelerators or working from home. Jabari and Krieger were the one team that expanded enough they needed a real office. It was still tough. They accepted lower quality for a lower cost. Noah and Dante were continuing the cycle. In six months, they would be begging AB accelerator to let them stay another six months.
> 124. Money spent on rent does not appear in the game. It doesn't sell games. If renting an office costs less than the benefits, then rent it. Otherwise, save the money. Efficiency, professionalism, and cooperation are the main benefits. Those are harder to measure than cash.
> 125. Group communication tools are useful if people want to use them. No one liked Basecamp. Hera used it. Once she left, it slowly faded as Juno used it less and less. The lockdown killed it (perhaps surprisingly since many communication tools like this became increasingly popular during lockdown).

In the end, of the original seven companies from the first cohort, two teams planned to go to a traditional office. Three teams planned to work from home. Two teams planned to join another accelerator. In the end, COVID-19 sent everyone home.

6.9 A Pandemic Emerges

Hera may have left as Digital Quarry manager months before, but the true end of Hera's version of the Quarry came with the convergence of COVID-19 and the planned departure of Quarry members. Two mentors, five Quarry companies, and the ethnographer were all scheduled to leave the Quarry at the end of March. There was a planned going away party on the 30th. We never made it.

Lockdown closed the Quarry. There was no official announcement on Basecamp about the Gymnasium closing due to the COVID-19 lockdown. Participants were informed in person or via email. All Basecamp activity stopped with the pandemic. Some people joined a Slack channel for local industry developers. In the early days, lockdown was only scheduled for two weeks. People left their computers and equipment at the Quarry. People assumed they would be back after a short break.

Lockdown stretched to months, and the Gymnasium stayed closed to Quarry members and others. Only one new company had moved into the Quarry when it closed. They lost access until it reopened. The three teams selected for Moonshot were not due to start until April. With the lockdown continuing, Juno launched the Moonshot program in an online form. The teams ran the six weeks of rapid prototyping virtually.

In the summer, the Gymnasium reopened with capacity restrictions. The first and second cohort picked up all their remaining equipment. The small third cohort moved into the Quarry. Like everywhere else, people tried to learn how to live in a pandemic world.

The lockdown plunged the Quarry into existential crisis. Was the Digital Quarry the physical place where developers worked? Was it the program that allowed access to mentors and special funding? Was it the central hub of video game developers in the region? What did it aspire to be? The lockdown closed the physical place, broke up the community, and forced part of the program online. It did not stop the Quarry. It suspended parts of it temporarily.

In several ways, the timing of the lockdown made things easier for Juno, BAT, and the Quarry to face the existential crisis. Many of the institutional actors were leaving the Quarry anyway. There were fewer people to worry about. The one new team hadn't fully moved in. The Moonshot teams could have been postponed until after lockdown. The Quarry could have closed for months and affected very few people. Juno chose to run Moonshot anyway. I was not privileged to how it was done, so I cannot say if she embraced a virtual version or made the best of it.[6] The main point is that Juno and BAT answered the existential crisis by trying to continue the Quarry in some form. As such, the Digital Quarry was not a place. The lack of continued connection to previous members hurt the argument for it being a community. It was a program.

Quick Lesson

126. It can happen here or anywhere. As far as I could tell, no one prepared for the possibly of the Quarry or the Gymnasium closing. I had heard about "draconian quarantines" in China starting in 2019. In the Quarry, there was no mention of COVID-19 until March. A Quarry member encouraged people to "remember to wash your hands for 20 seconds" and "don't come in sick." What should we do if we can't access the physical space? Asking the question as a hypothetical diminishes the existential risk.

- Also, preparation is better than disregard.

6.10 Conclusion

This chapter features two crux events. The first was the introduction of a powerful social actor. Tied to this was the departure of the final original members. The new Quarry manager acted immediately on starting. She saved the second cohort and allowed some members of the first cohort to depart. She developed a new vision of the Quarry as a hybrid space. She

---

[6] I assume she tried to work within the confines of the situation. I participated in a week-long hard science accelerator in May 2020 during lockdown. It was surprisingly well done considering the circumstances, but it did not embrace the online environment many events would as lockdowns became normal.

delayed implementing it until the next cohort began. There was hope that the new space would bring new promise to the Quarry.

The second crux event was the existential crisis of a pandemic lockdown closing the physical location of the Quarry. BAT reacted by launching Moonshot online. Once lockdown lifted after several months, the Quarry continued within a new normal. The Quarry was tested. A new conceptual understanding emerged. The organization persevered.

The loss of physical space was a common theme during the lockdown era of the global pandemic. Whether BAT followed the lead of others or independently decided to move Moonshot online, it was not alone in going virtual (Isabelle & Del Sarto, 2020).

6.10.1   Reflections on Practical Lessons

1. The COVID-19 lockdowns proved that the Quarry was not solely a coworking space. The program was able to continue despite having no access to a shared physical space. In contrast, the self-inflicted crisis proved that people were essential to the Quarry. Crises will test different things and raise existential questions. An organization can mimic a crisis by doing disaster preparedness. It does not need to be a global pandemic. It can be a new regulation, a financial issue, a people issue, or anything else that threatens to take away an everyday aspect. What would you do without it? The answer will tell you if the thing is essential.
2. Would a hybrid space work for the Quarry? I do not have the data to give you the answer. Even so, the next year featured multiple lockdowns and so it was not a typical representation of the possibility of a hybrid space. By the time the Quarry was allowed to stay open consistently, the original Moonshot cohort had already finished. It is hard to know, after a year of lockdown, if people were going to be eager to join the coworking space either via the Moonshot accelerator or the hot desk option. The answer lies in the importance of identity and community in the Quarry. Identity was important. Expanding membership weakened the shared identity (of video game developers). A hot desking approach combined with a two-class structure should also have weakened the community bonds; however, the Quarry community was not tightly bonded

because of physical proximity. Therefore, I estimate the hybrid space had an even chance to be more successful than the original structure.
3. BAT needed to save the second cohort. Why did BAT have responsibility? The companies pitched their company, not a project, to enter the Quarry; however, they all had existing projects that were put on hold for the rapid prototyping. After being in the Quarry for six months, they had nearly abandoned the original projects. They had received none of the training or pressure to seek contract work that BAT had put on the first cohort. Their only viability as companies rested on making the prototypes a success (i.e. securing external funding or releasing the game). The residual funding was a stay of execution—temporary, too little, and too late to make a difference.
4. Introducing a new manager led to better use of intern(s). BAT could not fire Felix (not that they gave any indication they wanted to). Juno realized quickly he could be better utilized. First, Juno started by changing his role. She used him as an expert on the Quarry to speed up her onboarding process. Once that was complete, she changed the structure of the Quarry to require people to go to Felix. In this way, he was transformed from an unused asset into an available feature of the program.

References

Garrett, L. E., Spreitzer, G. M., & Bacevice, P. A. (2017). Co-constructing a sense of community at work: The emergence of community in coworking spaces. *Organization Studies, 38*(6), 821–842. https://doi.org/10.1177/0170840616685354

Isabelle, D. A., & Del Sarto, N. (2020). How can accelerators in south America evolve to support start-ups in a post-COVID-19 world? *Multidisciplinary Business Review, 13*(2), 66–79.

Montgomery, L. M. (2020). A rejoinder to body bags: Indigenous resilience and epidemic disease, from COVID-19 to first "Contact". *American Indian Culture and Research Journal, 44*(3), 65–86.

Paul, I., Mohanty, S., & Sengupta, R. (2022). The role of social virtual world in increasing psychological resilience during the on-going COVID-19 pandemic. *Computers in Human Behavior, 127*, 107036.

Taylor, N., Jenson, J., & De Castell, S. (2009). Cheerleaders/booth babes/Halo hoes: Pro-gaming, gender and jobs for the boys. *Digital Creativity, 20*(4), 239–252.

CHAPTER 7

Postmortem: Practical Lessons in Incubating Creative Development

7.1 Introduction

This chapter develops several practical lessons based on the ethnography of crux events. The lessons learned come in two forms. First, the lessons are based on the importance and why the practitioner should care. These may not tie directly to a single crux event. Second, the chapter offers recommendations on how (not) to address them. These are based on crux events. The six main lessons are based around membership, resistance, interns, mentor meetings, feedback, and institutional knowledge.

7.1.1 Membership

The first lesson discusses the importance of defining and managing membership. Members entering or exiting can (or not) become a crux event. Examples are provided from arrivals (second cohort), departures (first and second cohort), and potential expanded membership.

Managing the entry of new members is important. This is especially true in two instances: when an innovation space has existing members and when membership is temporary. Both situations were true in the Quarry with the introduction of the second cohort (see Chap. 2) and the expanded team sizes during the rapid prototyping (see Chap. 3). The second cohort offers a planned example, and the expanded teams offer an unplanned, but expected example. How BAT introduced the second cohort offers several lessons.

From a new member perspective, the introduction can provide a *sense of membership in a community*. Garrett et al. (2017) identified the importance of building community in coworking spaces. The introduction of the second cohort to the Quarry did not do this. The initial induction did not set expectations for life in the Quarry. The induction did not even tell the new members where to sit. That was left to the surprised existing members. Unmet expectations can become a major source of contention (Gidley & Palmer, 2024). Additionally, BAT did not add the three new companies' information to the Quarry website until almost nine months after they started. One developer brought this up specifically in an unrelated meeting, and it still was not done for several months. Finally, the Quarry manager waited until the end of the week to "formally" introduce the second cohort to the rest of the Quarry. It made sense—give the new teams time to settle in. But at the same meeting, the Quarry manager announced a desire to hold biweekly game demo sessions. The split focus diminished the significance of introducing new members.

From an existing member perspective, the introduction can seamlessly integrate new members into existing institutional norms and structures (Zucker, 1977). The introduction of the second Quarry cohort was nearly a surprise. There was an announcement on Basecamp on day one, and rumors had been floating around for a while. Otherwise, the open space and small new teams of the new members hardly created a ripple for existing members. On the other hand, team expansion during the RPP illustrated the potential for new members to disrupt current members by their presence alone. An entire company abandoned the Quarry due to the increased activity. This is extreme without necessarily being an outlier. Even the people staying sought additional space and quiet outside of the Quarry proper. The first Quarry manager leaving makes it hard to explain small changes, or not, that BAT made for introducing the third cohort (see Chap. 6). In contrast to the second cohort, there was an announcement in advance on Basecamp. The second Quarry manager told some members about changing membership options coming with the new fiscal year, but probably because they were not eligible, did not mention the Moonshot program. Inevitably, this created confusion when existing members were asked about it from outside people.

At the other end of the life cycle, managing the exit of members is also important. Since membership was temporary, a planned exit can *provide meaning to the whole experience*. In the Quarry, all the exits were unplanned or confusing.[1] It started with the first Quarry manager—which may have set the tone for the rest. She (understandably) told no one in advance; however, after most people found out, she still did not tell everyone directly. Three weeks later, at least one person was still uncertain. Next, there was hours of discussion about a clean break for cohort one. The "need" for the companies to leave for a week always seemed like bureaucratic nonsense. Then, when some of the first cohort did leave, it was under the cover of proverbial darkness. They were there on Friday and gone on Monday without a word. Finally, the second Quarry manager scheduled a two-hour lunch party to mark the rest of cohort one leaving after eighteen months in the Quarry. We spent longer attending a time management seminar. In a classic twist of fate, COVID-19 canceled the event.

The exits were an anti-climax. Accelerators typically end with a "demo day" that accumulates the experience (Cohen et al., 2019). For the individual members, the exits should have capped a significant experience in their growth as game developers. Instead, the performance stumbled on the landing. Some teams were allowed to walk quietly away. Others were told to leave and fought to stay. The original exit plan became a source of controversy and frustration that at least somewhat poisoned the experience before it. The exits should have been a chance to celebrate the accomplishments of the Quarry program at developing talent. It could have justified the time and money investment. Instead, it served to highlight the lost opportunity. It could have reinforced the connection with members or established the place of the Quarry in the community at large. It could have begun the development of an alumni network that could have further bolstered the Quarry going forward. At best, an exit can enhance the experience. At worst, it can ruin it.

All this leads to the question: who is and can be a member? *Defining membership* can become critical. It is tied to identity, such as indie game developers (Phillips, 2015). Initially, the Quarry defined members by profession (indie video game developers) and potential (competitive application). No real distinction was made between the companies in the first cohort. The introduction of the second cohort (of younger companies) suggested levels of development. The first Quarry manager made this

---

[1] The one possible exception (the end of marketing internship) was overshadowed by the first Quarry manager leaving and the news around the end of the first year for cohort one.

explicit in a presentation. She planned for the Quarry to house companies at three maturity levels. Each would be treated differently. The fallout from the second round of RPP funding showed the consequences for not doing this. After the first manager left, the second Quarry manager went in a different direction. Membership both expanded and splintered into types. BAT abandoned the initial tenets around video game developers and selectivity. Now, anyone in the wider interactive sector could join the Quarry. The hot desking approach significantly lowered the bar for membership. The Moonshot program retained some level of competitiveness while seemingly segregating those members from the rest. What does the Quarry become when membership changes?

At no point did BAT attempt to change the financial-legal relationship between the companies, BAT, and each other. They were not a collective. They did not work for BAT. They were all officially independent except for working in the same office. It is interesting to wonder what would have happened if BAT had taken a small ownership stake in the companies, such as might happen in an incubator (Bruneel et al., 2012). Presumably, some of them would have refused. For the ones that accepted, would a stronger link to BAT and the other companies have changed things?

If I were to run my own version of the Quarry—let's call it Q2—what would I do about membership? I would take inspiration from universities' rituals (Dacin et al., 2010). Membership is competitive (although the degree of competitiveness can change over time). Membership is defined by why participants are there. In universities, it is to learn. In Q2, it is to make games and grow as game developers. There would be different levels of membership depending on achievement. In universities, this generally means years finished (freshman, sophomore, so on). In the Q2, this would be defined by games released, team size, or funding raised. I would celebrate every achievement but modulate the celebration level to the success level (i.e. big success, big celebration). The Quarry companies had successes—securing publishing deals, releasing games internationally, raising additional funds—but none of these were celebrated within the Quarry. Universities also do well at encouraging members to advertise their membership. This can be either material (branded swag) or social (public announcements of affiliation). The closest the Quarry came to branded swag were a few lanyards some people received for holding their Gymnasium keycard. Socially, some companies played up their residence in the Quarry. They appeared to do this in an attempt to leverage legitimacy (Leblebici & Shah, 2004). That is also one of the points of a university degree (Hurley & Sá, 2013). On the other hand, BAT didn't even list all Quarry companies on the Quarry website. There should have been pride on both sides.

Many accelerators already do this with "graduation events" (Cohen, 2013). I would make a big deal out of introducing new people. I would do it on a schedule, setting expectations for both new and existing members. Many universities provide new students with a guide thereby pairing introducing new members to the institution. Some hold events such as "freshers week," to help new students acclimatize to their new environment. I do not condone hazing or forcing new members to "earn" their place. They did that by being selected. Despite what one peer reviewer told me, I don't think the literature knows everything about these different types of incubators and accelerators. The Quarry companies with previous experience in accelerators, or even with BAT programs, did not know exactly what to expect on entering the Quarry. On the other end of the journey, exits require the same if not more delicacy and ritual.[2]

The end of membership should be the climax of the experience. It is the chance to provide final meaning to those involved. The Quarry allowed multiple companies to leave without even the hint of a graduation type event. There was a planned event for the remaining first cohort companies leaving, but COVID-19 canceled that. One final point of a graduation is to launch the individuals to the next stage of their relationship with the organization—as alumni. Universities gain many benefits from alumni—financial support, mentorship, networking, and reputation (Gallo, 2012). All those things can apply to an incubator or accelerator. The time in Q2 sows the seeds that will be reaped after participants leave. Membership changes after exiting, but there is still a type of membership.

7.1.2 Resistance

The second lesson discusses the role of resistance and crux events. Conflict is inevitable; however, some types of conflict possess more potential to change things than others. Collective resistance and public resistance, depending on how they are handled, can greatly influence crux events. In the Quarry, resistance either failed or succeeded only on a small scale. I

---

[2] Despite three university degrees, I have never attended my own graduation. I didn't notice the absence of ritual on the bachelor's or master's degrees. Missing graduation for the doctorate degree did contribute to the existing anti-climax that marks finishing a PhD.

will discuss three types of resistance. Examples are provided from the announcement of the RPP, a canceled leadership workshop series (LWS), and confrontational feedback by one company.

The announcement of the RPP showed both collective and public resistance. Well, not so much collective resistance as a collection of resistance. The companies were not coordinating their objections to the program. They were voicing individual issues. When they were together and in public, they built off each other—one company director brought up a scheduling issue, so another jumped in as well. In the room, it was the Quarry manager (admittedly with the backing of BAT) against the group. In the moment, the manager tried to placate the individual concerns or push them off. Once the meeting ended, the manager began immediately working on some of the lead dissenters. With just the Quarry manager and a single company's issues, she elicited what it would take to bring the company on board—the bribe cost. In this example, most of the companies were not fundamentally against the idea. They were more against the timing and execution. Compromises or outright brides provided additional advantages to joining.

In contrast, companies demonstrated more collective resistance against the LWS with a limited amount of public resistance. The type of resistance (mostly non-compliance) was not too different, but there were three nuances. First, multiple companies were fundamentally against the LWS. They didn't think they needed it, nor did they see the benefit. In the case of the RPP, I think every company would have participated if the conditions were right. But also, it seemed unlikely that there were conditions in which all teams would willingly participate in the LWS. Second, participants thought of each other. For example, one developer mentioned that other developers already had similar training. The identification with others' circumstances creates tighter collective resistance. Third, individual negotiations failed, if there were any at all. With the Quarry manager gone, BAT had no one responsible or capable of working with the companies to find a compromise. Partly, it seemed BAT didn't believe one was warranted. The impression was that BAT felt the companies should be grateful not insolent.

Robin's rebellion represented a different kind of resistance (Chap. 4). It played out over a series of events, both public and private, and it appeared that he basically went it alone. Privately people supported him. Robin's rebellion failed for a number of reasons. There was a vast power imbalance between single participants and BAT. The first Quarry manager was around then not, BAT management appeared then stepped away, and the second Quarry manager arrived. Robin had to begin the rebellion anew each time. His issues were numerous and far reaching. As such, a meeting on volunteering for a few hours for a university outreach event could be connected to the larger issue of BAT requiring "free work" from Quarry members (see Chap. 5). In the heat of the public complaints, others didn't have time to reflect on the issues. This made it hard for people to join him, for BAT to compromise, or for a clean outcome to be reached. I imagine some people (participants that were there or readers of this book) think it failed because of *how* he went about it. I agree that was part of it, but I think his attempts were hindered by societal norms, local attitudes, and institutional rules.

What can we learn from the resistance seen in the Quarry? The events illustrated the intersection of public/private and individual/collectives. Imagine a classic two by two grid. Collective public resistance can be greatly effective.[3] As I noted above, there is a difference between collective resistance and a collection of resistance. Unity and coordination define collectivity. Collective private resistance, if the reasons are made clear, can be effective. Individual public resistance often fails since there is little support and little room for compromise. Open conflict creates the feeling of zero-sum games and ultimatums. Individual private resistance depends on the other party being available for compromise. In the case of Robin's rebellion, the resistance went public because the first Quarry manager was no longer available for private dialogue.

How can we react to resistance to avoid crux events from going the wrong direction? There are two lessons. First, deterrence is the best defense. BAT took this route in launching the rapid prototyping successor Moonshot with more rigid structure, stricter rules, and possible punishment. Preventing or avoiding conflict before it becomes public or gathers people together reduces the likelihood of encountering a crux event. Continuous dialogue and feedback among participants create a feeling of togetherness and "being heard." Second, if a crux event does appear, an effective way of mitigating the resistance is by separating individuals and taking the conflict private. The first Quarry manager demonstrated this technique during and after the initial RPP announcement. Instead of negotiating with the group, she was able to address individual issues with

---

[3] Of course we already know this from any number of world public peace movements—although for an exception, see Gidley and Lubit (2023) or Lubit and Gidley (2021).

only the most vocal dissentients. By doing this, she was able to prevent the resistance from unifying and escalating to an untenable position, such as in the way it would later with the LWS (after she left).

7.1.3   Interns

The third lesson discusses the role of paid interns. I use the term interns since there was an element of learning to the roles in the Quarry. All the comments here could apply to other types of support people as well. The story of the interns is somewhat muted in this account because they were mostly an example of non-utilization. BAT hired interns for marketing and quality assurance testing. The interns could do work for any company in the Quarry. The logic was solid. None of the companies had a particular expertise in marketing. Some were actively against it. An intern could help get them started. All the teams could use QA game testing. No one had the budget to pay for testers, and the hope for testing by fellow developers never gained momentum. There was the need for the roles and others (accounting, legal, HR) that could be shared among the teams. Initially, neither intern succeeded. After some changes were made for each, they ended serving some purpose. What happened, and what could have been done differently?

First, there was not a solid plan for the interns. The marketing intern only ended up working for four of the ten companies. The QA intern thought he was hired to do one thing and found out he was supposed to be doing something different. Like a great many things in the Quarry, the companies were not consulted on the hires (either the role or individual). The marketing intern was introduced to the Quarry and her role laid out clearly. The QA intern, not so much. Companies mostly chose not to use the services either in advance or after an initial meeting.

Second, BAT could not force the companies to do something they didn't want to do. As I discussed above with the example of the leadership workshop, the companies used a variety of techniques for non-compliance including obfuscation and outright resistance. Working in advance with the companies, such as by consulting them on the hires, helps with smoothing the way for cooperation. One of the main reasons, and an easily preventable one, for the companies not utilizing the interns was due to limited strategic vision. Each company saw game development in a particular way based on their own philosophies and experience. Any intern roles were slotted into this structure. Take QA as an example. Many of the companies seemed to view QA as something that was done after the first game build was complete. Therefore, the companies did not need to use the QA intern until they had developed their game to a certain extent. By not engaging with the companies, BAT let them decide how to use and ultimately underutilize the interns.

Third, the companies may have been uncooperative on the whole, but they did want the help. They were uncooperative for two reasons. First, they didn't know what the intern was supposed to do. Countering this involves both clearly defining the role and being flexible to individual companies' needs. Second, they didn't think they needed whatever the intern was doing. Consulting participants in advance is the easiest way to achieve buy-in. If that is not available, then draw a Venn diagram of what the intern can offer and what the companies want. In the case of the Quarry, the obvious one was free labor.[4] Instead of providing knowledge (like the mentors), the interns should have provided labor. The people in the Quarry were game developers. They may have accepted the need to know about quality assurance or user testing, but none of them wanted to become marketers. Instead of teaching them something they didn't want to know, the interns could have just done the work—a valuable service that would have fostered collaboration.

As a final point, I will use myself (the ethnographer) as an example (see also final chapter in Gidley, 2021a). I used vague references to how I could help companies in the Quarry deal with business matters. I didn't know what I could do or what they needed. I also didn't want to influence the research too much. The vagueness meant I did very little. The people that did 'accept' my offers of help told me 'not right now.' In the end, the largest role I played was the confidant. Of course, I had to first overcome some people's belief that I was a spy for BAT. The QA intern definitely faced this same issue.

7.1.4 Mentor Meetings

The fourth lesson creates a typology of mentor meetings and follows this with ways to improve them. Mentors are a common feature of incubator and accelerator style spaces (Bruneel et al., 2012; Cohen, 2013). They are one of the main differences between those spaces and coworking spaces

---

[4] Most of the companies were against Ludic labor, but this did not preclude them from accepting labor paid by someone else (e.g. BAT).

(Clayton et al., 2018). Mentors are supposed to provide something intangible (knowledge) that participants can take with them after the space and funding are gone. What do mentor meetings do, and how could they be done better?

The Quarry offered up (loosely) four types of mentor meetings: null, social, strategic, and feedback. The first type is less a type than something that must be noted. Participants did not always attend mentor meetings when mentors were available (and occasionally it was the other way around). Recall one mentor asking who a company director was since they had never met. Obviously, there were instances where participants were sick or out of town, but there were a fair number where participants simply did not feel they needed the mentor that given week. Toward the end of the fieldwork, Juno arranged for more and more outside companies to utilize the mentors. Even so, some mentors questioned why they were coming in if only to sit around. In these null meetings, no knowledge was shared.

The second type of meetings were social ones. I do not use the term "social" in a negative sense. These meetings were not insubstantial just because they did not focus on traditional areas of knowledge sharing. They focused more on the individual. The mentor may assume any number of roles: friend, confidant, cheerleader, and therapist. Despite being in a coworking space, it seemed like some company directors needed to confide their hopes and fears in someone without judgment. Since other companies were technically competitors and BAT was potentially a cruel overlord, the mentors were the remaining option. Social meetings served debriefing sessions for all the challenges and promises of working as an indie game developer.

The third type of meetings were strategic. These meetings focused on company and strategic direction. The most obvious examples involved funding—whether to apply for funding (e.g. BAT, UK Games Fund, or Creative Europe), how to deal with publishers when trying to secure a distribution deal, or how to maximize trade show attendance. Occasionally, the meetings might also focus on the company ethos—what kind of game developer did they want to be? Almost all the company directors were in the Quarry for the love of making games. Balancing the love of creation and the business of making money was a significant topic. The main difference between this type and the others was a focus on the company as entity separate from the current game being developed and the individual director.

The final type of mentor meetings was feedback. These meetings discussed products—ideas, prototypes, demos, features, final games, and so on. Participants sought feedback on how to develop the game(s) they were working on. Developers might share artwork, videos, a playable version,[5] or code. Feedback meetings might crossover with strategy mentor meetings. A feedback meeting considered ways to improve a game—like a developer brainstorming how to fix a feature causing player nausea. A strategy meeting debated choosing two games to continue developing—like a developer asking how to allocate effort between two prototypes. BAT seemed to expect these would be the dominant type of meeting. In my observation, they were no more common than the others.

Mentor meetings could have been improved in three ways: agendas, follow-up, and accountability. All three ideas are interconnected. Agenda and follow-up are two sides of the same concept—the mentor meeting should not be an island. Before and after matters. Accountability holds participants and mentors to task.

An agenda is as straightforward as it sounds. What is the purpose of the meeting? What will be discussed? Unless the mentor has something specific, like a theme for the week, then the participant should make up the agenda. It should be shared with the mentor at least one business day in advance of the meeting. The mentor should read it and prepare as necessary. Creating an agenda obviously serves several purposes. It helps the participants consider what they need at the moment. It helps maximize the limited meeting time. It allows the mentor to prepare in order to provide the best mentoring.

Follow-up involves two steps. At the end of the meeting, the participant and mentor should agree on follow-up tasks for each. I previously described mentors as like comets (Gidley, 2021a). They fly in and disrupt things on a scheduled basis and then leave. It is too easy to forget about them until the next scheduled meeting. In these cases, the opportunity is lost. So, assuming that tasks have been agreed, at the beginning of the next meeting (and as part of the agenda), the items should be reviewed. Were the tasks completed? What was discovered? If there are not clear answers on a regular basis, then there must be some accountability.

Accountability goes two ways. Participants must follow through on creating an agenda and completing the tasks and actions agreed on in the meeting. Mentors must do the same. Time outside of meetings should be

---

[5] Very rarely did I personally observe playtesting by the mentors.

allotted as part of the mentor's contract for completing follow-up tasks. Quarry participants were grateful when mentors responded to queries outside of mentor days; however, mentors should not be expected to do the work for free. On the other hand, I heard complaints from participants and mentors that agreed follow-up never materialized. In this situation, it seems that the program manager must play the role of judge and enforcer.

7.1.5 *Feedback*

The fifth lesson discusses the role of feedback. Obviously, I have mentioned feedback several times already. Building on those initial thoughts, I propose three more aspects of feedback: the importance of feedback, the risk of ignoring feedback, and the consequences of divergent goals among various social actors.

First, following on from my previous statements about collaboration, feedback is important. Primarily in the Quarry, this meant feedback from the participants to BAT. Participants were willing to give it. On my first day, one participant asked about a formal anonymous feedback mechanism. He never got one. The first Quarry manager was willing to listen—to the extent that she felt she could change things. In order for the Quarry to succeed, at least some of the companies must succeed. It reasons that the companies would have some insight into how best to help them do so. The relationship between BAT and the Quarry companies could never have been a true partnership, but it could have been more collaborative.

The three main complaints on feedback were lack of desire for feedback, lack of anonymity, and lack of response to feedback. They are not necessarily steps in progression, but certainly desire is the first step. Lack of anonymity was a big issue in the Quarry context. The power imbalance between BAT and the Quarry companies made it dangerous to provide some types of feedback. To the extent that I succeeded in gathering insight from the different social actors (participants, mentors, BAT employees), it was heavily based on the promise of anonymity. People complained to me because I was confidential (and nonpartisan). Without it, people only provide unfavorable feedback if they possess certain personalities (like Robin) or security (like a contract). Although I will note that anonymous feedback works better if the people intend to stay—that is, if they have a vested interest in actual change rather than simply being mean (obviously a major problem with student reviews of teachers at the end of term). Lack of response is tied to the next theme.

Second, once feedback is solicited, there is enormous risk in ignoring it. There are three problematic ways to ignore feedback: being slow to respond, not drawing direct connections, and actively rejecting. Individuals expect quick change, and bureaucracies do slow change. The same applies to feedback. Being slow to respond gives the appearance and consequences of ignoring. BAT did this, and the consequences were the escalation of Robin's rebellion. Setting expectations can mitigate this risk. Not drawing a direct connection between feedback and change risks the response becoming lost. Half the purpose of responding to feedback is to satisfy those giving the feedback. Without closing this loop, people may feel nothing has been done. Some first cohort participants left because the changes to the Quarry were uncommunicated and unclear. Finally, actively rejecting feedback risks bringing to the forefront the inherently divergent goals of the social actors in the space. In some cases, rejection is the only option, so the way rejection is presented becomes important. For example, BAT was hindered by bureaucratic rules that prevented the implementation of certain changes the Quarry companies wanted. Quickly and directly connecting hindrances to feedback might have led to more positive outcomes.

Third, divergent goals may simply mean that no amount of feedback and response can reconcile all issues for all social actors. As groups, the companies, mentors, and BAT all had different reasons for participating in the Quarry. Within the groups, individuals had other motivations and experiences. Divergent goals are not inherently negative. Plus, the nature of competition necessitates divergence. One issue that appeared in the Quarry was zero-sum thinking. BAT encouraged[6] this by funding only two rapid prototyping projects and attempting to gaslight participants to how much money was available. Instead of having a difficult conversation about why a prototype was not good enough, BAT insisted there was never enough money for everyone. The path of "enough money, not enough quality" pits BAT against the unfunded companies. The path of "only some will be funded" pits the companies against each other in a zero-sum game. Interestingly, some people in the Quarry experienced both.

---

[6] Inadvertently, I think.

7.1.6 Institutional Knowledge

The sixth lesson discusses the importance of institutional knowledge to smooth surfing during crux events. Institutional knowledge—either individually or collectively—can serve as a stabilizing force during tumultuous events. Without institutional stability, social actors may try to fill the void. In the Quarry, two examples are the original Quarry manager leaving, and a mentor attempting to make a power play behind the scenes.

The first Quarry manager departing left a void. Two factors impacted institutional knowledge, one social and one material. The Quarry manager served multiple purposes. She was usually everyone's first contact with the Quarry. She set the initial expectations, laid out the rules, and introduced new social actors to the space. All other actors had a formal relationship with her. She was the problem solver, question answerer, and the final arbitrator. In my solar system analogy (Gidley, 2021a), she was the sun around which everyone else revolved. Without her, it was as if gravity behaved differently. People were not extremely lost on an everyday basis. They didn't stop making games after she left. They were unsure of the bigger things—the moments that might define the fate of the game or the company or themselves. Maybe the Quarry could have reorganized in time to compensate for the lack of her presence, but people knew that someone would replace her after a time, so nothing happened. There was no attempt to self-organize to fill the void.

The second factor, and this was entirely preventable, was the lack of material institutional knowledge. By this, I mostly mean the written word—rules, procedures, reports, action plans, helpful tips. BAT had a strategic plan. The Quarry did not. Hera didn't write notes for the next person (or at least that's the impression BAT projected). She kept it all in her head. It was probably safer that way, with less risk of accountability. This makes her absence felt even more. It also means: the transition to the next manager will be bumpy, the remaining members must fill in this knowledge gap, and vital institutional knowledge may need to be relearned (or lost forever). It appeared to stunt the growth of some Quarry members by several months or completely disillusion them to the experience.

What is the lesson? People will leave, and their absence will be felt. First, have a plan. Second, communicate the temporary solution. Third, some people will try to take advantage of the situation. Fourth, fill the void quickly but also smartly. The new person will lack institutional knowledge at the start, so the material must serve as a transitional aid.

There is a saying (and cliché) that nature abhors a vacuum. The period after the Quarry manager announced her leaving illustrated this socially. She was the dominant social force in the life of the Quarry due to her position, history, and social relationships with other actors. The impending departure created a void that at least one actor saw as an opportunity. As I briefly mentioned in Chaps. 4 and 5, one of the mentors was unsatisfied with some of the companies and by extension the Quarry. He saw the manager leaving as an opportunity to make a power play to remake the Quarry. He failed. The exact reasons were outside of my observational points, but I can speculate. Probably he simply overestimated his own influence, or he underestimated the people at BAT. One possibility is that his institutional knowledge was limited and out of date. Mentors saw a very thin slice of the Quarry and the companies. It is useful to solicit their view, but the constraints of the view should limit the impact. The main point is that some people see vacuums as opportunities. They are decision events that could significantly impact the future.

As one final thought, I wondered what became of the Quarry after people returned following the first period of COVID-19 lockdown. No one from the first two cohorts would be in residence. The only holdovers from pre-pandemic would have been the new Quarry manager, the QA intern, a mentor or two, and a company that had yet to fully move in. The institutional knowledge of "how things work" would have been scattershot. It would have been an interesting time.

7.2 Conclusion

The two common repeated ideas running through the above themes are plan and collaborate. Plan for crux events. Collaborate with stakeholders. Some crux events are obvious and expected, like the entry and exit of cohorts. These should have organizational plans independent of individuals. But some things are so unexpected, like say a global pandemic, that how do you plan for them? First, realize that many things are only unexpected because we didn't pay attention to the signs. Almost everyone agreed that the Quarry manager leaving was unexpected, but there were a couple people that hinted they knew she was unsatisfied for a while. It was a months-long process of applying and acquiring the new position. Second, the specifics are less important than the consequences. What did the pandemic do to the Quarry? It closed the physical location. It could have been a fire, construction, or gas leak. So, you don't plan for a pandemic. You plan for the physical location to be closed. Then you plan for the place to reopen (even if it never does). Like insurance, not all plans will be used, but they should be available if needed. Collaborating with stakeholders may seem obvious, but as this book demonstrated, that is not always the case. Collaboration and stakeholders require a certain philosophical outlook. A stakeholder approach breaks down barriers between groups. BAT, mentors, and companies are no longer divided by their individual roles. Instead, they can view themselves as having a stake in the greater outcome. This is the foundation for true collaboration. The Quarry had occasional consultation (such as BAT asking for feedback) rather than true collaboration (as BAT decided independently what to do with the feedback). There was always an aura of us versus them. Collaboration would mean working with each other to co-create the Quarry. It means giving up some power and control for the greater good.

The final lesson—if you can call it that—is more a series of short thoughts. Some are my own. Some are from my informants.

Making video games as an indie developer is hard. This is how you succeed.

(a) You should love making games because you will need something to sustain you in moments of doubt and rejection (because someone is not paying you to keep going).
(b) Getting money requires doing a lot of things you don't want to do, such as appreciating marketing, networking all the time, and considering an audience beyond people like you.
(c) Then you must find the balance between A and B.
(d) Get lucky.

A legendary video game developer (to be left unnamed here) offered the following advice during an industry meetup event. *Make a lot of games. Admit when you have a loser and drop it.* I would add, trust you will come up with another brilliant idea. This one isn't the only one.

Felix told me about a friend in Sweden. He hired his girlfriend, an artist, to work for his game company. They were pumping out a game a day. Yes, one per day.

Felix: They are all reskins. She is happy about it because they are doing so many games. I can see it's crushing his soul.

Aslani: That is the kind of thing that is ruining it for indie games. It may keep a company alive for a short time, but it brings everyone down in the long run.

References

Bruneel, J., Ratinho, T., Clarysse, B., & Groen, A. J. (2012). The evolution of business incubators: Comparing demand and supply of business incubation services across different incubator generations. *Technovation, 32*(2), 110–121. https://doi.org/10.1016/j.technovation.2011.11.003

Clayton, P., Feldman, M., & Lowe, N. (2018). Behind the scenes: Intermediary organizations that facilitate science commercialization through entrepreneurship. *Academy of Management Perspectives, 32*, 104–124. https://doi.org/10.5465/amp.2016.0133

Cohen, S. (2013). What do accelerators do? Insights from incubators and angels. *Innovations: Technology, Governance, Globalization, 8*(3–4), 19–25.

Cohen, S., Fehder, D. C., Hochberg, Y. V., & Murray, F. (2019). The design of startup accelerators. *Research Policy, 48*(7), 1781–1797.

Dacin, M. T., Munir, K., & Tracey, P. (2010). Formal dining at Cambridge colleges: Linking ritual performance and institutional maintenance. *Academy of Management Journal, 53*(6), 1393–1418.

Gallo, M. (2012). Beyond philanthropy: Recognising the value of alumni to benefit higher education institutions. *Tertiary Education and Management, 18*, 41–55.

Garrett, L. E., Spreitzer, G. M., & Bacevice, P. A. (2017). Co-constructing a sense of community at work: The emergence of community in coworking spaces. *Organization Studies, 38*(6), 821–842. https://doi.org/10.1177/0170840616685354

Gidley, D. (2021a). *An ethnographic study of institutional work in a creative proto-institutional place*. Doctoral dissertation, Queen's University Belfast.

Gidley, D., & Lubit, A. J. (2023). The dual institutional work of Lyra's Walk: Partisan violence and peace protest in Northern Ireland. *Journal of Organizational Ethnography, 12*(2), 141–161. https://doi.org/10.1108/JOE-01-2023-0003

Gidley, D., & Palmer, M. (2024). Institutional policing work in a constellation of labels and spaces of place: Video game development management insights. *International Journal of Organizational Analysis*, Vol. ahead-of-print No. ahead-of-print. https://doi.org/10.1108/IJOA-03-2024-4765

Hurley, P., & Sá, C. M. (2013). Higher education policy and legitimacy building: The making of a new academic credential in Ontario. *Higher Education Quarterly, 67*(2), 157–179.

Leblebici, H., & Shah, N. (2004). The birth, transformation and regeneration of business incubators as new organisational forms: Understanding the interplay between organisational history and organisational theory. *Business History, 46*(3), 353–380. https://doi.org/10.1080/0007679042000219175a

Lubit, A. J., & Gidley, D. (2021). Becoming part of a temporary protest organization through embodied walking ethnography. *Journal of Organizational Ethnography, 10*(1), 79–94.

Phillips, T. (2015). "Don't clone my indie game, bro": Informal cultures of video-game regulation in the independent sector. *Cultural Trends, 24*(2), 143–153.

Zucker, L. G. (1977). The role of institutionalization in cultural persistence. *American Sociological Review, 42*(5), 726–743. https://doi.org/10.2307/2094862

CHAPTER 8

A Conceptual Crux Events Framework

In this chapter, I build a theoretical framework around crux events, incubator development, and indie video game creation. The theory is process based (Langley, 1999). It starts with the crux event, followed by the reaction, and ends with the outcome. I will show how my theory builds or compares to other theories. Like all ethnography, it is specific and particular to the context and circumstances. I believe it has some transferability—both to other similar places and to less similar ones—and I will suggest how.

> **For Students**
>
> 1. The crux events discussed in this section are grand concepts for either organizations or larger social structures; however, the conceptual framework could be applied on a personal level. For students, it might be useful to remember that things may seem significant in the moment, but they do not always end up significant in the end. An interesting exercise might be to apply the crux event perspective to your personal life and see if it changes your view of something in the past. The prologue of
>
> *(continued)*

> (continued)
>
> this book provides one example in the context of this research. Alternatively, consider the example of deciding to pursue a PhD. I faced this choice as did at least two members of the Quarry. One member joined the Quarry and is still making games five years later. The other accepted a fully funded PhD (but I don't know what happened to him). In my case, the PhD was personally significant, but it did not change my career trajectory (in the way I thought it would). I worked for a few months for a game developer, but I never found traction in academia (outside of a few published articles). What is an example from your life?

Based on my ethnography, I propose three types of crux events: gateways; surprises; and crises. Social actors react to the events in three main ways: embrace, resist, or ignore. In turn, this leads to several possible outcomes: distraction, inspiration, questions, or hope. Since I have spent a long time telling the story and discussing crux events in the Quarry, this chapter will only briefly mention the ethnography. I will use the ethnography as a jumping off point to theorize.

8.1 Crux Events

8.1.1 Gateways

Gateways are the first type of crux event. A gateway is an entry or exit for social actors. Most obviously, a gateway is the introduction of new members or the departure of existing members. It can also mean entries or exits within the organization such as a collective graduation to the next level.

It is important to differentiate between gateways for individual social actors (solo people or organizations) and gateways for the group. Each social actor will have at least one entry and at least one exit (eventually, since no one lives forever). The innovation space, in this case the Quarry, will have multiple members enter and exit. A gateway as a type of crux event requires the membership entry or exit to potentially substantially influence the environment. The quantity and quality of the gateway members affects whether the entry or exit could be considered a crux event.

For example, in the Quarry, there were several crux gateway events: second cohort starting, Hera leaving (although discussed later as a surprise), part of first cohort quitting, and remaining first cohort departing (although discussed later as a crisis). Entries and exits that were not crux events include the QA intern starting, the marketing intern starting and departing, and companies moving on from temporary employees.

Entry gateways can be seen in what Goffman (1961) called "total institutions." Extremes allow for more easily seeing the framework. Starting university, entering prison, or enlisting in the military all feature entry gateways; however, not every entry is a crux event. These total institutions are too institutionalized for the usual introduction of new members to potentially make an impact on the institution. There are exceptions related to the *quality* of the members entering the gateway. In the American military, the two prominent examples are racial desegregation and allowing women to enlist in new roles (Moore, 2017; Moskos Jr., 1966). There continue to be crux events as the American military only recently allowed women unrestricted access to combat roles (Kamarck, 2016). This class of BUDS (Navy Seal training school) was a crux event because it had the potential to change the institution.

Total institutions also provide excellent examples of exit gateways. University graduation, prison release, and military discharge are all significant exit gateways for the individuals involved. They are also common, in some cases every day, occurrences. What would make a total institution exit into a crux event? It could be a certain quality of the members' exit. The release of high-profile political prisoners can reshape the space they depart as well as wider society. For example, Nelson Mandela's release from Robben Island after 26 years (Cascio & Luthans, 2014). It could also be the *quantity* of members. The mass release of political prisoners or people unjustly imprisoned represents a crux event. Some cases are mostly about quantity, such as the closure of prisoners of war camps after peace. Other cases feature a combination of quantity and quality of the members, such as the liberation of concentration camps and the documentation of the full scope of the Holocaust (Michalcyzk, 2016). In these cases, the members exiting also ends the organization.

8.1.2 Surprises

Surprises are the second type of crux event. A surprise is an unexpected incident impacting a substantial part of the institution. Surprises may appear by addition or subtraction. Like gateways, the quantity and quality of the surprise addition or subtraction matters. I would also argue *how* it came about matters as well. Were there hints (like foreshadowing in a story)? Was it completely unexpected (like a twist no one saw coming)? Or did new information change the view on a situation (like a character catching up with the reader's dramatic irony)? Let us consider surprises by addition followed by surprises by subtraction.

Surprise by addition occurs when something new and unexpected is added to the organization. Things can take on many forms (rules, objects, structures), but they are not people or social actors. In the Quarry, most surprises, as such workshops or funding opportunities, did not rise to the level of a crux event. On the other hand, the announcement of the RPP was a crux event surprise by addition. The RPP was a twist that redefined the Quarry structure from an incubator and coworking space into an accelerator. New policies or regulations are an obvious point of comparison, although those are usually foreshadowed. A couple examples of surprise rules or policies by addition include Europe's introduction of a carbon trading scheme (Cartel et al., 2019), Ireland's lifting of an abortion ban (Fischer, 2019), and the US Supreme Court allowing gay marriage (Tankard & Paluck, 2017). On the object side, bringing new technology into an industry can become a crux event. Barley (1986) famously showed how the introduction of new radiology machines changed the relationship and roles of two professions.

Surprise by subtraction occurs when an organization loses something. For the loss to become a crux event, it must be significant and usually sudden. In the UK, the best recent example is Brexit. Although it took several years to accomplish the full process, the original vote was a crux event. Much has been written on the topic (Liew et al., 2020; Walter, 2021), so I focus the point here on Britain leaving the European Union was a surprise. In the Quarry, there was a direct comparison with Hera leaving. I said above the surprise cannot be a social actor, so we must think about Hera leaving as the loss of the *role* of Quarry Manager rather than the loss of Hera the person. Staying in the UK, we can compare surprise by subtraction to the monarchy. The death of a monarch, especially one as old as Queen Elizabeth II, was not a surprise. Furthermore, there is a clear line of succession to fill the role vacated by the person. The abdication of Edward VIII was a surprise crux event. British monarchs rarely abdicated (Zajac, 2017), and not voluntarily, so the vacating of the role created uncertainty.

8.1.3 Crises

Crises are the last type of crux event. A crisis is a threat to the foundation of an organization or institution. They are seismic disruptions to the way things are. Like an earthquake, the magnitude matters. The foundation can handle minor or trivial rumblings. It might even be able to withstand major shaking, but existential threats are crux events where things may shake out in different ways. There are two subtypes of crisis: self-inflicted or externally instigated.

Self-inflicted crises come from within the organization. This can be through the actions of organizational actors or structural flaws that are exposed. In the Quarry, the largest self-inflicted crisis arose when BAT cut the secondary funding for the rapid prototyping. The crisis threatened the viability of the second cohort companies, and by extension, the Quarry as a nurturing innovation space. One example of a self-inflicted crisis comes from the Northern Ireland Renewable Heat Initiative (RHI). As detailed in Gharib et al. (2024), the RHI had inherent financial flaws that were exposed in time. Legitimacy attacks led to the collapse of the devolved government (Gharib et al., 2022). The crisis was self-inflicted because social actors created the scheme, ignored the warnings, and in some ways willingly pursued actions directly leading to the crisis. Another similar example is the 2008 global financial crisis (Jessop, 2012).

External crises arise from outside the organization. A crisis as crux event potentially impacts the existential foundation even if it did not start there. Consider a hurricane. They always start offshore and happen multiple times per year. They can cause a crisis, like with Hurricane Katrina and FEMA, when they impact the essence of an organization. In the Quarry, and much of the world, the largest recent crisis has been the COVID-19 pandemic, or syndemic (Horton, 2020). Lockdowns threatened the very idea of shared spaces. The Quarry, like many other physical places (e.g. museums in Agostino et al., 2020), closed the physical location for months. Could the Quarry be the Quarry without the physical building? The question speaks to identity. There are similar questions asked about the "American Dream" in relation to the "migrant crisis" on the southern US border (Russo, 2014) and liberal democracy in relation to the "Syrian refugee crisis" across Europe (Kornberger et al., 2019).

8.2 Reactions

Social actors may respond to crux events in three ways. Some actors may embrace the change or disturbance inherent in the event. Other actors may resist the potential disruption and fight it. Others may ignore the significance of the event. Each reaction may happen in response to any type of crux event. It is important to remember that individual reactions may not rise to the level of impacting the organization. While a social actor may embrace a crux event, depending on their position within the organization, this may create barely a ripple.

8.2.1 Embrace

What are the reasons social actors might embrace a crux event? People might see the event as an opportunity to change something either for the organization as a whole or themselves. There may be other, perhaps nefarious reasons, but change appeared to be the main motivation in the Quarry. Let us consider a few examples and different types of crux events.

Embracing a gateway accepts transitions as a part of advancement and growth. Individuals and organizations must move from one stage to the next, or else leave or be left behind. Those embracing the gateway do so willingly. In the Quarry, there were examples of social actors embracing both entries and exits. A mentor described how one company rapidly absorbed all available knowledge in only a few months after joining the Quarry. Alternatively, one first cohort company decided to use leaving the Quarry as a restart. They both embraced the opportunity provided by the gateway. Obvious parallels can be drawn to the university experience. Some university freshmen embrace the collegiate experience via "Freshers Week" and other activities (Palmer et al., 2009). There is also substantial research on the importance of graduation rituals (Magolda, 2003). Virtual ceremonies during COVID-19 demonstrated how this can become a crux event. From a personal standpoint, I have never participated in my own graduation. I never embraced the gateway.

Embracing a surprise is a reflection on how people view the surprise—as either beneficial or detrimental. In the parlance of business, is it an opportunity or a threat? Unlike a gateway which is usually expected, a surprise comes fast and may not allow time for consideration before reacting. What does it feel like in the moment? In the Quarry, companies embracing the RPP focused on being paid to develop intellectual property. This was a beneficial surprise by addition ("free money!"). There is some transference to the individual level with being laid off or fired from a job. Some people are able to embrace this surprise by subtraction as an opportunity. Popular culture, and academic literature (Zikic & Klehe, 2006), seems littered with examples of people "going back to school" after an unexpected termination. For commercial organizations, a trade show represents an attempt to embrace surprises in the form of a chance "hot lead" or unearthing unknown prospects (Blythe, 1999). Relatedly, a product announcement may be the chance to create surprises for customers as both companies and customers seek that "wow" moment. Steve Jobs and the announcement of the iPod and iPhone spring to mind.

Embracing a crisis seems counterintuitive. Crisis involves facing a significant threat to social actors' everyday life or worldview. Things previously taken-for-granted are no longer certain. As such, some things may be easier to change, even some things that didn't appear like they could change. Embracing a crisis means abandoning old constraints while allowing new ones to appear. Accepting the challenge allows for change. In the case of the Quarry, one long held assumption was that the physical space partly defined the Quarry. BAT talked about the essentialness of the coworking aspect and participants talked about the importance of the material aspects of the building. At the very least, a physical space of some kind was an important aspect of the Quarry. The COVID-19 lockdowns closed shared spaces like the Quarry. This plunged the Quarry into an existential crisis. BAT embraced the crisis by separating the Quarry as a program from the Quarry as a physical space. A great many other organizations tried similar tactics during the pandemic, including schools (Pokhrel & Chhetri, 2021), government (Williamson et al., 2020), and commercial organizations. In her thesis chapter on the COVID-19 pandemic, Lubit (2023) showed how a mosque, a women-only refugee and asylum seeker meeting space, and a social group attempted to address the loss of physical space. Of the three organizations, only the women's only space embraced the crisis as an opportunity to redefine the relationship between organization and members.

8.2.2 *Resist*

Resisting a gateway is not unusual. Many parents are familiar with children not wanting to begin the first day of school. Resisting a gateway is complicated by perspective. There are three perspectives: those leaving, those staying, and those on the other side. In the Quarry, the first cohort being told to leave at the end of the first year can be viewed from the first two perspectives. Many in the first cohort resisted leaving. Partly this was how it was proposed—a one-week clean break. Partly it was being unprepared for what came next. For those staying, BAT leaned toward embracing the gateway, and the other companies leaned toward ignoring it; however, the first cohort demonstrated the strongest reaction to the crux event.

Resisting a surprise usually indicates the social actor views the surprise as detrimental. If we consider the RPP again, several companies initially resisted signing up. They did so because they knew the RPP would hinder their other projects. They were not against the RPP in principle—rather it was the timing. In this case, there was resistance to only one aspect of the crux event. Elsewhere in the literature, we see many examples of resistance to the surprise introduction of new credentials or roles for certain professions. Trish Reay et al. (2017) examined how doctors initially resisted moving from single providers to working with a team of health care professionals.

Resisting a crisis seems natural. Unlike a gateway (which should be expected) or a surprise (which may be beneficial), a crisis usually comes unannounced and with potential dire consequences. Resisting means defending the status quo against significant threats. In the Quarry, companies and mentors resisted the mini-production funding cut by lobbying BAT for relief. Resistance aimed to keep the companies working full time in the Quarry. Resistance to a crisis can be seen as defensive work such as seen in Wright et al. (2020). Infectious disease represents an existential threat to delivering emergency medical care. As such, resisting can mean striving to maintain values in the face of the threat.

8.2.3 Ignore

Social actors may ignore the crux event. They may act as if it did not happen or that it is irrelevant. In some cases, the crux event may not impact some organizational actors or at least, they do not think it will impact them and so they act that way. Let us consider some examples.

Ignoring a gateway must be considered from both sides of the gateway. Which social actors are likely to ignore a gateway? For entries, existing members might ignore new members. This was the approach taken by many of the first cohort on the introduction of the second cohort. On the other end, remaining members or departing members may ignore the exit gateway, at least mentally. For Mario, exiting the Quarry meant little change in everyday life. For those remaining, the exit of the three initial first cohort companies passed with an observation and nothing else. In some cases, the gateway may lose some of its importance based on future circumstances. For example, a university student moving onto graduate school may ignore the bachelor's degree gateway.

Ignoring a surprise means being aware of the surprise but choosing to disregard it. In some cases, social actors may react to part of the surprise but ignore other aspects. For example, when Hera announced her intention to leave, BAT posted her job opening, solicited feedback from Quarry members, and arranged a small farewell party. They ignored the transition process and the liminal space Hera's leaving would likely create. In relation to the RPP, two non-participating companies ignored the surprise and went on as if nothing had changed. In the surprise crux events mentioned earlier (carbon trading, abortion rights, and gay marriage), it is likely many social actors ignored the change.

Ignoring a crisis may seem more difficult than ignoring a gateway or surprise. Indeed, the ethnography did not provide strong support for social actors ignoring a crisis. BAT initially appeared to ignore the self-inflicted crisis of not funding any of the second cohort companies. In time, it was revealed that BAT was simply pushing off dealing with the crisis until later. A purer form of ignoring a crisis can be found in the myth of Nero playing the fiddle while Rome burned. In recent times, the COVID-19 pandemic provides many examples. Many politicians ignored the consequences of the crisis and insisted on going on as normal (Duarte, 2020).

8.3 Outcomes

Crux events do not lead in a straight line to predetermined outcomes. Any crux event and reaction may lead to any of the four possible outcomes. First, the crux event may end up a distraction from everyday routines. Second, the crux event may serve as inspiration for a new direction forward. Third, the crux event may raise existential questions for the organizations involved. Fourth, a crux event might end with hope. These four outcomes are an initial list. Some paths are more likely than others, and some paths are very unlikely. For example, a crisis ignored is unlikely to end up a distraction, but a gateway embraced likely leads to hope or inspiration.

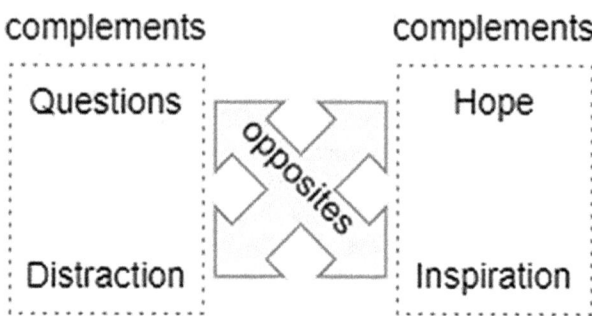

Fig. 8.1 Theoretical positioning of initial outcomes

Figure 8.1 below illustrates the theoretical positioning of the initial outcomes. Hope and inspiration are complements. Distraction and hope are opposites. Distraction and questions are complements. Questions and inspiration are opposites.

8.3.1 Distraction

A crux event may be a distraction to everyday life. In the end, the crux event may be a temporary distraction where nothing much changes afterward. When looking back, the crux event may seem less important or momentous than it did at the time. It may be somewhat forgotten how things were perched on a proverbial knife's edge. In the Quarry, Hera's leaving ended up a distraction. For a relatively short period of time after Hera left, everyday routines were disrupted. From some perspectives, the fate of the Quarry hung in the balance. Then the role of Quarry manager was filled, and, on the surface, life returned to familiar rhythms. Let us consider another example.

The Y2K computer bug dominated late-twentieth-century concerns (Kratofil & Burbank, 1999). Then the century rolled over, and nothing happened. The world did not end. Life went on as it had after any other new year. People quickly forgot the mania around it. When it is thought about, it is usually considered a case of 'much ado about nothing' (Adams, 2001).

8.3.2 Questions

The crux event may leave social actors with existential questions. What does it all mean? What is the point? Why are we doing this? For the social actors involved, there may be a feeling that things have been knocked off axis. Depression might set in. There is uncertainty about the organization and participation in the organization (assuming it's a choice). In the Quarry, the funding cut left multiple social actors with existential questions. Akira questioned whether he would continue as a video game developer. A mentor planned to tell BAT that the entire second cohort would fail without help. Others questioned how the Quarry could continue if they lost all the companies.

Very often, crisis crux events lead to existential questions. The FEMA response to Hurricane Katrina led to existential questions around its purpose and values. The failure of the RHI in Northern Ireland led to the collapse of the devolved government for almost three years (Gharib et al., 2024). In turn, this threatened the power sharing at the heart of the Good Friday Agreement and peace in the region. Indeed, these questions were raised by participants in Lyra's Walk—a temporary organization advocating for the reforming of the government, among other things (Gidley & Lubit, 2023; Lubit & Gidley, 2021). The COVID-19 crisis forced social actors and institutions across the world to consider the very foundation of public spaces, health, and social interaction. Unlike with the threat of Ebola (Wright et al., 2020), the COVID-19 pandemic left lasting existential questions among people. One final example is the Cuban Missile Crisis which brought the world to the brink of nuclear war. The philosophy (or policy) of mutually assured destruction left many questioning the philosophy of war, but also life itself.

Existential questions need not arise from only negative events.[1] The Apollo 11 moon landing is considered one of the great achievements of humanity. It was also the pinnacle of the "space race." Once it was achieved, the question inevitability became: what next? Would the landing propel humans to explore the rest of the solar system, or was it the climax? As far as manned space flight, it was the finish line. Yes, humans went back to the moon several more times, built the International Space Station, and sent tourists to space, but people have not gone further, yet (Eyles, 2018).

---

[1] Negative is a matter of perspective. The Apollo moon landing was not positive for the Soviet Union. The country was the first to put an object into space and land an object on the moon, but they never did land a person on the moon.

8.3.3 Hope

Crux events may result in hope. In these cases, not much visibly changes, but the promise of change empowers those involved. Alternatively, an organization faces a threat and demonstrates resilience thereby affirming faith in the system. In the Quarry, hope was the least observed outcome. The one example of hope after a crux event was the introduction of Juno as the new Quarry manager. The hope was "cautiously optimistic" rather than unbridled expectation. It some ways, it may be difficult to differentiate between distraction and hope since both demonstrate less visible impacts. Hope may appear after gateways where social actors wait for change without actively pursuing it.

The threat of Ebola in Wright et al. (2020) represents an interesting example. The story is about the work to maintain the value of providing health care to those needing it. The crisis was limited (only a handful of suspected cases). It appears at first glance to be a distraction; however, the COVID-19 pandemic offers additional context. The Ebola response was a story of success. When the organization was confronted with an external crisis, it stood up. It was a test where the response mattered. American democracy faced a similar test during the January 6 insurrection at the Capitol. The outcome was hope—in that the institution demonstrated resilience to the self-inflicted crisis.

8.3.4 Inspiration

A crux event may serve as inspiration for the social actors impacted. Inspiration results in a change and a new direction forward. In these cases, the crux event served as a launching pad for the next stage. In the Quarry, the obvious example is the RPP. The companies involved were inspired to pursue original intellectual property. In some cases, the companies pursued IP created during the RPP. Based on the prototyping experience feedback, BAT reshaped the Quarry to include a version of the RPP as a foundational piece. The crux event led to lasting transformation. An outcome of inspiration differentiates from an outcome of hope by the change enacted. Inspiration, as a crux event outcome, requires change.

One obvious example of a crux event leading to an inspiration outcome was the release of Nelson Mandela from prison. The move helped inspire the end of decades of apartheid and ushered in full democracy in South Africa. Another example is the first crux event of the "space race" when the Soviet Union launched Sputnik (Eyles, 2018; Siddiqi, 2000). For both America and the Soviet Union, the crux event led to inspiration. The first artificial satellite broke the barrier for what was humanly possible. Furthermore, it inspired enormous investment in time, resources, and knowledge to surpass the achievement.

8.4 Conclusion

This chapter provided a conceptual framework for analyzing crux events, reactions, and outcomes. The framework is preliminary and hopefully useful for others to build on. Three types of crux events were identified—gateways, surprises, and crises. Social actors reacted to crux events in three ways—embrace, resist, ignore. This led to four types of outcomes—distraction, questions, hope, or inspiration.

I will end by letting the reader ponder the following as possible crux events.

- The dropping of the first (or second) atomic bomb on civilians.
- Sean Connery quitting the role of James Bond (for the first time).
- Roman Abramovich purchasing Chelsea Football Club.
- The invention of CRISPR/Cas9 gene editing techniques.
- The first COVID-19 lockdown in China.
- The opening of Facebook membership beyond colleges.

Perhaps inspiration will arise from the possibilities of using a crux event framework.

References

Adams, A. R. (2001). *Notes on a non-event: Y2K as social construction and its discontents.* Master's thesis, The University of Arizona.

Agostino, D., Arnaboldi, M., & Lampis, A. (2020). Italian state museums during the COVID-19 crisis: From onsite closure to online openness. *Museum Management and Curatorship, 35*(4), 362–372.

Barley, S. R. (1986). Technology as an occasion for structuring: Evidence from observations of CT scanners and the social order of radiology departments. *Administrative Science Quarterly, 31*(1), 78–108. https://doi.org/10.2307/2392767

Blythe, J. (1999). Visitor and exhibitor expectations and outcomes at trade exhibitions. *Marketing Intelligence & Planning, 17*(2), 100–110.

Cartel, M., Boxenbaum, E., & Aggeri, F. (2019). Just for fun! How experimental spaces stimulate innovation in institutionalized fields. *Organization Studies, 40*(1), 65–92.

Cascio, W. F., & Luthans, F. (2014). Reflections on the metamorphosis at Robben Island: The role of institutional work and positive psychological capital. *Journal of Management Inquiry, 23*(1), 51–67. https://doi.org/10.1177/1056492612474348

Duarte, T. R. (2020). Ignoring scientific advice during the Covid-19 pandemic: Bolsonaro's actions and discourse. *Tapuya: Latin American Science, Technology and Society, 3*(1), 288–291.

Eyles, D. (2018). *Sunburst and luminary: An Apollo memoir.* Fort Point Press.

Fischer, C. (2019). Abortion and reproduction in Ireland: Shame, nation-building and the affective politics of place. *Feminist Review, 122*(1), 32–48. https://doi.org/10.1177/0141778919850003

Gharib, A. M., Palmer, M., Gidley, D., & Zhang, M. (2024). Transitioning through a crisis: Industrial customer responses to a green technology innovation scheme. *Industry and Innovation*, 1–31.

Gharib, A. M., Palmer, M., & Zhang, M. (2022). Maintaining legitimacy: An institutional cooptative analysis of a green technology innovation scheme crisis. *Innovations, 26*(2), 278–308. https://doi.org/10.1080/14479338.2022.2116641

Gidley, D., & Lubit, A. J. (2023). The dual institutional work of Lyra's Walk: Partisan violence and peace protest in Northern Ireland. *Journal of Organizational Ethnography, 12*(2), 141–161. https://doi.org/10.1108/JOE-01-2023-0003

Goffman, E. (1961). *Asylums* (p. 84). Anchor Books.

Horton, R. (2020). Offline: COVID-19 is not a pandemic. *The Lancet, 396*(10255), 874.

Jessop, B. (2012). Narratives of crisis and crisis response: Perspectives from North and South. *The Global Crisis and Transformative Social Change*, 23–42.

Kamarck, K. N. (2016). *Women in combat: Issues for Congress.* Congressional Research Service Washington United States.

Kornberger, M., Leixnering, S., & Meyer, R. E. (2019). The logic of tact: How decisions happen in situations of crisis. *Organization Studies, 40*(2), 239–266.

Kratofil, B., & Burbank, K. (1999). The impact of the y2k bug. *Business Economics*, 39–43.

Langley, A. (1999). Strategies for theorizing from process data. *The Academy of Management Review, 24*(4), 691–710.

Liew, T., Goodwin, R., & Walasek, L. (2020). Voting patterns, revoking article 50 and antidepressant trends in England following the Brexit referendum. *Social Science & Medicine, 255*, 113025.

Lubit, A. (2023). *"I would love people to realise that I call this my home": Migrant Muslim women's everyday visibility, movement and placemaking strategies in Northern Ireland.* Doctoral dissertation, Queen's University Belfast.

Lubit, A. J., & Gidley, D. (2021). Becoming part of a temporary protest organization through embodied walking ethnography. *Journal of Organizational Ethnography, 10*(1), 79–94.

Magolda, P. M. (2003). Saying good-bye: An anthropological examination of a commencement ritual. *Journal of College Student Development, 44*(6), 779–796.

Michalcyzk, J. J. (2016). *Filming the end of the holocaust: Allied documentaries, Nuremberg and the liberation of the concentration camps.* Bloomsbury Academic.

Moore, B. L. (2017). Introduction to armed forces & society: Special issue on women in the military. *Armed Forces & Society, 43*(2), 191–201. https://doi.org/10.1177/0095327X17694909

Moskos, C. C., Jr. (1966). Racial integration in the armed forces. *American Journal of Sociology, 72*(2), 132–148.

Palmer, M., O'Kane, P., & Owens, M. (2009). Betwixt spaces: Student accounts of turning point experiences in the first-year transition. *Studies in Higher Education, 34*(1), 37–54.

Pokhrel, S., & Chhetri, R. (2021). A literature review on impact of COVID-19 pandemic on teaching and learning. *Higher Education for the Future, 8*(1), 133–141.

Reay, T., Goodrick, E., Waldorff, S. B., & Casebeer, A. (2017). Getting leopards to change their spots: Co-creating a new professional role identity. *Academy of Management Journal, 60*(3), 1043–1070.

Russo, C. (2014). Allies forging collective identity: Embodiment and emotions on the migrant trail. *Mobilization: An International Quarterly, 19*(1), 67–82.

Siddiqi, A. A. (2000). *Challenge to Apollo: The Soviet Union and the space race, 1945–1974* (Vol. 4408). US National Aeronautics & Space Administration.

Tankard, M. E., & Paluck, E. L. (2017). The effect of a supreme court decision regarding gay marriage on social norms and personal attitudes. *Psychological Science, 28*(9), 1334–1344. https://doi.org/10.1177/0956797617709594

Walter, S. (2021). Brexit Domino? The political contagion effects of voter-endorsed withdrawals from international institutions. *Comparative Political Studies, 54*(13), 2382–2415. https://doi.org/10.1177/0010414021997169

Williamson, S., Colley, L., & Hanna-Osborne, S. (2020). Will working from home become the 'new normal' in the public sector? *Australian Journal of Public Administration, 79*(4), 601–607.

Wright, A. L., Meyer, A. D., Reay, T., & Staggs, J. (2020). Maintaining places of social inclusion: Ebola and the emergency department. *Administrative Science Quarterly*. https://doi.org/10.1177/0001839220916401

Zajac, A. C. (2017). *"Something Must Be Done!": Edward VIII's abdication and the preservation of the British monarchy.*

Zikic, J., & Klehe, U. C. (2006). Job loss as a blessing in disguise: The role of career exploration and career planning in predicting reemployment quality. *Journal of Vocational Behavior, 69*(3), 391–409.

Afterword

Was the Quarry a success? That was the most common question I received during fieldwork. I will consider the question in two ways. First, what happened to the ten companies in terms of their material output? Did they release games or at least schedule a release? Did they acquire funding or abandon the industry? Second, I will consider the question from a holistic view of time and perspective. Undoubtably some companies and individuals improved from the experience, but it is uncertain if their creativity was accelerated. I remember reading this tweet: "It may have taken the last seven years, but my game is finally out. Consider retweeting this. It will help me justify wasting all these hours making a silly arcade game." It seems to capture all the hard work, relief, hope, and ambiguity.

Here is the two-sentence summary of what happened to the first two cohorts of companies in the Quarry. No name or even aliases. Just random numbers. I mostly rely on publicly available information.

1. Continued to work on an existing project. They secured university partnership funding for the experimental narrative game. They continue to work on getting it ready for release.
2. Returned to work as a data analyst. About 18 months after leaving the Quarry, they released a game based on a prototype created during the RPP.

3. Secured further funding for an RPP game while continuing to work on a second game. They grew the company to nine people after a couple years.
4. Released their RPP game a year after leaving the Quarry. They released a further couple games.
5. Released several mobile games before taking a job in IT management. One of the prototypes is still in development.
6. Released (via a commercial publisher) their BAT funded game a year after leaving the Quarry.
7. Released (via a commercial publisher) a game for multiple consoles about one year after leaving the Quarry. They continued to provide updated content for the game for several years.
8. Moved into freelance work. The company is dormant.
9. Signed a subcontract to develop a game (released in early 2023) for a commercial publisher. Their own original game was rescheduled for early access in 2024.
10. Dissolved company in 2022. It's not clear if a game was released. Unfortunately, the company director passed away suddenly in 2023.

There is not a simple answer. The two main considerations are time and viewpoint (perspective). By time, I am thinking about temporal scale and temporal orientation. As I argued elsewhere about the rapid prototyping program (Gidley & Palmer, 2022), the temporal scale may change how we view success. Are we judging a week, a month, a year, a decade? In the case of orientation, are we judging the past, present, or future? Viewpoint can become even more complex. There were multitudes of social actors interacting with the Quarry as a concept. Starting with the obvious—the Quarry game developers, mentors, BAT, interns, and going a step further—the ethnographer, visitors, consultants, members of the Gymnasium coworking space, students, other game developers in the region, local government, industry players in the region and beyond. It is a thankless task to consider all that, so I will limit viewpoints to BAT, Quarry participants during the ethnography, and potential future participants.

The past, in this case, refers to the time before the Quarry launched. According to one mentor, the game developers in the region were a disparate collection of individual companies. The Quarry's goal was to bring them together. The Quarry did that reasonably well; however, it did not form a collective. The Quarry became a focal point for game developers in the region. It helped to build a regional identity, but it was a long way from finished.

The present, in this case, refers to the one year of ethnographic time chronicled in this book. Since the reader has just finished reading this book, I think I can leave it up to you to decide if the Quarry was a success during the time covered.

The future, in this case, refers to the indefinite time after the ethnographer left the Quarry. Obviously, I have not told the reader, nor do I fully know, what happened since I left. The Quarry manager's plan indicated a desire to lean into the idea of the Quarry as central hub while at the same time vigorously supporting the most promising small teams. The plans were immediately complicated by pandemic lockdowns. The community part was severely hit and delayed, but the fast-track program admirably shifted online. BAT had made a commitment to a further two years of funding the Quarry. One key indicator of success would be extending this support.

Second, there are multiple viewpoints on which to judge the success of the Digital Quarry. To do that, I would consider the goals and experiences of the various social actors. Success is usually judged against expectations versus outcome. That being said, I was not privileged to all expectations or experiences. Therefore, I will warn the reader that some of this is speculation and extrapolation.

For BAT, I believe the goal was to develop the video game industry in the region by drawing in outside investment and making existing companies sustainable. The goal, as one participant noted, was not to make all the Quarry teams into million quid companies. If that had happened, I think everyone would have agreed the Quarry was a resounding success. None of the companies came close to this figure, but that is beside the point. So, did the Quarry (1) develop the video game industry in the region, (2) draw outside investment, and (3) make sustainable companies? The Quarry did a bit of all three, but not to the level that I imagine BAT expected. We could point to things impacting the Quarry as excuses (the manager leaving, a pandemic), or we could look at the success of companies outside of the Quarry during the same period. The Quarry was an experimental drug, but the placebo seemed to work just as well and maybe even better.

For the initial Quarry companies featured in this book, expectations and experience defined success. I briefly mentioned the outcomes above. I think the companies with low expectations ("free office" types) considered it a success. Those expecting secrets, special access, or a transformational experience were disappointed. They could see the potential of the Quarry, but this also made them aware of how it fell short. Returning to the comparison of the Quarry to a university. How many of the team felt they had learned something? Most. How many felt like they had taken the next step because of the Quarry? Maybe a couple. How many would have paid for the experience? I want to say none, but that sounds harsh.

For some potential future participants, I think the Quarry held an allure. I think some wanted to join the Quarry. At the same time, I don't think any of them would expect joining the Quarry to guarantee success or to significantly lower the barriers to success. It may have made the struggle slightly easier or been a nice bonus to existing plans. From this perspective, it is hard to call the Quarry a success since people were not pushing to get in. It was not essential, but it could have been.

Appendix

Possible discussion questions for each chapter. These are intended for a college or university classroom setting. There are some general questions that could apply to any chapter:

- What do you think of the story?
- What lessons did you take away?

Prologue
- What would you have done in this situation?
- Does this story belong in the book?
- What does the story say about the author? Prompts:
  - He writes in the third person.
  - He starts the book with a story about himself.

Chapter 2
- How would you feel about different working arrangements?
  - Solo developer.
  - Even partnership.
  - Working as the sole artist/programmer for a small studio.
  - Working in a big studio.
- Would you be worried about people stealing your game ideas?

- What should BAT have done differently for the start of the second cohort?

Chapter 3
- Would you have participated in the rapid prototyping at the terms laid out? Would it make a difference if you were the first or second cohort?
- How would you run a rapid prototyping program? Why did you make those choices?
- Pick a week's theme (e.g. climate change). Come up with a game idea—characters, gameplay, style. How would you pitch it?
- What sessions should have been in the bootcamp? Schedule six sessions.
- What is commercial viability? How would you measure it?
- Would you like a placement as an intern in the Quarry? If not, why? If yes, justify a role.

Chapter 4
- What do you think about how Hera handled leaving?
- Which program would you rather participate in—Kofi's mentoring/knowledge transfer or the Quarry?
- Would you apply for the production funding after the reduction?
- If you ran the Quarry, would you kick out companies that no longer fit your vision?
- If you took a job, like Felix, that ended up different than you expected, what would you do?
- What feedback would you give BAT at this point?
- How should BAT have solicited feedback?
- What do you think of Robin's Rebellion?

Chapter 5
- Would you order the financing hierarchy differently? Is anything missing?
- What criteria would you use to judge a pitch for additional funding?
- If you ran a studio, how many projects would you make simultaneously? Why?
- What factors would influence your decision on staying or leaving the Quarry?

Chapter 6
- If you were hired to fix the Quarry, what changes would you make? And how?
- Did Juno's changes sound like an upgrade on the existing Quarry?
- Should BAT have tried to keep the entire first cohort for another six months?
- Did BAT save the second cohort or just keep them on life-support? What could they have done differently (assuming there was no money available until April)?
- Would you participate in Moonshot at those terms?
- What could have been done to prepare for an external crisis, like a global pandemic?

Chapter 7
- What is the most important practical lesson and why?
- If you ran your own version of the Quarry—what would you do about membership, resistance, interns, mentor meetings, feedback, and institutional knowledge?
- What lessons were missed by the author? Which ones were wrong?

Chapter 8
- Apply the crux event framework to an example (the end of the chapter provides some).
- What are some other crux events, reactions, and outcomes?
- Is the framework useful? What are its advantages or flaws?

Chapter 1—Website List
https://www.gamefounders.com/
https://theoctopus.com/
https://www.ubisoft.com/en-us/company/about-us/innovation/startup-programs
https://gamebcn.co/
https://spielfabrique.eu/Thunderfox/#anchor-about
https://games-i.com/
https://carbon-incubator.com/
https://corelabsaccelerator.com/
https://pixelles.ca/
https://www.dutchgamegarden.nl/incubation/
https://www.thefamily.co/

https://sites.disney.com/accelerator/
https://tranzfuser.com/2024competition/
https://gamecenter.nyu.edu/about/incubator/
https://indiesworkshop.com/
https://burngameven.com/
https://www.daestudios.be/
https://www.globaltopround.com/
https://developersonair.withgoogle.com/events/indie-games-accelerator
https://www.madridingame.es/
https://www.rngfoundry.com/
https://ukie.org.uk/games-accelerators
https://basecampmalta.com/
https://gamecity-hamburg.de/company-index/games-lift-incubator/
https://code.mcit.gov.sa/en/accelerator-incubator/gamefounders-ksa-2
https://games.brussels/coworking-spaces-for-game-developpers-in-brussels/
https://www.indieasylum.com/
https://newmediamanitoba.com/
https://www.rit.edu/magic/make-publish
https://www.dutchgamegarden.nl/
https://games.london/accelerator/
https://colognegamelab.de/about/cgl-cologne-game-incubator/alumni/
https://www.brinc.io/gaming/
https://www.ltu.edu/magazine/2024/unreal
https://gaming-edih.hr/en/product/training-in-the-field-of-video-game-development/
https://aie.edu.au/about-us/incubator-program/
https://gamejamplus.com/incubation/
https://www.massdigi.org/
https://www.bicaraba.eus/en/the-campus-accelerator-of-video-games-evolves-in-game-eus-a-firm-bet-for-the-creation-and-retention-of-local-talent-and-for-the-impulse-of-the-sector-in-araba-and-euskadi/
https://www.creativescotland.com/news-stories/latest-news/archive/2024/02/indielab-games-launches-its-uk-wide-accelerator-programme-2024
https://www.piszczor.com/accelerator/
https://babyghosts.fund/grant-and-accelerator

https://bluebyte.ubisoft.com/en/our-engagements/entrepreneurs/indie-camp/
https://levelupacceleratorprogram.com/
https://www.indiegameacademy.games/
https://www.madridinnova.es/en/espacios/madrid-in-game-en/
https://www.helika.io/accelerate/
https://www.wulum.com/gca
https://so-fu.jp/#igi
https://www.f2pcampus.com/faq/
https://www.iepro.com/
https://alberta.scaffold-institute.com/
https://narwhal.ax/
https://accelerator.digitaldragons.pl/
https://www.digitalartsandentertainment.be/page/327/Game+For+Thought
https://www.gamehub.org.il/english
https://www.screenwest.com.au/funding-incentives/digital-games-funding/
https://www.thegamecircle.com/en/hakkimizda

REFERENCES

Abanazir, C. (2019). Institutionalisation in E-sports. *Sport, Ethics and Philosophy, 13*(2), 117–131.

Adams, A. R. (2001). *Notes on a non-event: Y2K as social construction and its discontents*. Master's thesis, The University of Arizona.

Agostino, D., Arnaboldi, M., & Lampis, A. (2020). Italian state museums during the COVID-19 crisis: From onsite closure to online openness. *Museum Management and Curatorship, 35*(4), 362–372.

Barley, S. R. (1986). Technology as an occasion for structuring: Evidence from observations of CT scanners and the social order of radiology departments. *Administrative Science Quarterly, 31*(1), 78–108. https://doi.org/10.2307/2392767

Battilana, J., Leca, B., & Boxenbaum, E. (2009). How actors change institutions: Towards a theory of institutional entrepreneurship. *The Academy of Management Annals, 3*(1), 65–107.

Baum, J. A., & Silverman, B. S. (2004). Picking winners or building them? Alliance, intellectual, and human capital as selection criteria in venture financing and performance of biotechnology startups. *Journal of Business Venturing, 19*(3), 411–436.

Blake, J. (2019, January 6). How the UK became a major player in the gaming world, BBC. Retrieved from https://www.bbc.co.uk/news/newsbeat-46757989.

Blythe, J. (1999). Visitor and exhibitor expectations and outcomes at trade exhibitions. *Marketing Intelligence & Planning, 17*(2), 100–110.

Bouncken, R. B., Laudien, S. M., Fredrich, V., & Görmar, L. (2018). Coopetition in coworking-spaces: Value creation and appropriation tensions in an entrepreneurial space. *Review of Managerial Science, 12*, 385–410. https://doi.org/10.1007/s11846-017-0267-7

Britannica, T. Editors of Encyclopaedia (2016, January 18). *band. Encyclopedia Britannica.* https://www.britannica.com/topic/band-kinship-group

Bruneel, J., Ratinho, T., Clarysse, B., & Groen, A. J. (2012). The evolution of business incubators: Comparing demand and supply of business incubation services across different incubator generations. *Technovation, 32*(2), 110–121. https://doi.org/10.1016/j.technovation.2011.11.003

Bueno Merino, P., & Duchemin, M. (2022). Contribution of Psychological Entrepreneurial Support to the Strengthening of Female Entrepreneurial Intention in a Women-Only Incubator. *M@n@gement, 25*(4), 64–79. https://doi.org/10.37725/mgmt.v25.4556

Cabras, I., Goumagias, N. D., Fernandes, K., Cowling, P., Li, F., Kudenko, D., Devlin, S., & Nucciarelli, A. (2017). Exploring survival rates of companies in the UK video-games industry: An empirical study. *Technological Forecasting and Social Change, 117*, 305–314.

Capoccia, G., & Kelemen, R. D. (2007). The study of critical junctures: Theory, narrative, and counterfactuals in historical institutionalism. *World Politics, 59*(3), 341–369.

Cartel, M., Boxenbaum, E., & Aggeri, F. (2019). Just for fun! How experimental spaces stimulate innovation in institutionalized fields. *Organization Studies, 40*(1), 65–92.

Carpenter, M., Daidj, N., & Moreno, C. (2014). Game console manufacturers: The end of sustainable competitive advantage? *Communications and Strategies*, (94), 39–60.

Cascio, W. F., & Luthans, F. (2014). Reflections on the metamorphosis at Robben Island: The role of institutional work and positive psychological capital. *Journal of Management Inquiry, 23*(1), 51–67. https://doi.org/10.1177/1056492612474348

Casper, S., & Storz, C. (2017). Bounded careers in creative industries: Surprising patterns in video games. *Industry and Innovation, 24*(3), 213–248.

Clayton, P., Feldman, M., & Lowe, N. (2018). Behind the scenes: Intermediary organizations that facilitate science commercialization through entrepreneurship. *Academy of Management Perspectives, 32*, 104–124. https://doi.org/10.5465/amp.2016.0133

Cohen, S. (2013). What do accelerators do? Insights from incubators and angels. *Innovations: Technology, Governance, Globalization, 8*(3–4), 19–25.

Cohen, S., Bingham, C. B., & Hallen, B. L. (2019b). The role of accelerator designs in mitigating bounded rationality in new ventures. *Administrative Science Quarterly, 64*(4), 810–854. https://doi.org/10.1177/0001839218782131

Cohen, S., Fehder, D. C., Hochberg, Y. V., & Murray, F. (2019a). The design of startup accelerators. *Research Policy, 48*(7), 1781–1797.

Comunian, R., Faggian, A., & Jewell, S. (2015). Digital technology and creative arts career patterns in the UK creative economy. *Journal of Education and Work, 28*(4), 346–368.

Dacin, M. T., Munir, K., & Tracey, P. (2010). Formal dining at Cambridge colleges: Linking ritual performance and institutional maintenance. *Academy of Management Journal, 53*(6), 1393–1418.

Darchen, S., & Tremblay, D. (2015). Policies for creative clusters: A comparison between the video game industries in Melbourne and Montreal. *European Planning Studies, 23*(2), 311–331. https://doi.org/10.1080/09654313.2013.865712

DCMS. (1998). *A new cultural framework.* HMSO.

Dorobantu, S., Henisz, W. J., & Nartey, L. (2017). Not all sparks light a fire: Stakeholder and shareholder reactions to critical events in contested markets. *Administrative Science Quarterly, 62*(3), 561–597.

Duarte, T. R. (2020). Ignoring scientific advice during the Covid-19 pandemic: Bolsonaro's actions and discourse. *Tapuya: Latin American Science, Technology and Society, 3*(1), 288–291.

Emerson, R. M., Fretz, R. I., & Shaw, L. L. (1995). *Writing ethnographic fieldnotes.* University of Chicago Press.

Eyles, D. (2018). *Sunburst and luminary: An Apollo memoir.* Fort Point Press.

Fischer, C. (2019). Abortion and reproduction in Ireland: Shame, nation-building and the affective politics of place. *Feminist Review, 122*(1), 32–48. https://doi.org/10.1177/0141778919850003

Fisher, S. J., & Harvey, A. (2013). Intervention for inclusivity: Gender politics and indie game development. *Loading..., 7*(11).

Fowler, A., & Khosmood, F. (Eds.). (2023). *Game jams-history, technology, and organisation.* Springer International Publishing.

Fuzi, A. (2015). Co-working spaces for promoting entrepreneurship in sparse regions: The case of South Wales. *Regional Studies, Regional Science, 2*(1), 462–469. https://doi.org/10.1080/21681376.2015.1072053

Gallo, M. (2012). Beyond philanthropy: Recognising the value of alumni to benefit higher education institutions. *Tertiary Education and Management, 18*, 41–55.

García-Sánchez, P., Mora, A. M., Castillo, P. A., & Pérez, I. J. (2019). A bibliometric study of the research area of videogames using Dimensions.ai database. *Procedia Computer Science, 162*, 737–744.

Garnham, N. (2005). From cultural to creative industries. *International Journal of Cultural Policy, 11*(1), 15–29.

Garrett, L. E., Spreitzer, G. M., & Bacevice, P. A. (2017). Co-constructing a sense of community at work: The emergence of community in coworking spaces. *Organization Studies, 38*(6), 821–842. https://doi.org/10.1177/0170840616685354

Gaudl, S. E., Nelson, M. J., Colton, S., Saunders, R., Powley, E. J., Ferrer, B. P., Ivey, P., & Cook, M. (2018). Rapid game jams with fluidic games: A user study & design methodology. *Entertainment Computing, 27*, 1–9.

Gharib, A. M., Palmer, M., Gidley, D., & Zhang, M. (2024). Transitioning through a crisis: Industrial customer responses to a green technology innovation scheme. *Industry and Innovation*, 1–31.

Gharib, A. M., Palmer, M., & Zhang, M. (2022). Maintaining legitimacy: An institutional cooptative analysis of a green technology innovation scheme crisis. *Innovations, 26*(2), 278–308. https://doi.org/10.1080/14479338.2022.2116641

Gidley, D. (2021a). *An ethnographic study of institutional work in a creative proto-institutional place*. Doctoral dissertation, Queen's University Belfast.

Gidley, D. (2021b). Creating institutional disruption: An alternative method to study institutions. *Journal of Organizational Change Management, 34*(4), 810–821.

Gidley, D., & Lubit, A. J. (2023). The dual institutional work of Lyra's Walk: Partisan violence and peace protest in Northern Ireland. *Journal of Organizational Ethnography, 12*(2), 141–161. https://doi.org/10.1108/JOE-01-2023-0003

Gidley, D., & Palmer, M. (2021). Institutional work: A review and framework based on semantic and thematic analysis. *M@n@gement, 24*(1), 49–63.

Gidley, D., & Palmer, M. (2022). The impact of video game prototyping in an accelerator as viewed via spatial, temporal, and product scales. *International Journal of Innovation, 10*(3), 410–433.

Gidley, D., Palmer, M., & Gharib, A. (2023). Suffering, recovery and participant experience in a video game development accelerator. *Journal of Organizational Ethnography, 12*(1), 31–45. https://doi.org/10.1108/JOE-07-2022-0023

Gidley, D., & Palmer, M. (2024). Institutional policing work in a constellation of labels and spaces of place: Video game development management insights, International *Journal of Organizational Analysis*, Vol. ahead-of-print No. ahead-of-print. https://doi.org/10.1108/IJOA-03-2024-4365

Goffman, E. (1961). *Asylums* (p. 84). Anchor Books.

Gong, H., & Hassink, R. (2017). Exploring the clustering of creative industries. *European Planning Studies, 25*(4), 583–600.

Gong, H., & Hassink, R. (2019). Developing the Shanghai online games industry: A multi-scalar institutional perspective. *Growth and Change, 50*, 1006–1025. https://doi.org/10.1111/grow.12306

González-Piñero, M. (2021). How to launch new talent into the video game market? The case of GameBCN. In REDINE (Coord.), *Medios digitales y metodologías docentes: Mejorar la educación desde un abordaje integral* (pp. 165–174). Adaya Press.

Goswami, K., Mitchell, J. R., & Bhagavatula, S. (2018). Accelerator expertise: Understanding the intermediary role of accelerators in the development of the Bangalore entrepreneurial ecosystem. *Strategic Entrepreneurship Journal, 12*, 117–150.

Grandadam, D., Cohendet, P., & Simon, L. (2013). Places, spaces and the dynamics of creativity: The video game industry in Montreal. *Regional Studies, 47*(10), 1701–1714. https://doi.org/10.1080/00343404.2012.699191

Guevara-Villalobos, O. (2013). *Cultural production and politics of the digital games industry: The case of independent game production.* Doctoral dissertation, University of Edinburgh.

Hallen, B. L., Cohen, S. L., & Bingham, C. B. (2020). Do accelerators work? If so, how? *Organization Science, 31*(2), 378–414.

Harvey, A., & Fisher, S. (2013). Making a name in games. *Information, Communication & Society, 16*(3), 362–380. https://doi.org/10.1080/1369118X.2012.756048

Hausmann, A., & Heinze, A. (2016). Entrepreneurship in the cultural and creative industries: Insights from an emergent field. *Artivate, 5*, 7–22. https://doi.org/10.1353/artv.2016.0005

Hensel, P. G. (2018). Organizational responses to proto-institutions: How the semi-edited and unedited accounts clash. *Journal of Management Inquiry, 27*(2), 224–245. https://doi.org/10.1177/1056492616688086

Horton, R. (2020). Offline: COVID-19 is not a pandemic. *The Lancet, 396*(10255), 874.

Høvig, Ø. S. (2016). Co-evolutionary dynamics and institutions: Innovation in a guild community in Norway. *Norsk Geografisk Tidsskrift - Norwegian Journal of Geography, 70*, 152–161.

Hurley, P., & Sá, C. M. (2013). Higher education policy and legitimacy building: The making of a new academic credential in Ontario. *Higher Education Quarterly, 67*(2), 157–179.

Isabelle, D. A., & Del Sarto, N. (2020). How can accelerators in south America evolve to support start-ups in a post-COVID-19 world? *Multidisciplinary Business Review, 13*(2), 66–79.

Izushi, H., & Aoyama, Y. (2006). Industry evolution and cross-sectoral skill transfers: A comparative analysis of the video game industry in Japan, the United States, and the United Kingdom. *Environment and Planning A: Economy and Space, 38*(10), 1843–1861. https://doi.org/10.1068/a37205

Jessop, B. (2012). Narratives of crisis and crisis response: Perspectives from North and South. *The Global Crisis and Transformative Social Change*, 23–42.

Johns, J. (2006). Video games production networks: Value capture, power relations and embeddedness. *Journal of Economic Geography, 6*(2), 151–180.

Johnson, R. S. (2013). Toward greater production diversity: Examining social boundaries at a video game studio. *Games and Culture, 8*(3), 136–160.

Johnson, M. R., & Woodcock, J. (2019). 'It's like the gold rush': The lives and careers of professional video game streamers on Twitch.tv. *Information, Communication & Society, 22*(3), 336–351.

Jørgensen, K. (2019). Newcomers in a global industry: Challenges of a Norwegian game company. *Games and Culture, 14*(6), 660–679. https://doi.org/10.1177/1555412017723265

Kamarck, K. N. (2016). *Women in combat: Issues for Congress*. Congressional Research Service Washington United States.

Kennedy, H. W. (2018). Game jam as feminist methodology: The affective labors of intervention in the ludic economy. *Games and Culture, 13*(7), 708–727. https://doi.org/10.1177/1555412018764992

Kerr, A. (2020). Decoding and recoding game jams and independent game-making spaces for diversity and inclusion. In *Independent videogames* (pp. 29–42). Routledge.

Kornberger, M., Leixnering, S., & Meyer, R. E. (2019). The logic of tact: How decisions happen in situations of crisis. *Organization Studies, 40*(2), 239–266.

Kratofil, B., & Burbank, K. (1999). The impact of the y2k bug. *Business Economics*, 39–43.

Langley, A. (1999). Strategies for theorizing from process data. *The Academy of Management Review, 24*(4), 691–710.

Lawrence, T., Hardy, C., & Phillips, N. (2002). Institutional effects of interorganisational collaboration: The emergence of proto-institutions. *The Academy of Management Journal, 45*(1), 281–290.

Leblebici, H., & Shah, N. (2004). The birth, transformation and regeneration of business incubators as new organisational forms: Understanding the interplay between organisational history and organisational theory. *Business History, 46*(3), 353–380. https://doi.org/10.1080/0007679042000219175a

Lee, M. (2015). Fostering connectivity: A social network analysis of entrepreneurs in creative industries. *International Journal of Cultural Policy, 21*(2), 139–152. https://doi.org/10.1080/10286632.2014.891021

Liew, T., Goodwin, R., & Walasek, L. (2020). Voting patterns, revoking article 50 and antidepressant trends in England following the Brexit referendum. *Social Science & Medicine, 255*, 113025.

Lifshitz-Assaf, H., Lebovitz, S., & Zalmanson, L. (2021). Minimal and adaptive coordination: How hackathons' projects accelerate innovation without killing it. *Academy of Management Journal, 64*(3), 684–715.

Locke, K. (2011). Field research practice in management and organization studies: Reclaiming its tradition of discovery. *The Academy of Management Annals, 5*(1), 613–652.

Lubit, A. (2023). *"I would love people to realise that I call this my home": Migrant Muslim women's everyday visibility, movement and placemaking strategies in Northern Ireland*. Doctoral dissertation, Queen's University Belfast.

Lubit, A. J., & Gidley, D. (2021). Becoming part of a temporary protest organization through embodied walking ethnography. *Journal of Organizational Ethnography, 10*(1), 79–94.

Mac, S. D. (2014). Multiplayer games: Tax, copyright, consumers and the video game industries. *European Journal of Law and Technology, 5*(3).

Magolda, P. M. (2003). Saying good-bye: An anthropological examination of a commencement ritual. *Journal of College Student Development, 44*(6), 779–796.

Malone, N. (2021). *Temporality, selfhood and sociality: Experiences of the emergent indie game developer.* Doctoral dissertation, Edge Hill University.

Michalcyzk, J. J. (2016). *Filming the end of the holocaust: Allied documentaries, Nuremberg and the liberation of the concentration camps.* Bloomsbury Academic.

Mikami, K., Nakamura, Y., Ito, A., Kawashima, M., Watanabe, T., Kishimoto, Y., & Kondo, K. (2016). Effectiveness of game jam-based iterative program for game production in Japan. *Computers & Graphics, 61*, 1–10. https://doi.org/10.1016/j.cag.2016.07.006

Montgomery, L. M. (2020). A rejoinder to body bags: Indigenous resilience and epidemic disease, from COVID-19 to first "Contact". *American Indian Culture and Research Journal, 44*(3), 65–86.

Moore, B. L. (2017). Introduction to armed forces & society: Special issue on women in the military. *Armed Forces & Society, 43*(2), 191–201. https://doi.org/10.1177/0095327X17694909

Morgeson, F. P., Mitchell, T. R., & Liu, D. (2015). Event system theory: An event-oriented approach to the organizational sciences. *Academy of Management Review, 40*(4), 515–537.

Moskos, C. C., Jr. (1966). Racial integration in the armed forces. *American Journal of Sociology, 72*(2), 132–148.

Nieborg, D. B. (2015). Crushing candy: The free-to-play game in its connective commodity form. *Social Media + Society.* https://doi.org/10.1177/2056305115621932

Palmer, M., O'Kane, P., & Owens, M. (2009). Betwixt spaces: Student accounts of turning point experiences in the first-year transition. *Studies in Higher Education, 34*(1), 37–54.

Papavlasopoulou, S., Giannakos, M. N., & Jaccheri, L. (2017). Empirical studies on the maker movement, a promising approach to learning: A literature review. *Entertainment Computing, 18*, 57–78.

Parker, F., Whitson, J. R., & Simon, B. (2018). Megabooth: The cultural intermediation of indie games. *New Media & Society, 20*(5), 1953–1972.

Parkman, I. D., Holloway, S. S., & Sebastiao, H. (2012). Creative industries: Aligning entrepreneurial orientation and innovation capacity. *Journal of Research in Marketing and Entrepreneurship, 14*(1), 95–114. https://doi.org/10.1108/14715201211246823

Patten, T. (2016). "Creative?"... "Entrepreneur?" – Understanding the Creative Industries Entrepreneur. *Artivate, 5*(2), 23–42. https://doi.org/10.1353/artv.2016.0006

Paul, I., Mohanty, S., & Sengupta, R. (2022). The role of social virtual world in increasing psychological resilience during the on-going COVID-19 pandemic. *Computers in Human Behavior, 127*, 107036.

Pauwels, C., Clarysse, B., Wright, M., & Van Hove, J. (2016). Understanding a new generation incubation model: The accelerator. *Technovation, 50–51*, 13–24. https://doi.org/10.1016/j.technovation.2015.09.003

Phillips, T. (2015). "Don't clone my indie game, bro": Informal cultures of videogame regulation in the independent sector. *Cultural Trends, 24*(2), 143–153.

Plum, O., & Hassink, R. (2014). Knowledge bases, innovativeness and competitiveness in creative industries: The case of Hamburg's video game developers. *Regional Studies, Regional Science, 1*(1), 248–268. https://doi.org/10.1080/21681376.2014.967803

Pokhrel, S., & Chhetri, R. (2021). A literature review on impact of COVID-19 pandemic on teaching and learning. *Higher Education for the Future, 8*(1), 133–141.

Pottie-Sherman, Y., & Lynch, N. (2019). Gaming on the edge: Mobile labour and global talent in Atlantic Canada's video game industry. *The Canadian Geographer / Le Géographe canadien, 63*, 425–439.

Rajani, N. B., Weth, D., Mastellos, N., & Filippidis, F. T. (2019). Use of gamification strategies and tactics in mobile applications for smoking cessation: A review of the UK mobile app market. *BMJ Open, 9*, e027883. https://doi.org/10.1136/bmjopen-2018-027883

Reay, T., Goodrick, E., Waldorff, S. B., & Casebeer, A. (2017). Getting leopards to change their spots: Co-creating a new professional role identity. *Academy of Management Journal, 60*(3), 1043–1070.

Rodgers, D. (2007). Joining the gang and becoming a broder: The violence of ethnography in contemporary Nicaragua. *Bulletin of Latin American Research, 26*(4), 444–461.

Ruffino, P., & Woodcock, J. (2020). Game workers and the empire: Unionisation in the UK video game industry. *Games and Culture.* https://doi.org/10.1177/1555412020947096

Russo, C. (2014). Allies forging collective identity: Embodiment and emotions on the migrant trail. *Mobilization: An International Quarterly, 19*(1), 67–82.

Scarbrough, H., Panourgias, N. S., & Nandhakumar, J. (2015). Developing a relational view of the organizing role of objects: A study of the innovation process in computer games. *Organization Studies, 36*(2), 197–220. https://doi.org/10.1177/0170840614557213

Scott, W. R. (2008). *Institutions and organizations: Ideas and interests* (3rd ed.). Sage Publications.

Siddiqi, A. A. (2000). *Challenge to Apollo: The Soviet Union and the space race, 1945–1974* (Vol. 4408). US National Aeronautics & Space Administration.

Smolka, K. M., & Heugens, P. P. M. A. R. (2019). The emergence of proto-institutions in the new normal business landscape: Dialectic institutional work and the Dutch drone industry. *Journal of Management Studies*. https://doi.org/10.1111/joms.12540

Spinuzzi, C. (2012). Working alone together: Coworking as emergent collaborative activity. *Journal of Business and Technical Communication, 26*(4), 399–441. https://doi.org/10.1177/1050651912444070

Storz, C., Riboldazzi, F., & John, M. (2015). Mobility and innovation: A cross-country comparison in the video games industry. *Research Policy, 44*(1), 121–137. https://doi.org/10.1016/j.respol.2014.07.015

Styhre, A. (2020). *Indie video game development work: Innovation in the creative economy*. Springer Nature.

Tankard, M. E., & Paluck, E. L. (2017). The effect of a supreme court decision regarding gay marriage on social norms and personal attitudes. *Psychological Science, 28*(9), 1334–1344. https://doi.org/10.1177/0956797617709594

Taylor, M. (2020). *UK games industry census: Understanding diversity in the UK games industry workforce (Research Report UKIE)*. Retrieved from UKIE website: https://ukie.org.uk/resources/uk-games-industry-census-2021

Taylor, N., Jenson, J., & De Castell, S. (2009). Cheerleaders/booth babes/Halo hoes: Pro-gaming, gender and jobs for the boys. *Digital Creativity, 20*(4), 239–252.

Thompson, D., & Hebblethwaite, L. (2020). *Think global, create local: The regional economic impact of the UK games industry (Research report UKIE)*. Retrieved from UKIE website: https://ukie.org.uk/resources/think-global-create-local-the-regional-economic-impact-of-the-uk-games-industry

Tsang, D. (2021). Innovation in the British video game industry since 1978. *The Business History Review, 95*(3), 543–567.

UKIE. (2018). *UK video games industry fact sheet* [white paper]. The Association for UK Interactive Entertainment.

Vervoort, J. M. (2019). New frontiers in futures games: Leveraging game sector developments. *Futures, 105*, 174–186. https://doi.org/10.1016/j.futures.2018.10.005

Vu, N. Q., & Bezemer, C. P. (2021). Improving the discoverability of indie games by leveraging their similarity to top-selling games: Identifying important requirements of a recommender system. In *Proceedings of the 16th international conference on the foundations of digital game* (pp. 1–12).

Walter, S. (2021). Brexit Domino? The political contagion effects of voter-endorsed withdrawals from international institutions. *Comparative Political Studies, 54*(13), 2382–2415. https://doi.org/10.1177/0010414021997169

Webber, N. (2020). The Britishness of 'British Video Games'. *International Journal of Cultural Policy, 26*(2), 135–149. https://doi.org/10.1080/10286632.2018.1448804

Whitson, J. R. (2020). What can we learn from studio studies ethnographies?: A "Messy" account of game development materiality, learning, and expertise. *Games and Culture, 15,* 266–288. https://doi.org/10.1177/1555412018783320

Williamson, S., Colley, L., & Hanna-Osborne, S. (2020). Will working from home become the 'new normal' in the public sector? *Australian Journal of Public Administration, 79*(4), 601–607.

Wright, A. L., Meyer, A. D., Reay, T., & Staggs, J. (2020). Maintaining places of social inclusion: Ebola and the emergency department. *Administrative Science Quarterly.* https://doi.org/10.1177/0001839220916401

Xia, S., Xiong, Y., Zhang, M., Cornford, J., Liu, Y., Lim, M. K., Cao, D., & Chen, F. (2020). Reducing the resource acquisition costs for returnee entrepreneurs: Role of Chinese national science parks. *International Journal of Entrepreneurial Behavior & Research, 26*(7), 1627–1657.

Zajac, A. C. (2017). *"Something Must Be Done!": Edward VIII's abdication and the preservation of the British monarchy.*

Zietsma, C., & McKnight, B. (2009). Building the iron cage: Institutional creation work in the context of competing proto-institutions. In *Institutional work: Actors and agency in institutional studies of organizations* (pp. 143–176). Cambridge University Press.

Zikic, J., & Klehe, U. C. (2006). Job loss as a blessing in disguise: The role of career exploration and career planning in predicting reemployment quality. *Journal of Vocational Behavior, 69*(3), 391–409.

Zilber, T. B. (2002). Institutionalization as an interplay between actions, meanings, and actors: The case of a rape crisis center in Israel. *The Academy of Management Journal, 45*(1), 234–254. https://doi.org/10.2307/3069294

Zucker, L. G. (1977). The role of institutionalization in cultural persistence. *American Sociological Review, 42*(5), 726–743. https://doi.org/10.2307/2094862

Index[1]

A
AB accelerator, 156, 163, 165
Accelerators, xi, xiii, 1–3, 8–16, 19, 26, 40, 46, 53, 61, 66, 78, 93, 132, 135, 136, 142, 144, 151, 155, 157, 163–166, 167n6, 168, 173, 175, 179, 192
Announcement (communication), 110
Audience, xi, xii, 8, 61, 69, 70, 76, 91, 134, 148, 159, 186

B
Basecamp, v, vii, viii, xvii, 29, 30, 39, 40, 47, 67, 74, 78, 103, 118, 124, 142, 153, 157, 161, 163–166, 172
BAT management, 97, 99, 100, 104, 105, 121, 135, 177

Bootcamp, 46, 53, 55, 58–62, 78, 79, 90, 95, 114, 210
British Artistic Technologists (BAT), v, xiv, 7, 26, 47, 82, 112, 141, 172, 193, 206
Business, xi, xviii, 3, 9, 10, 28, 34, 40, 41, 51, 53, 54, 65, 67, 68, 85, 87, 95, 105, 113–115, 121, 135, 142, 145, 153, 163, 179–181, 194

C
Clients, 35, 55, 57, 60, 63, 65, 139
Code, 39, 51, 113, 181
Cohorts, vii, xv, xvi, 9, 19, 26, 27, 30–42, 47, 52, 54, 68, 88, 89, 95, 103, 106, 112, 113, 115, 116, 121–124, 126, 128, 129,

---

[1] Note: Page numbers followed by 'n' refer to notes.

131, 132, 135–138, 141, 144, 146–151, 153, 155–164, 166–169, 171–173, 173n1, 175, 183, 185, 191, 193, 194, 196, 197, 199, 205, 210, 211
Collaboration, 10, 11, 89, 179, 182, 186
Commercial viability, 56, 74–77, 210
Committees, v, vi, viin4, xv, 29, 89, 91, 92, 106, 117, 117n6, 128, 132, 134, 136
Community building, 27, 172
Consoles, 4, 7n1, 147, 206
Consultants, xv, 27, 53, 59, 62, 86, 88, 107, 153, 206
Content, 41, 57, 107, 206
Continental Gymnasium (the Gym), xiv
Contracts, xv, 28, 101, 107, 112, 119, 150, 164, 182
Contract work, 53, 57, 131, 164, 169
COVID-19 pandemic (lockdown), 11, 193, 195, 197, 199, 200
Coworking spaces, xi, xiii, xiv, 1, 3, 8–12, 27, 53, 61, 78, 142, 147, 151, 152, 162, 164, 168, 172, 179, 180, 206
Creative industries, xi, xii, xiv, xviii, 2, 6
Creativity, 2, 19, 47, 49, 130, 205
Crunch, 52, 119, 135
Crux events, v, viii, ix, xii, xiii, xvii, 1–19, 26, 29, 32, 42, 46, 53, 77, 78, 82, 109, 112, 137, 141, 158, 159, 167, 168, 171, 175, 177, 184, 185, 189–201, 211

D

Demo Friday, 39–40, 42
Departures, 62, 82–84, 90, 95, 98, 109, 112, 141, 147, 166, 167, 171, 185, 190

Developers as gamers, v, xvi–xviii, 2, 3, 7, 12, 26, 27, 32, 33, 36, 40, 41, 47–58, 61, 70, 79, 112, 117n6, 129, 151, 152, 154, 162, 166, 168, 173, 174, 179, 180, 186, 190, 199, 206
Development process, 73, 154
Digital Quarry, v, vi, xi, xiii, 10, 12, 17, 19, 29, 31, 37, 39, 83, 85, 92, 95, 101–106, 108, 109, 113–115, 114n2, 129, 132, 135–137, 144–145, 151–155, 157, 159, 161, 163, 164, 166, 167, 207
Discoverability, 62, 64

E

Ethnographer, vi–viii, xvi, xvii, 26–29, 31–38, 40, 54, 57, 67, 69, 71, 77, 85, 88, 101–106, 108, 109, 116–119, 123–127, 131, 143, 145, 146, 149–151, 156, 159, 166, 179, 206, 207
Ethnographer (Devon), 40, 71
Ethnography, ix, xvi–xviii, 3, 7, 8, 11, 18, 19, 171, 189, 190, 197, 206
Ethos, 36, 56, 58, 65, 127, 180
Exit interviews, 121–123, 133
Expectations, 7, 12, 29, 66, 83, 98, 106, 107, 135, 142, 155, 160, 172, 175, 183, 184, 200, 207
External crisis, 159, 200, 211

F

Feedback, xi, 10, 35, 40–42, 47, 51–53, 64, 67, 71, 71n4, 78, 83, 86, 87, 91, 100–103, 108, 108n7, 109, 113, 115, 118, 120, 121, 125, 128, 134–137, 142, 149, 152, 154, 171, 176, 177, 180–183, 186, 197, 200, 210, 211

Free labor, 105, 107, 179
Freelancers, xiii, 35, 148, 152
Fun, 32, 70, 71, 74, 104, 148

G
Game release, 205
Gamescom, 49, 50, 56, 60, 64, 65, 74, 77, 78, 82–86, 90, 125, 127
Greater Data Protection Regulation (GDPR), vi, 31

H
Hotdesking, 162
Hybrid space, 150–158, 165, 167–169

I
Incubators, xi, xiii, 1, 2, 8–16, 19, 46, 53, 78, 132, 142, 144, 165, 174, 175, 179, 189, 192
Indie video game companies, 134
Innovation, xi–xiii, xvii, 1–19, 142, 144, 171, 190, 193
Intellectual property (IP), 2, 48, 57, 59, 76, 194, 200
Interns, xi, xv–xvii, 26, 27, 32, 35, 67, 68, 70–72, 84, 89n3, 96, 98, 108, 113, 115, 142, 155, 169, 171, 178–179, 185, 191, 206, 210, 211
Introduction of newcomers, 26, 38, 42

K
Key performance indicators (KPI), 113, 115, 136
Kitchen, xiv, 34, 37, 123, 149

L
Leadership workshop, 86, 107, 178

M
Mandatory, xv, 53, 54, 86, 107
Marketing, xvii, 8n2, 27, 53, 67, 68, 70, 76, 91, 96, 113, 115, 134, 160, 173n1, 178, 186, 191
Membership, xi, xiii, xiv, 10, 31, 40, 107, 152, 153, 168, 171–175, 190, 201, 211
Mentors, vi, xi, xv–xvii, 9, 30, 38, 40, 41, 47, 49, 51–58, 65, 67, 74, 75, 77, 82–86, 88, 91, 92, 95–98, 100, 102, 103, 108, 109, 113, 114, 116, 122, 127–129, 131–134, 136, 137, 142–145, 148–151, 154–156, 158, 163, 166, 171, 179–186, 194, 196, 199, 206, 211
Mini-production Funding, 90–94
Mobile Games, 4, 5, 7n1, 31, 55, 58, 116, 206
Monetization, 54, 125, 134, 137
Moonshot, 151, 155–160, 162, 166–168, 172, 174, 177, 211

O
Office space, xiii, 10, 37, 115, 122, 147, 152, 153, 163, 164

P
Physical proximity, 38, 169
Pitching, 41, 61, 63–65, 112, 115–120, 126, 137, 138
Practical Lessons, ix, xi, xvii, 1, 19, 26, 42, 46–47, 79, 82–83, 109–110, 112–113, 138–139, 142, 159, 168–169, 171–187, 211

Presentations, 31, 47–49, 60–62, 74, 78, 94, 113, 116, 120, 128, 174
Process research, 18
Project management, 48, 49
Prototypes, 48–50, 52, 56, 60, 64–66, 69, 70, 72–75, 77, 78, 90, 94, 117, 119n7, 124–126, 133, 139, 148, 149, 151, 160, 169, 181, 183, 205, 206
Publisher, 4, 48, 50, 52–54, 58, 63, 65, 74, 77, 90, 91, 94, 99, 117, 119, 124, 126, 130, 131, 139, 149, 151, 159, 160, 164, 180, 206

Q

Quality assurance (QA), 145–146, 155, 178, 179
The Quarry Manager, xv, xvi, 27, 38, 40–42, 46, 47, 60, 62, 82–110, 112, 113, 162, 172, 176, 184, 185, 207
Quick lessons, xi, 29, 33, 34, 36, 38, 41, 49, 51, 53, 55, 58, 59, 61, 62, 66, 68, 70, 73, 78, 84, 86, 89, 94, 96, 98, 100, 103, 107, 120, 123, 124, 126, 129, 130, 132, 134, 136, 137, 144–147, 149, 150, 152, 154, 155, 158, 160–163, 165, 167

R

R&D, 50
Rapid prototyping program (RPP), 7, 11, 40, 46, 52–54, 58, 60, 62, 68, 76, 78, 90, 102, 115, 132, 148, 172, 174, 176, 177, 192, 194, 196, 197, 200, 205, 206, 210
Rebellion, 98–100, 103–108, 176, 177, 183, 210
Residual funding, 150, 157, 169

Resistance, xi, 11, 36, 42, 78, 86, 88, 175–178, 196, 211
Rules, xvi, 3, 11, 28, 29, 31, 46–79, 86, 96, 107, 112, 132, 134–136, 142, 177, 183, 184, 192

S

Self-inflicted Crisis, 112–139, 168
Sick (illness), vii, 40, 41, 52, 72, 103, 159, 180
Six games in six weeks, 60–77, 151, 160
SME, 37
Students, xi, xii, xvi, xvii, 12, 26, 27, 32, 35, 39, 49, 68, 69, 72, 98, 99, 175, 182, 189–190, 197, 206

T

Trust (protectedness), 37

U

UK Department of Culture, Media and Sports (DCMS), 2
UKIE, 2–4
University job fair, 103, 107
User experience (UX), 69, 70

V

Vertical slice, 74, 75, 77, 117, 126, 132, 150
Video game industry, xiv, xv, 1, 144, 207
Volunteer, 103

W

Welcome, 33, 34, 114
Women (gender), 5, 65, 191, 195
Written agreements, 29

GPSR Compliance

The European Union's (EU) General Product Safety Regulation (GPSR) is a set of rules that requires consumer products to be safe and our obligations to ensure this.

If you have any concerns about our products, you can contact us on

ProductSafety@springernature.com

In case Publisher is established outside the EU, the EU authorized representative is:

Springer Nature Customer Service Center GmbH
Europaplatz 3
69115 Heidelberg, Germany

www.ingramcontent.com/pod-product-compliance
Lightning Source LLC
LaVergne TN
LVHW021336080526
838202LV00004B/189